D1724253

K. Ludwig Pfeiffer
From Chaos to Catastrophe?

Buchreihe der ANGLIA/ ANGLIA Book Series

Edited by
Lucia Kornexl, Ursula Lenker, Martin Middeke,
Gabriele Rippl, Hubert Zapf

Volume 59

K. Ludwig Pfeiffer

From Chaos to Catastrophe?

—

Texts and the Transitionality of the Mind

DE GRUYTER

For an overview of all books published in this series, please see
http://www.degruyter.com/view/serial/36292

ISBN 978-3-11-057934-5
e-ISBN (PDF) 978-3-11-058183-6
e-ISBN (EPUB) 978-3-11-057947-5
ISSN 0340-5435

Library of Congress Cataloging-in-Publication Data
A CIP catalog record for this book has been applied for at the Library of Congress.

Bibliographic information published by the Deutsche Nationalbibliothek
The Deutsche Nationalbibliothek lists this publication in the Deutsche Nationalbibliografie;
detailed bibliographic data are available on the Internet at http://dnb.dnb.de.

© 2018 Walter de Gruyter GmbH, Berlin/Boston
Printing: CPI books GmbH, Leck
♾ Printed on acid-free paper
Printed in Germany

www.degruyter.com

―――――

"Oh it is all about mind!" (Max Ackerman in Mosley 2000: 458)

"[...] consciousness creates things: but for us to become used to this, we have to become used to some breaking up, reforming, breaking up, of ourselves" (Mosley 2000: 473)

"[...] scientific language was a tool of consciousness when it looked at the outside world; it was not one much fitted to the process of consciousness looking at itself" (Mosley 2000: 537)

Foreword

Some years ago, I found myself in Vienna, meeting and talking to my friend and former student Ralph Kray on ultimately failing university business. Thinking back to those lectures of mine which he had attended in former times, he had the idea, flattering for me, that these lectures, old as they were, should be published. Extensive scanning activitities took place, resulting in a digital collection established by Ingo Berensmeyer (whom Ralph had persuaded of or browbeaten into the enterprise), another friend, former student and now very successful colleague of mine, at the University of Giessen.

A few glances into the collection brought me to the ungrateful and unpleasant conclusion that the plan was doomed to failure. The texts were old, without aura, at best clad with pleasant patina. To save face, we mumbled something about subjecting them to a rejuvenating treatment which might be performed in the perspective, fashionable at the time, of the resilience of the mind. For that purpose, I plunged (or rather replunged) into studies of neurobiology which I had started about ten years before for another research project with Klaus Vondung, called "Mysticism and Modernity". Strangely enough, although I ignored both lectures and mysticism, one chapter after another got written until my confusion about the connections between these chapters was complete. I turned to other friends and colleagues (Peter Gendolla, Ralf Schnell and the aforementioned Klaus Vondung) and forced them to read that stuff with special attention to the 'logic', absent or present, of and between the chapters. Their criticisms, in turn, forced me to do something about that. As a consequence I rewrote large parts of the text sometimes up to ten times. I then sent the text to Wolfgang Wicht, among other things one of the two best reviewers I know (the other was the late Ulrich Schulz-Buschhaus).

Fortified with Wicht's blessing, I tried my luck with the publishers and had the incredibly good fortune to run into Hubert Zapf who not only wrote a detailed (and very flattering) evaluation, but also suggested the Anglia Book Series as a suitable publishing platform.

My sincere thanks go to all the names mentioned so far and, in one of these paradoxes we know, with special intensity to those who do not want to be mentioned. I should now extend my thanks to the people at the publishing company Walter de Gruyter, in particular Katja Lehming and Olena Gainulina.

Kronberg/Ts., October 2017 K. Ludwig Pfeiffer

https://doi.org/10.1515/9783110581836-001

Contents

Introduction: Processes and Products: Claims, Goals, Risks —— 1

Part I Consciousness Studies: Neurosciences and 'Literature'

1   The Transitionality of Consciousness —— 15

2   Universalism *vs.* Particularism —— 23

3   Patterns of Consciousness, Language, Discourse —— 31

4   James, James and the Structure of Fluctuations —— 37

5   Neurobiology: Intricacies and Implications —— 49

6   Dramatic Narratives —— 62

7   Transitionality and the Obsession with Form —— 76

8   Existential Impressionism and Cultural Status: Dorothy Richardson
        (1873 – 1957) —— 90

9   An Interlude, Or, From Richardson to Richardson —— 102

Part II Consciousness and History: Biographical 'Novels' and
        their 'Liberal' Extensions

1   Biography on the Rebound —— 115

2   Biographical Patterns, Models of Consciousness and Historical
        Significance in Dickens —— 127

3   Diagnostic Power and Practical Relevance: Some Further
        Steps —— 132

4   The Pseudo-Freedom of Consciousness and its Cost-Benefit Analysis
     in the Twentieth Century —— 141

5   The RAF, a Twentieth-Century Reality Shift, and a Contemporary
     German 'Novel' —— 155

6   The Drama of 'Liberalism' —— 164

7   What Does Enlightenment Enlighten Us About? —— 171

8   The Paradox of Liberty and Authority —— 185

Part III A Case Study: Chaotic Consciousness
          and Catastrophic History, Discordant Evolution and
          Political Overreaction: Oswald and Nicholas Mosley

1   Catastrophe Practice: Frameworks and Presuppositions – From
     Individuality to Scripts —— 191

2   Catastrophe Practice: Routines – Individuality Manufactured and
     Medialized —— 197

3   Hopeful Monsters: Discordant Evolution and Steps towards
     Mutation —— 203

4   Hysterical Consciousness and the Beginnings of Institutional
     Degeneration in Autobiographical Writings —— 210

5   The Failure of Rules and the Unleashing of Hysterical Consciousness:
     Oswald Mosley and Fascism —— 214

6   Tentative Conclusions —— 219

Works Cited —— 221

Index —— 232

Introduction: Processes and Products: Claims, Goals, Risks

My title may be too dramatic, my subtitle rather uninspiring. Even so, the mixture might yield a suitable discursive working temperature. This should happen especially if one brings the terms chaos and catastrophe close to their technical 'philosophical' meaning in which, for catastrophe, sudden discontinuities, mostly called bifurcations (subtle, catastrophic, explosive) are seen as the result of a slow underlying evolution, or where, in the case of chaos, small changes of initial operating conditions and parameters in nonlinear systems bring about unexpectedly radical results.[1] It goes without saying that this take-over of technical terms is a pretty loose one. In this book, chaos, feeding on the technical sense, refers to the workings of consciousness, catastrophe, also profiting from the technical sense, to real consequences for which symptomatic, typical or far-reaching significance can be claimed. I assume, as it were, elective affinities between chaos and catastrophes, between the processes and the products of the mind. Chaos and catastrophe, in whichever sense, are couched in an atmosphere of highly charged drama. This is because they are produced by the hysterical (sometimes also called schizophrenic) consciousness. The term 'hysterical consciousness' is derived from Edgar Morin's evolutionary anthropology (see part I, chapter 6); with the term 'schizophrenic' I align myself more or less with Julian Jaynes' notion of the old bicameral mind which has survived, both as a term and as a phenomenon, in its far too narrow pathological meaning. I am very much relieved, however, to see that the term 'hysteria' appears meanwhile to have made its way also into historical studies. In his new book on failed predictions, Joachim Radkau characterizes various periods in German after-war history as periods of hysteria (because of the Sputnik shock, dying forests, nuclear dangers etc). I am sure it would be easy to find many more, especially since Radkau, in an earlier book, has described the later nineteenth and early twentieth centuries as an age of nervousness. In other words: The use of 'hysteria',

---

1 The heyday of chaos and catastrophe theories and their application in the humanities and social sciences has surely been over for about 20 years. While I hope for some originality in my ways of application, I use the theories more like general orienting signposts only. Still, I would like to acknowledge a few books from which I have taken some inspiration: See Brown 1995; Briggs and Peet 2001 (on catastrophe theory according to René Thom 119–121); Gregobi and Yorke 1997: 300–304 (on sociology and catastrophe theory according to Thom and Zeeman), 363, 372–374; Ruelle 1991: 41, 122–125.

In this book, all translations from languages other than English are mine.

https://doi.org/10.1515/9783110581836-002

'hysterical' and 'schizophrenic' as general (some would say: metaphorical) concepts, not just as systematic concepts for special pathological cases of persons and societies might not be as absurd as it looks at first sight. In fact, similar or analogous notions show up in many theoretical contexts: Konrad Lorenz assumes that in a certain sense "we are all psychopaths" because we pay heavily for the many of our unfulfilled desires. Arthur Koestler traces human tendencies toward self-destruction back to the evolutionary blunder of a "schizophysiological disposition", with evolution failing to integrate the old (limbic) and the new (neocortical) brain. The list could be continued. [2]

The book, in what could easily look like overreaching itself, is rather like a bet on the possibilities of describing both *processes* and to assess the achievements or the functional deficits of *products* of consciousness. It does not ignore so-called realities, historical, social and otherwise. But they are considered in fairly general forms only, in which they may be said to modulate the relations between processes and products (more on history towards the end of this introduction). Processes of consciousness (called thoughts, ideas, images or something else) often appear chaotic in the conventional and the technical sense. Products of consciousness like total conceptions of the world and human beings, worldpictures, theories, models of thought and a lot of products in between (doctrines, dogmas, ideologies, opinions) spring from the activities with which consciousness tries to make sense of itself and the world. In order to ease and yet to

---

[2] Radkau 2017. See also Radkau 1998. See further Lorenz 1963: 375–376, Koestler 1978: 10–11. In orthodox psychiatry (if there is such a thing), the relativistic consequences of any attempt to define pathological forms of both schizophrenia and hysteria, and especially a differential diagnosis of the two, are all too obvious. See for instance Redlich and Freedman 1966, chapter 14. The only thing which is certain (according to the authors!) is the suffering of countless people diagnosed in these terms. For a contemporary literary text in which most of my central terms are used in ways very similar to mine see Genazino 2011 (19: "Hysteriker des Ichs", 131: "schizoid", 134: "Depressionen und Erlebnishysterie", 136: "Katastrophen"). Even more pointedly, the constraints of life and the narrow boundaries of full consciousness tend to produce, in the context of profit and income maximization, following closely on the heels of historical events and characters, hysterical and schizophrenic figures of thought and emotion in Goetz 2015: 271–272, 277, 298. The gallery of British authors and literary characters treated in a book of essays by Levin Ludwig Schücking (1878–1964), perhaps the greatest of early German representatives of English philology, seems to be characterized by the duality of hysterical tendencies and efforts towards self-control and self-discipline. See Schücking 1948: 58, 85, 127, 129, 137, 146, 159, 161, 163, 164, 172, 284, 290, 293, 298, 335–355 (the insufficiency and deceptiveness of ‚Biedermeier' emotional restraint especially in Dickens). In Garcia 2016, a 'hystericization', inspired in the last resort by electricity in the eighteenth century, imparts another turn of the screw to the modern life value of intensity. It would appear that intensity, 'nervously' pursued, is in itself a form of hysteria.

structure these transitions (adding up to the concept of *transitionality*) I have looked at texts mostly, but certainly not always called literature. In spite of that, this book is *not* about literary techniques of representing consciousness variously called (authorial) thought report, narrated monologue, free indirect style, interior monologue or stream of consciousness. I rather follow older theorists like Eliseo Vivas for whom literature was searching for "the primary data of human experience", or contemporary ones like Terence Cave who see the best parts of the literary area as "the signature of cognition in action". In that capacity, it is among the richest of our cognitive artefacts. The kind of thinking it offers may come close to philosophical, scientific, political, everyday and other modes. But it also develops cognitive surplus values.[3] Such surplus values, in their turn, do have practical importance, even if this is not immediately obvious. They tend to appear with particular force in the elaboration of the *transitions* built into conscious processes, transitions elusive and evanescent, hard to grasp, to describe or to define, yet crucial for the formation of realities we are likely to accept, desire or reject. Starting out from the incessant dynamics of the basic elements of consciousness (which we may or may not call 'thoughts'), a conscious space is being built up all the time in which the more or less internal patterning of conscious processes is ultimately confronted, for better or worse, with what consciousness conceives of as realities out there. Given the multitude and partial vagueness or lack of communicative fitness of conscious processes, linked with more or less unknown unconscious ones, there must be a certain degree of 'freedom' of conscious activities (which may or may not be related to the notorious problem of freedom of the will). Given the pressures from 'out there', there will also be restrictions to that freedom. Consequently, the intention, on a second level, is to set up a *cost-benefit analysis* for the relations between the processes of consciousness and its products, from an inner dynamics of what looks like a liquid mass of conscious events, where thoughts are barely identifiable, to the most elaborate finished products. Such an analysis is surely crucial for the future of especially Western societies. Since this book is *not* an exercise in *cultural criticism* (German "Kulturkritik")[4], however, this analysis will show up in

---

3 For Vivas (1901–1993) see Krieger (in whose life work Vivas has a crucial place) 1994: 58; for Cave see Cave 2016: 1, 12, 20. Cave's book and my own, while sharing quite a few ('cognitive') interests, differ with respect to their main object. In my concentration on consciousness I am less inclined to set up and delimit unified fields of discourse like 'literature'. I accept the use of this and other delimiting concepts, but also go beyond them whenever this appears worthwhile.

4 For a model history of cultural criticism see Bollenbeck 2007, for a competing one, also with Rousseau in a crucial position, Konersmann 2008. In positioning cultural criticism within the

repeated, fairly simple (hopefully not simplistic) assertions only, not in the form of a really elaborated argument. Even so, an *evolutionary logic* will hopefully emerge within the range of products of thought. This logic should show implications and consequences, risks, main and side effects in the transitions from total conceptions like cosmologies to worldviews, from dogmas to theories and finally down the supreme reign of inflationary and inflated opinions, today digitally created, sustained and multiplied.[5]

Obviously, histories of types of thought, including their 'origins' in psychological, intellectual, social and other dispositions and traditions, have often been written. Very often, the *history of ideas* is seen as the professional field in which such inquiries mainly take place. It would be silly to deny how much one must profit by them. Yet the history of ideas seems to be plagued by one central problem, namely an unresolved wavering between historical specificity and typological generality. Intellectual currents must be given names (idealism, materialism, gnosticism, apocalyptic, utopian or dystopian thought etc). The impression that such currents show up repeatedly or even permanently, that they are fixed parts of typological inventories of human thought is hard to ward off. The impression collides, however, with the conviction that these currents of thought are much more enmeshed in and determined by the web of history or histories, so that their typological generality turns out to be an illusion.[6] I am therefore trying out an approach which, first, confronts the dynamics of the (as we will see: 'hysterical' or 'schizophrenic' tendencies of the) mind with its products, that is to say types of thought, but, second, reduces the generality of these types by a limited and selective interpretation of their functional value with respect to satisfactory explanations of the world, individual situations and the orientation of action.

In the digital age, it would be possible to use the metaphor of interfaces of the mind for the transitional spaces envisaged here. Such terminological tricks would not, however, dispel the impression, easily gained and hard to get rid of, that the enterprise faces discouraging risks. At first glance, the transitional dynamics seems to veer towards a multitude of arbitrary or the limitations of

---

relativism of Western cultures, their cult of change and of permanent commentary, together with the disappearance of stable life forms (15, 44, 132 etc), Konersmann is somewhat systematically closer to the concerns of the present enterprise.

5 In principle, this work is related to Dux 1982. This "logic of worldpictures" concentrates, however, to a very large extent on 'primitive' thought, ('primitive') religion (up to the development of monotheism) and the role of the natural sciences.

6 A good discussion of that problem especially with respect to the work of Eric Voegelin can be found in Vondung 2016: 119, 126, 131.

conventional forms. The idea of transitionality, in the way it is developed here, might appear to be useless because I do not adopt the quasi-natural starting point for such investigations which are broadly called *creativity studies*. Such studies have been pursued for quite a while within disciplines and approaches like editorial science, brain research, as well as investigations into textual genesis as a complex process triggered by rough concepts, sketches, schemes as well as linguistic, musical and image stimuli, and handled in practice more easily with the blessings of the digital age. The force of such approaches is hard to deny, conclusive results, however, even harder to attain.[7] On all levels, the evidence is rather fragmentary. I have shifted therefore, much like a traditional literary scholar, my attention back to elaborate finished products appearing mostly in the shape of published books. Method and manner of this investigation, collecting and exploiting all kinds of evidence from philosophy, neurobiology and evolutionary anthropology may appear rather arbitrary. As always, they must be judged by their fruits which I intend to gather especially in the second and third parts.

Very roughly, as far as products of consciousness are concerned, I will make use of mainly, though not exclusively, four types: Total conceptions of the world and human beings, worldpictures (for which I will use, for reasons to be explained later, the German term *Weltanschauungen*), theories, and models of thought. Although these are types which, to all intents and purposes, overlap and can be found at all times, they are characterized also and, I hope to show, preeminently by degrees of suitability and functionality but also deficits with respect to the situations in which people find themselves. Certainly, the categories named present rough distinctions only. In any period for which I assert the hegemony of one of these terms, a stronger or weaker presence of others can also be detected. Moreover, overlaps and forms in-between certainly occur frequently. Consequently, the point is not that products appear at a certain time; it is rather the relative role they play in configurations of products of thought in varying situations within longer periods of time.

Twentieth-century German Nazism, to take one of the worst examples of what one would call a *Weltanschauung*, certainly saw itself and was frequently seen as an irresistible rhetorical-cognitive machine. But the writing for this product was on the wall early on. In terms of ideas, it was a botched concoction.

---

7 I am thinking in both respects for instance of the very promising project "Brain I Concept I Writing which started around 2008 at the RWTH (= Technological University) Aachen and which I had to review. It is difficult to say how that project has been doing meanwhile. The difficulty is probably not only due to the fact that the project coordinator Axel Gellhaus died a few years after the start of the project.

Christopher Ricks for instance has understandably called Fascist 'ideology', in this case the ideas of the British Fascist leader Sir Oswald Mosley, as being dedicated, devoted, pledged and doomed to "nullity" (Ricks 1983: 3).[8] In terms of action, Nazism was primitively politicized. It did not really deserve the name of *Weltanschauung* in comparison with those gestures towards totality which one can find in the nineteenth century, the period which I would like to proclaim the most important historical area for this product of thought. Why so many people went along with the Nazi ideology (here the term would make sense in spite of my reservations to be spelled out below) for such a long time must be due to very extraordinary factors which keep fueling an immense amount of historical explanation. The ambition of this book does not go so far.

However, in spite of a lack of historical specificity, the distinctions between products of thought should be instructive with respect to the risks and side effects in the interplay of the ways of consciousness and the ways of the world. In spite of overlaps, it should be possible to distinguish, for instance, between medieval religious *dogma* and the *dogmatism* of opinions in later times. Sometimes, the Reformation is seen as a crucial event in this development: "Before, one could manage with a minimum of dogmas. Now, distinctions in the doctrines of the Church(es) became of utmost importance. The progressive intellectualization of the articles of faith drove Protestant theologians into quarrels concerning the interpretation of Luther's teachings." This 'intellectualization' goes hand in hand with the narrowing range of the world picture behind the quarrels. In a general form, Bishop George Berkeley may have had something like that in mind when he wrote: "Few men think, but all insist on having opinions." Berkeley presents this as a general human tendency. I assume it is. Also, in order to suggest the fairly general way in which history enters the picture let me suggest that the way in which such a tendency shows up depends also on characteristic arrangements of knowledge. Thus, Schopenhauer, who quotes the Berkeley phrase, attributes an obsession with disputes, due to a lack of real knowledge, already to the Middle Ages. (This is not a contradiction, but a variation on the Reformation thesis above.) The obsession seems to have been brought under control, though, by elevating Aristotelian logic into the center of all knowledge. Whether correct or not, this would be an example for a configuration of thought not to be found at all times, but not restricted to one short period either. It is clear that this medieval 'solution' of knowledge control could not assert itself

---

8 Similarly, Gehlen has quoted Hannah Arendt to the effect that Hitler was producing a purely imaginary world and less concerned with asserting any specific interests (Gehlen 1973: 119).

anymore today.[9] Whatever configuration for W. B. Yeats' "The Second Coming" (1919) we may assume, we cannot ignore the modern implications of a phrase like "the centre cannot hold" especially in its conjunction with "Things fall apart" (l. 3). These phrases look as if they were comparable to John Donne's "Tis all in pieces, all coherence gone" ("The Anatomy of the World", 1611). But in contrast to the latter, there is no cushioning transcendent(al) faith in Yeats which softens and ultimately neutralizes the fall into incoherence.

The (very) general historical pattern, perhaps I should say: my evolutionary scheme concerning products of thought looks like this: We find *total conceptions* (of human beings and the world, including cosmologies and cosmographies like the great chain of being) mainly from antiquity to the eighteenth century; we meet *Weltanschauungen* as *totalizing efforts* at a comprehensive worldview mainly in the nineteenth century. The plurality of *theories* with greater or smaller range dominates the twentieth century. I interrupt to admit that the history of theory goes back of course to ancient Greece. Yet it seems equally clear that ancient *theoria* represents a life form which, while using thought as its rational basis, preserves visionary elements and the inclusion of *eudaemonia*, that is to say the unfolding of the rational parts of the *soul* which the twentieth century concept has more or less completely lost. *Theoria* is intimately concerned with the orientation of life, theory is not or at best loosely so. Where twentieth century theory ventures into the field of recommendations for action (like Arnold Gehlen's anthropology telling us to let ourselves be consumed by institutions), it is doubtful whether the recommendation really follows from the theory. That is why the twenty-first century can enjoy, but also has to wrestle with what we might call *models of thought* and their implications. Models of thought are risky in a double sense. They enjoy the freedom to sketch *bold* projections, but they also run the *risk* of being dislodged from 'realistic' contexts of action altogether. In its turn, *Weltanschauung* in German implies already a somewhat strained effort to order the world in spite of its resisting complexity.

---

9 For the quote concerning the impact of the Reformation see Borek 2017: 115 (text by Katja Neubauer). The Berkeley phrase occurs in different wordings. I have used www.earlymoderntexts. com/assets/pdfs/berkeley1713.pdf (accessed 04/22/2017). Schopenhauer quotes the sentence ("Few men think; yet all will have opinions") in his *Die Welt als Wille und Vorstellung* (Schopenhauer 1977: vol. 1, 71). This volume has also the thesis on the obsession with disputes in the Middle Ages (82). Concerning the term *Weltanschauung:* There is, as far as I know, one monumental history (Meyer 1947–1950) where the term is used in sovereign and unambiguous fashion for the achievements and less for the liabilities of Western thought. For a modern mixed picture see for instance Joas and Wiegandt 2005. See also fn. 5.

With many other theories I share the conviction that the Western eighteenth century represents the great historical divide which radically changes the fate of the *central problem* of all these types (and the many in between), namely the question if and to what extent these products of thought are able to imply or present *norms and orientations of action*. My overall thesis is that the products of thought have progressively lost that power in the West. The orientation of action is included or taken for granted in total conceptions, it encounters difficulties in *Weltanschauungen*, it is lost more or less in theories and rather more than less in models of thought. Today, it appears therefore that the West, blocked by a huge amount of self-criticism anyway, looks fairly helpless in the many situations in which it is confronted, by groups large and small, with strict demands for social organization and action of one and only one kind. This helplessness becomes all the more conspicuous when such demands are made in the name of a higher, especially religious order. We will encounter this judgment, embodied particularly by Georges Devereux, more often later on. By contrast, Arnold Gehlen (1973: 76 – 77) has described Schopenhauer as the last important philosopher with a "total view" or perception of life (including the life of animals and plants). Gehlen's characterization must be qualified, however, since Schopenhauer's total view does not direct action; it rather contains the strong recommendation to negate the will, that is to say to renounce action as much as possible altogether. Modern efforts to set up total conceptions (theories of everything, grand unified theories and the like) have met more with mockery than with serious discussion. Most of them are restricted to the range of objects normally tackled by physics anyway.

Competitive configurations of products will be analyzed in fairly minute detail. They are embedded in a loose historical framework taken over from E. J. Hobsbawm. He holds that "the revolution which broke out between 1789 and 1848 [...] forms the greatest transformation in human history since the remote times when men invented agriculture and metallurgy, writing, the city and the state. This revolution has transformed, and continues to transform, the entire world." Strictly speaking, Hobsbawm has in mind two revolutions, the rather more political French and the industrial British. Their early phase was thus tied to "a specific social and international situation". But its "long-range results [...] cannot be confined to any social framework, political organization, or distribution of international power and resources". For Hobsbawm, these results consist mainly in the development of capitalist industry and of middle class or 'bourgeois' liberal society propagated ultimately "across the entire world" (Hobsbawm 1962: 1–2). My emphasis will be on cognitive implications relevant for the orientation of action.

In this respect, Hobsbawm's picture translates into a Western world which has given in to a *compensatory need*, severing the justification of action from its older context as part of total conceptions and *Weltanschauungen* and turning them into separate systems of *ethics*. This is an unfortunate situation, because the ensuing plurality of ethical systems cannot really cope with its logical consequence, the plurality and arbitrariness of motivating and legitimizing action. This state of things differs radically from what Arnold Gehlen had in mind when he urged the need for pluralistic ethical projects. Gehlen argued that this pluralism must take at least four levels of ethical or moral relevance into account: ethical norms emerging from relations of mutuality, a number of physiological regulations of behavior including well-being and happiness, ethical forms of behavior related to the family and ultimately extended into global humanitarianism, and the ethical demands of institutions including the state (Gehlen 1973: 47).

This ethical pluralism does not amount to general tolerance; it is rather its opposite. Societies proclaiming general tolerance must assume to have no internal or external enemies or believe that their formulae for appeasement and pacification work sufficiently well. We know meanwhile that this is not the case. In the West, the confusion of ethical pluralism and general tolerance was facilitated and encouraged by the progressive moral disqualification of the state. From there, the transition from tolerance to a "nihilistic acceptance of everything" is easy (Gehlen 1973: 40 with 38–41). Ethics was meant to reintroduce norms of action as a discourse of its own after world picture and action had been severed in the later eighteenth century. This severance is also responsible for the compulsion to invent or reorganize legal discourse (see part II, chap. 4). This necessity, in its turn, explains the frequency of legal discourse in eighteenth-century texts, including those called literature. In recent times, numerous studies have been devoted to this interpenetration. The severance also shows up on other levels, for instance those described in cheerful resignation by Nicholas Mosley who will be examined at greater length in the third part: "My reason tells me what theories are the most possible, the most likely, the most desirable; but it needs more than Reason to put any theory across, it needs a great Faith. And my Reason tells me that it is dangerous to trust in Faith, for how does one know that one's Faith is Right? And so I'm stuck, and likely to remain so." Similarly, even where chains of action, as in the military, are hierarchically ordered, the order of orders is not enough: "(...) what was required was more than a reliance upon orders; it was a two-way trust that had something of the nature of love" (Mosley 2007: 57, 66).

Obviously, ethics, like theory, can and must be traced back to antiquity. For a long time, however, it was plausibly classified as applied anthropology and not as a discourse of its own. Right from the beginning I am thus flaunting my conviction, to be corroborated by evidence later on, that systems of ethics do not heal but rather cement the separation of world pictures and the legitimation of action. Legitimation is then progressively pushed aside by questions of motivation, with disastrous results. The contingency and arbitrariness, the hollowness and ensuing stretchiness of motivation cannot be controlled. For Gehlen, in an analogous development, family morality together with its extension into global humanitarianism have failed. Family morality may be necessary for individual psychic health. But anything possessing "greatness" (state, religion, the art and sciences and even economic life) gained that greatness only after leaving the dimension of the family behind (Gehlen 1973: 93).

Such situations do not need specific historical causes to be brought about; they can be triggered by a lack of logical connection between a world structure, postulated by a product of thought, and the drive towards or necessity of action. Empirically ('historically'), from day to day, cultural life is "short-winded" (Gehlen 1973: 9), marked by what Luhmann has called opaque complexity. Logically and conceptually, total conceptions and *Weltanschauungen* are unstable at any time. Subjecting all or most of what can be called real to their dictates, they inevitably push their claims too far and turn into extravagant or overwrought metaphors of reality. This does not at all rule out shorter or longer periods of stability. The elements, for instance, of the relations between humans and nature, of hunger and food, of mother and child, moon and darkness, the sequence of birth and death impose themselves as a kind of "empirical Apriori". Yet they remain ambiguous because, although touching human life profoundly, they also seem to be independent of it. Their processes seemingly following cycles of their own, we cannot calculate, control and figure them out completely. In spite of the happiness they can offer, they also remain sources of anxiety (Gehlen 1973: 55–56).[10]

The difficulty of the conceptual situation can be exemplified with the term *ideology*, which I have tried to keep out of this book as much as possible. Its conceptual history from a descriptive to a polemical combat term appears to me to be too unfortunate for use. It has become both overly complex and terribly simplistic. For the latter, indeed the dominant trend we just have to think of the usual implication that the ideology is always the doctrine, thought and opinion of the other. Contradictory connotations of the term are remarkable right away in Marx who starts out with the meaning of *Weltanschauung* and then moves away

---

10 More on the promises and threats of basic worldpictures can be found in Gehlen 1975: 164–170. On the transparent/opaque complexity issue see Luhmann 1984: 8–9.

into the murkier regions of false consciousness. (Incidentally, to quite a considerable extent Marxists themselves classify Marxism as a *Weltanschauung* and thereby support my typology.) It is helpful, however, to follow a tendency in conceptualization which sees the totalizing *Weltanschauung* as the *effort*, frequently doomed to obvious failure, to bring a broad range of phenomena, say from the economy to aesthetics, under conceptual control. It is also helpful to keep in mind the fruitful convergences between this typology and the one formulated by Hans Blumenberg in terms of *reality concepts* ("Wirklichkeitsbegriffe"; Blumenberg 1964). My total conceptions will largely be found in what Blumenberg calls reality of momentary evidence and guaranteed reality. To a much reduced degree, they may still float around in his third concept which he calls reality as the realization of a homogeneous context. This type is on its way to *Weltanschauungen*, because, as we will see, *Weltanschauungen* are in most cases marked, in contrast to total conceptions, by efforts and (often obvious) difficulties of construction. Blumenberg's fourth concept, again, reality as resistance, is tied up in various ways with *Weltanschauungen* (if realization requires an obvious effort or is noticeably difficult), but may also be related to the more relativistic atmosphere in which theories and models of thought are couched.[11]

Products of thought are the end result of processes of thought. We therefore have to find ways of connecting these two domains. The first part of the book is supposed to take care of that task. It might appear as one long detour since the evidence which I try to collect from neurobiology, evolutionary anthropology, philosophies of consciousness and literature does not lead to the products in any straightforward way. Yet it has seemed imperative to me to find out how far one can get with what can be called the internal logic of for instance and mainly neurobiology in order to be able to go beyond. The main result (the 'hysterical' or 'schizophrenic' consciousness and its immediate extensions) should reward the trouble. For purposes of illustration, I have inserted confrontations with literary texts along the way.

---

11 For the term conceptions I am indebted to Lovejoy, who uses mostly this term to designate the great chain of being in the preface to his famous book *The Great Chain of Being* (Lovejoy 1936). Unfortunately, the term is somewhat neutral. *Weltanschauung* takes it inspiration from Jaspers (1960), but restricts its historical applicability. Feyerabend has encouraged the idea to use theory as a key form of thought for the twentieth century (see chap. 4, second part), while models of thought were profitably used by Frank Witzel (see chap. 5, second part), but see also, very symptomatically, Adorno 1962: 7, where models of thought are used even for "the so-called great philosophical themes". For both an advocacy of models of thought and a criticism of the tendency towards a "Platonism of models" in economic theory see Albert 1998: 5, 110–142. For the reality concepts see Blumenberg 1964. The present topic will be continued in chapters 3 and 4 of the second part.

The second part exploits the biographical structure of many texts, especially so-called novels, in order to show the hysterical mind at work and to suggest, in the way of the cost-benefit analysis already mentioned, its more than biographical consequences. In order to get an idea of the central problem I am driving at the reader is asked to see the first and second part as a *confrontation:* The more, in the developmental logic of the main products of thought, these lose their overall cognitive and orientating power, the more that power can be and is replaced by the 'hysterical' and 'schizophrenic' forces of consciousness which then can elevate any product, however fragmentary and dogmatic, into a solution (sometimes a final one) for private and public woes. The first part attempts to describe the 'chaotic' workings of consciousness, but also to demonstrate layers of their attractiveness in the fascinating shapes they may gain in the obsessive, mostly 'literary' search for forms in which they can both be contained and display that fascination. The second part, by contrast, emphasizes the 'catastrophic' drift which the products of consciousness take on in the logic of their development. In very different forms, this is a massive problem for most modern societies. In the third part, this confrontation, namely the relations and conflicts between Oswald Mosley and his son Nicholas, is acted out in a *personalized political-religious paradigm.*

Finally, I have thought it appropriate to start out with three preparatory chapters in order not to be plagued with their problems throughout the book: Chapter 1, tacitly abandoning concepts like intentionality, introduces the notion of transitionality and assesses the range of conscious phenomena, thereby drastically limiting the relevance of the unconscious. Chapter 2 plays down the unavoidable oscillation of analyses like the present ones between universal and particular claims. Chapter 3 argues for the necessity of a plurality of competing, but also mutually supportive discourses and therefore for a methodological flexibility which is certainly not generally welcome.

Part I Consciousness Studies: Neurosciences and 'Literature'

1 The Transitionality of Consciousness

Before we can embark on an analysis of products of thought, then, a close and somewhat laborious look at processes is mandatory. We are rarely sufficiently aware that most of our conscious processes do not belong fully and intimately ('authentically') to our mind which seems to – and in fact does – bring them forth. As we will see especially in the third part on Nicholas (and Oswald) Mosley, there appears to be a certain distance, a dimension of alienation (which we could but do not have to attribute to the 'unconscious') built into everything which occupies our brains and minds. It is part of the logic of neurobiology from Julian Jaynes to Edgar Morin to see the mind make up for that alienating distance by charging and investing it affectively with a psychic energy similar to or indeed identical with what in psychopathological terms we would call hysteria. Such theses might strike most people as at least counterintuitive. I therefore want to show that they develop organically, as it were, from the neurobiological and evolutionary logic.

Handling processes of consciousness, tracing their transition into products and controlling these logically and/or historically is made still harder from the outset by two dilemmas. 'Cultural' matters appear soft in kind but they are rigorously universal in the range of phenomena where they play some role. We can normally distinguish them from what appears to impose itself as hard (scientific) facts. Yet upon closer inspection a large part of these facts too, to say nothing of mentalities, seems inextricably shaped by cultural forces. Distinctions must be made, but they are undermined all the time. The dilemma of being compelled both to distinguish and to see distinctions eroding is underpinned by a second cognitive dissonance, indeed a theoretical conflict which will make itself crucially felt throughout the present work. Many contemporary theories, especially varieties of systems theory, tend to assign a merely peripheral position to persons, individuals or, to use a more distinguished term, subjectivity within the domineering framework of social, economic and scientific 'systems'. Individual chances of intervening into, interfering with and perhaps even actively shaping larger processes playing by their own ('self-referential') rules have always been slim. They have diminished, or so it appears to many observers, to the extent that an awareness of the metastatic growth of the systemic control of life has come to rule more or less in undisputed form. Digital control appears as its most recent fashion, reducing constructive individual scopes to anarchic or chaotic episodes.[12]

---

12 Helmut Schoeck (1964: 85) has offered very interesting analyses of the slow, but inexorable

https://doi.org/10.1515/9783110581836-003

But the latest fashion rarely has the last word. Systemic self-reference cannot completely neutralize or eliminate the often so-called subjective or individual factor: In ways however residual or rudimentary, subtle or sophisticated, the self-reference (in former times called for instance the functional or institutional autonomy) of systems depends on some participation of people.

In order to gauge the possible role of subjectivity and individuality, however, we need an access, as good as possible, to consciousness where the energies of subjectivity are being shaped – and destroyed – all the time. To venture into the field of consciousness theory or merely the description of conscious processes and activities, on the other hand, is a very tricky undertaking. Access to our own, to say nothing of other minds is limited and, especially in the case of other minds, almost buried under heaps of speculation. Worse, even non-Freudians today will accept the diagnosis that large parts of our mental life are not enacted in what can reasonably be called consciousness. Ramachandran (2011: 249) simply asserts that "only a limited part of the brain is conscious. The conscious self is not some sort of 'kernel' or concentrated essence that inhabits a special throne at the center of the neural labyrinth, but neither is it a property of the whole brain." Earlier, Julian Jaynes (2000: 23 – 28) had listed, in an otherwise very controversial book, many examples of how little we are conscious of our ordinary behavior (playing the piano, generally the performance of skills, the genesis of scientific discoveries and the mostly unconsciously creative role of the three B's: Bus, Bed, Bath, finally a possible lack of consciousness even in making judgments or simple thinking). In fact, the most glaring omission this book may seem guilty of has to with its neglect of any (Freudian or similar) theory of the unconscious. My problem is just that I do not see how the impact of the 'contents' of the unconscious can be ascertained. In any case, consciousness studies must reckon today with what Tim Bayne has called, in a well-balanced article (Bayne 2015: 2/18), "introspective insecurity", with the difficulties of identifying "phenomenal states" (states that there is "something that it is like") from first-order judgments (like perceptual judgments) and visual imagery to feelings. The pessimist mainly discussed by Bayne, Eric Schwitzgebel, argues that Descartes had it "quite backwards when he said the mind – including especially current conscious experience – was better known than the outside world". In an older terminology, Arnold Gehlen (1973: 16, 18) has spoken of human beings

---

(de)formation of lived experience by social dimensions, indeed sociology itself, and an awareness of it, from at least the eighteenth century onwards.

as a "liquid mass" and of the inextricably involute form in which combinations of concrete things come close to people as their most profound feelings.[13]

It might help in this situation to try and keep Daniel C. Dennett's early precise conceptual work at least somewhere 'in our minds'. Dennett distinguishes and links consciousness and awareness. One could for instance say that we are not aware of the activities of the mind but conscious of the thoughts these produce. This consciousness is clearly targeting the capacity for an awareness newly defined. Dennett admits that his treatment of the term 'aware' may seem to some "like an admission of madness" [14], because he recasts the use of 'aware of' by 'aware *that*' in a double sense in order to make the propositional attitude clearer. 'To be aware that' can then either mean that the object of awareness is the content of somebody's speech perspective or that it can effectively direct current behavior (Dennett 1969: 118–119). The control of behavior is important also for the performance of skills: "We bring activities into awareness, to correct them and improve them. The pianist who keeps fumbling a trill starts paying attention to the particular motions of his fingers when trilling" (124).

This is a nice first example for what henceforth I will call the transitionality of consciousness. Dennett has more of such useful examples: A car driver swerving neatly around an obstacle must have been aware of it, we think. But he may say that (knowing the area well, for instance) he was more aware of the music he was listening to. Table-tennis players have been shown to be more aware of the sound of the ball striking the table than of the sight. But they themselves 'may have no idea' of *that* awareness (115–118). These examples do not refute Jaynes' remarks just quoted but they cut down on their general validity. It is doubtful whether there can be anything else but *ad hoc* conceptual work since the ordinary usage of the two words "is not remotely consistent" (130). Furthermore, I take a recent essay by Kenneth Williford as a confirmation of my point of departure (transitionality) and the very general direction in which it can be brought into concrete shapes. Williford (2015: 2/27 with 22/27) starts with the intuition that phenomenal consciousness is relational (his term for transitional) in

---

13 Bayne's article can be found in Metzinger's and Windt's very important and rewarding online collection of essays. For recent arguments to integrate the unconscious with conscious life and self-conceptions see Böhme 2017: 185–188. My doubts remain.

14 Dennett 1969: 119. Dennett's latest contribution to consciousness studies which I have seen does not contradict that earlier work. See Dennett 2015. See also Fauconnier and Turner 2002: "Conceptual blending operates largely behind the scenes. We are not consciously aware of its hidden complexities, any more than we are consciously aware of the complexities of perception involved in, for example, seeing a blue cup [...] Everyday thought seems straightforward, but even our simplest thinking is astonishingly complex" (v).

some sense (or involves a subject-object polarity). "If we identify the subject with the episode or stream of consciousness itself (however we individuate or ontologize these) and maintain that consciousness is immediately self-aware ("reflexively" aware), then the intuition of relationality and the Humean intuition of the missing subject [Hume's intuition that the subject-relatum is not phenomenologically accessible] can be reconciled." There is no self-entity, but the sense that one is an individual emerges in the self-acquaintance which characterizes the stream of consciousness at any moment.[15]

Consciousness, as Jaynes has said, does not copy experience. But the pressures of what appears as experience, in spite or rather because of introspective insecurity, must be transformed into some conscious form. These forms are productively, some would say: creatively connected not only to language, but also to socioculturally prestructured "vital relations and their compression" (Fauconnier and Turner 2002, chapter 6). We would consequently need a model of consciousness which does justice to the objections against a loose use of the term consciousness, which respects or at least does not deny the restrictions of conscious areas in the brain and which also circumvents the dead-end debates about other minds and the like. We certainly could do worse than exploiting a longer article of Niklas Luhmann for that purpose. Luhmann, grand master of systems theory, has banned individual persons to the periphery of systems in the most determined fashion. But he has also elaborated an intriguing model, in which the phenomenology of consciousness, especially in its self-observational modes, and the participation, via what is normally called socialization in sociology, of individual persons in social processes are made to (appear to) merge.[16]

Consciousness exists as self-transformation. The permanent decay of its basic elements, thoughts (*Gedanken*), especially in their observed forms as ideas (*Vorstellungen*), turns into a prerequisite of its continued existence. Any thought or idea remaining stable in consciousness would overtax its ordering capacities within minutes (Luhmann 1995a: 57, 62). Psycho(patho)logically, I would

---

15 Like all the other papers in this collection that I know, Williford does not and cannot move towards the dramas of consciousness I am interested here, but tries, very impressively, to untangle the (phenomeno)logical knots of his topic. In that respect, see also the introductory article by the editors, Metzinger and Windt 2015: "What Does It Mean to Have an Open MIND?" on intuitions, first-person experience reports, on the energy it probably costs the brain to accept the "intuitive soundness" of a theory it is supposed to accommodate plus the energy it takes to integrate such a theory into our pre-existing models of reality.

16 Luhmann 1995a. This article, presented here in drastically simplified form, omitting especially Luhmann's concern with paradoxes, should be seen in conjunction with Luhmann 1995b and Luhmann 1995c. See 167–168 for the individual-systemic periphery thesis.

add, obsessions, traumata and the like would then loom large. On the other hand, there must occur a "narrowing of choice" (58), making sure that thoughts, ideas and communications find themselves in some meaningful context and do not fall apart into an entropic and meaningless collection of arbitrary and equally valid probabilities (58). The autopoiesis of consciousness, in short, consists in the ongoing production of more or less clear thoughts. The extent of clarity is self-regulated, depending on the needs which thoughts must serve from dozing, daydreaming, working on mathematical formulas or preparing for the transition into communication (61). Communication in particular pushes ahead a certain control of probabilities: It is much slower than the processes of consciousness and therefore makes consciousness aware that it cannot articulate all the more or less clear or vague thoughts and ideas it is agitated by internally (60). Both self-observation and communication, in terms of evolution, must then be taken for granted. In both directions, the ego emerges as the product of self-limitation (70, 72). Referring both to itself and, in communication, to others, consciousness can build up more or less coherent stories which, in situations of pressure, may tempt us to ascribe forms of identity to ourselves and others.

Luhmann assumes that language and consciousness have developed in co-evolution. He can do without the assumption of a linguistic deep structure à la Chomsky. Nor does he have to posit a "language of thought" (Jerry Fodor) underlying and enabling concrete thought processes (76). Repetitions and variations of patterns build up what is called experiences and expectations to which relative senses of routine, success and failure can be attached (78). With increasing complexity, consciousness turns to language for help and then cannot get rid of it anymore. Possibilities of consciousness depending to a large extent on language have played a crucial role for social elites (or those aspiring to that status) and have pushed into being regulations like eloquence, rhetoric, *topoi*, quotations, aphorisms and more, in which consciousness and language seem to merge, in which thought appears to take on crystal-clear forms (81– 82).

Luhmann's essay is of prime importance here because it works with minimal assumptions concerning the form of consciousness (thought, idea, self-observation) and does not privilege any representation of consciousness as correct, adequate or modern. For him, a term like stream of consciousness, coined by William James and elevated by literary critics into the most 'realistic' (re)presentation of consciousness, is indeed misleading, because it obscures the role of self-observation and of communicational pressures, however indirect these may be in situations of individual self-intimacy (65). Before Luhmann, in a fascinating passage belonging to an essay on experience, Arnold Gehlen had tried to stop the overestimation of the stream of consciousness and to prepare the way for essential transitions. At the bottom, in the depths of the stream of consciousness, he said, there must be

> a consciousness, or rather a being with oneself, of a very different kind: an efficient presence of a basis for reactions, of horizons of abilities, of educated instincts of selection and avoidance, a tense readiness for what lies in the direction of our basic interests, and a trained disregard, in thought and feeling, of what we do not want and put on hold, a selective attitudinal norm.[17]

All the relevant terms here (reactions, abilities, instincts, readiness, disregard) refer to energies of changing what appears as basic conscious elements. Likewise, Luhmann's essay, in spite of describing consciousness as an operationally closed system, opens up all kinds of transitions between consciousness and larger 'realities' (cf. the topic of "socialization" from 86 onward). We might indeed overestimate 'literature' which concentrates, especially in its modern forms, so much on the minute (and therefore, people are tempted to assume, real) workings of consciousness. From a systemic perspective, given the many directions and choices which consciousness can use to develop forms of its own coherence, it is rather the distance between psychic and social systems which is characteristic of modernity (Luhmann 1995a: 99–100) – a thesis prefigured, as we will see, by William James in the criticism of his brother's *The Golden Bowl*.

The distance thesis, in its turn, does not give us the complete story either. In Luhmann, this distance is simply and suspiciously taken for granted. There is no sense, critically speaking, that the negotiation of that distance and the self-positioning efforts of the individual do not run along the lines of cool self-observation, but very often take the form of a *drama* (more on that in chapter 6 of part I). Its outcome, a possible impact of the intensity and affective charge of consciousness and the individuality which springs from it, is not all predetermined. For Luhmann, models of the self – fabricated by the joint workings of consciousness, communication and socialization – are simply sold and passed on by one discourse or medium to the next. The notion of a two-part self, for instance, discovered at the end of the eighteenth and fully developed during the last two decades of the nineteenth century, is bought from the novel and adopted by different sciences, especially psychiatry, psychology, social psychology and ultimately psychoanalysis as their own. Such models appear to proliferate in a completely arbitrary way; we seem to have lost any kind of controlling overview (97).

This may be more or less true. Still, one can try to do better than that. Certainly, no human being can be inserted or fitted into social systems so complete-

---

17 Gehlen 1961: 37.

ly that his or her 'reproduction' turns into a social operation performed by society or one of its subsystems. That would be the situation of Aldous Huxley's *Brave New World*. But it is also true that, as Luhmann admits, consciousness has to cooperate in communication. It is further true, as Luhmann does not admit, at least not explicitly, that the self-referential operations of social systems are not always defined in perfect clarity. Consequently, in many cases the cooperation, that is to say the resources and resilience of consciousness take on prime, not to say constitutive importance. They do so particularly once the problem of communicative control, formerly called understanding, gains an almost explosive complexity under the impact of evolutionary advances and media developments like the various writing systems and print.[18]

Beautiful models of dramatic transitionality have been built by Karl Jaspers (Jaspers 1960) into his psychology of worldviews ("Weltanschauungen").[19] The very concept of that psychology is described as a walk along the boundaries of our inner lives, as far as we can understand them (6). We find its sources in an immediate experience always transformed by conflict and consequences, by coming together with other personalities, by being absorbed in "experienced thought" ("erlebtes Denken", 7). The reality of experience, that is the most concrete thing we have, is also the most indefinite, ill-defined and the vaguest of vital possessions (21). Neither subject nor object are transparently given. It is only in mysticism where the paradox of the clarity of the unsayable might occur (21). Most worldviews, emerging in the tensions between experience, attitudes (contemplative, hedonistic, ascetic, aesthetic, rational and so on), types of spirit ('mentalities' like skepticism, nihilism, belief in the infinite) and of situation (boundary situations like fight, death, coincidence, guilt) are therefore shot through with mystic tendencies suppressed or out in the open.

For a striking initial example of two models of consciousness caught in transitional dramas of their own with very different, yet socially relevant results we could look at George Eliot's *Middlemarch* (1872). There is young Dorothea Brooke in whom the dynamics of thoughts and their observation has not yet been channeled into flexible routines. A raw psychic energy ("intensity") is at work which, grasping for abstract ("theoretic", "lofty") conceptions, does not find the stability of form: "For a long while she had been oppressed by the indefiniteness which hung in her mind, like a thick summer haze, over all her desire to make her life greatly effective." Casaubon's proposal of marriage throws her

---

18 Luhmann 1995b: 46 (concerning "immense thrusts in complexity") and 1995c: 166–167.
19 I am grateful to Josef Ludwig for more than just drawing my attention to this strangely important book.

into the rush of a solemn emotion "in which thoughts became vague and images floated uncertainly."[20] The consciousness of the scholarly clergyman Edward Casaubon, by contrast, is filled with and clings to finished, elaborate and seemingly well-ordered products of thought normally called "knowledge" and indeed "complete knowledge" (vol. 1, 17). Its prestige stifles the energy of dynamic self-observation. Casaubon keeps investing all his limited energies into the writing of a "Key to all Mythologies". Given what appears to others as Casaubon's sterility of mind and weakness of body (he develops heart disease), given also the dubious reputation of mythologies as collections of arbitrary stories, most readers of Eliot's text have had no trouble in predicting both the failure of marriage and of the mythological enterprise.

---

20 Eliot 1961: vol. 1, 2, 20, 34.

2 Universalism *vs.* Particularism

Dorothea's and Casaubon's modes of thought (with Dorothea a transitory one only) and the products of thought they mainly think with should also be seen as descendants of two old and basic orientations of thought. Given the many relations and affinities between elements of the same and of different kinds, consciousness often tends to become universalist. Confronted with what might also appear as an untamable diversity, thought is also tempted, however, to emphasize distinction, difference, empirical variety, multifariousness. It would appear that there are correlations between universalist modes and older products of thought like total conceptions and *Weltanschauungen* as well as between particularism and the more recent forms of theories and models of thought. But the impact of universalism and particularism on the functional logic of products of thought is difficult to assess. Their appearance is not historically determined. It might be best to view them as auxiliary programs weakening or strengthening the functional logic of products of thought. Since they will not be built systematically into the following analyses, a few comments here might be in order.

In *Middlemarch*, the failures of marriage and mythology duly happen. However: The irrelevance of mythologies in a broad sense as hegemonic, but illusory forms of knowledge is not at all established. To study mythologies, as Schelling's *Philosophie der Mythologie* (lectures published in 1856/57) tried to demonstrate in an effort not at all very different from Casaubon's, can amount to an awareness of their crucial role as figures of hidden, but universal philosophical truths.

Casaubon, more or less like Schelling, holds "that all the mythical systems or erratic mythical fragments in the world were corruptions of a tradition originally revealed. Having once mastered the true position [...], the vast field of mythical constructions became intelligible, nay luminous with the reflected light of correspondences" (Eliot 1961: vol. 1, 16). The twentieth and twenty-first centuries, in any case, have provided ample scope for the impulse to order processes of consciousness into bodies of knowledge with far-reaching claims and remarkable pathos. Our times have pushed ahead with the ambition, in Matthew Arnold's famous and slightly changed words, to see life steadily and to see it whole (cf. "To a Friend", 1849). The urge to catch and gather as much knowledge as possible and to *unify it in some coherent whole seems hard to quench*. Nicholas Mosley, whose work will be examined at length towards the end, called that the necessity "to see [reality] as a whole" if one was to understand it (Mosley 1991: 31).

In that noble enterprise, however, the risk to produce mythologies not in the shape of at least potentially universal knowledge but rather as scientific fiction

https://doi.org/10.1515/9783110581836-004

has drastically increased. Expanding its hegemony, science has also become liable to fall prey to its own standards and criteria. Unifying movements like physicalism or the supreme ambition of an *Einheitswissenschaft*, eagerly pursued as new models of rationality in the early twentieth century, quickly succumbed to the fiction-critical mythological suspicion. They did not stand, or so it appears, the slightest chance against the explosion, at more or less the same time, of pluralism in the sciences, in other discursive fields and even more so in the arts of the early twentieth century. Even in the universalizing discipline *par excellence*, philosophy, the impression has been hard to avoid that an anarchy of approaches has swept away not only universality, but even the modest claim of a convergence or relatedness of knowledge interests like the mapping of fields and 'interests' of knowledge in Habermas' conception of "Erkenntnisinteressen".[21]

And yet, for quite a while, we have been witnessing something like a physicalism *redivivus*, with universalizing tendencies, in what could certainly count as a contemporary core science – in neurobiology, more particularly in its special form as brain research. In fact, both in socio- and in neurobiology, we witness even more – the old ambition to procure and impart conclusive knowledge concerning a universal idea about human nature.[22] Neurobiology, as many of its practitioners have written and as one of its foremost representatives in Germany, Wolf Singer, re-emphasized to me in an interview, could not exist without the assumption that each and any conscious event (to say nothing of unconscious events) presupposes a material basis. Neurobiology has not yet found out precise correlations between material basis and conscious acts or processes. But the hope or the assumption is that it will one day.[23] That assumption has provoked

---

21 Cf. for an early example, Kröner 1929: 262 (Carnap on philosophy as poetry), 311–312 (Simmel likewise on philosophical systems as "quasi-aesthetic formations"). It comes as no surprise that Kröner isolated himself with this work, that he could not publish his Habilitationsschrift which, in its turn as an "essay in the logic of philosophy", tried to find its own way toward (re)unification. In her study on Freud, Conrad and Ford Enderwitz points out that Ford in particular might still have seen life steadily, but could not see it whole anymore. The mass of details craving for attention makes it impossible to see the figure in the carpet (Enderwitz 2015: 124).
22 Two examples must suffice here. For sociobiology see Wilson: 2004, for neurobiology Ramachandran 2011.
23 Singer is very careful. His most recent contribution is remarkable for two strong theses: (1) The more data ever more sophisticated tools will supply us with, "the more we are humbled by the mind-boggling and no longer intuitively graspable complexity of the brain's dynamics." (2) There are quite a few functional and evolutionary reasons which would argue for an increase of our fitness to live in a complex world with and through extended conscious processes. See Singer 2015: 22/30 – 31, 26/30.

others not so convinced into (re)launching a countermovement. That counter-movement has embraced diversity. But it also keeps paying tribute to the reunification of diversity in universal forms. Andrew L. Gluck, for one, grants physical monism for the natural sciences but insists upon a mind-body dualism for the social sciences which respects the phenomenological, that is non-material (mental, spiritual and similar) self-experience of consciousness. For that school, the materiality thesis is incapable of accounting for the ways in which subjective inner worlds, an experienced inner life are generated by the processing of a lump of neuronal sludge.

The dynamics and the tensions between competing universalizing world-views, between an appreciation of empirical diversity and the larger design in which diversity might be absorbed and brought to rest in universal structures have been beautifully and suggestively analyzed by Karl Jaspers in his psychology of worldviews already exploited. We encounter, Jaspers boldly asserted, the best philosophers, that is those concerned with both concrete and universal cognition, those reaching out for the universal by plunging fully into the concrete, we encounter them no longer within the ranks of professional philosophy, but rather in those excellent specialists who are driven into concrete universality or universal relatedness ("allseitig[e] Beziehungen der Erkenntnis [...] immer konkret") because the masterful investigation of what appears as empirical and concrete is replete with universal suggestions. Unfortunately, as Jaspers also saw, this drive often transforms itself into a form of theoretical absolutism. That transformation has found its most typical expressions in forms of materialism and spiritualism (Jaspers 1960: 2, 198–199. Cf. 1–4).

Both neurobiology and most of its critics illustrate and confirm Jaspers' position very clearly. Yet both suffer from equally obvious gaps. Neurobiology is haunted by a crucial *explanatory gap*. Gerald Edelman, who was one of its most prominent representatives, has provided a succinct characterization:

> The issue concerns the so-called explanatory gap that arises from the remarkable differences between brain structure in the material world and the properties of qualia-laden experience. How can the firing of neurons, however complex, give rise to feelings, qualities, thoughts, and emotions? Some observers consider the two realms so widely divergent as to be impossible to reconcile. (Edelman 2004: 11–12)

The "consciousness people", as Gluck occasionally likes to dub them, are plagued in their turn by what I would like to call *descriptive gaps*. One may grant, with the restrictions on consciousness areas and events mentioned before, an "ineluctable modality" (James Joyce) of inner, non-material consciousness. But that experience is far from offering itself with the transparency we might and normally do wish for. Consequently, the consciousness people often turn to "art, poetry, music, and other non-scientific disciplines", because these appear to have "the potential to reveal much about human consciousness".[24] Ironically, turning to the arts for help is precisely what the neurobiological materiality people (my term) also like to do. Jaspers saw both descriptive and explanatory gaps in most worldviews as well as the efforts of wiping them out by techniques of "Verabsolutierung" (making absolute) very clearly. He therefore acknowledged the need to build "images of totality" not only by adopting "rational", but also "intuitive" and "aesthetic" attitudes.[25] Jaspers did not bother about the question which types of discourse might live up to such expectations.

The need for images of totality has been felt by adherents and opponents of neurobiology, too. Both groups, indeed, arguing from and into opposed universal directions, align themselves with the grand universal claims which have been made for so-called poetry for instance by P. B. Shelley, for a somewhat broader array of textual kinds for instance by R. W. Emerson, or for a fairly narrow one for instance by J. G. Fichte. Shelley nominated poets as the unacknowledged legislators of the world (see chapter 6), Emerson presented authors from Plato via Shakespeare down to Swedenborg as the lawgivers of mankind, Fichte reserved that role for the "Gelehrte", a kind of combination of philosopher, scholar and scientist.

Aristotle elevated the universality of 'literary' fictions above the particularity of history. Many more names advocating one or the other variety of such universal claims could be proffered. But the evidence for contrary positions, banishing universalisms of all kinds into the curiosity shop of cultural and intellectual history, has been accumulating in even more massive form. The overall situation is blurred. Paul Johnson, in his often scathing criticisms of intellectuals, despises Shelley the man but remains deeply respectful of his poetry, of plays like *The Cenci* and, above all, of *A Defence of Poetry*, in which the legislator claim is staked (see below chap. 6). The most striking statement to my mind, however, has come from Jaspers again. In another seminal book of his which has become and remained a basic text of and for psychiatry, Jaspers disputed the materiality

---

24 Gluck 2007: 87. See xix, 13, 24, 46, 86 (I have followed the title page for the title and subtitle of Gluck's book. The front cover changes the subtitle into "An Inquiry into Epistemology, Metaphysics, and Consciousness". I hope this is not a bad omen for consciousness.) The Joyce quote is from *Ulysses* where the very beginning of chapter 3 insists on the "[i]neluctable modality of the visible: at least that if no more, thought through my eyes". The relationship between consciousness and the visible or other 'mediating agents' will have a strong impact on the arguments developed here.
25 Cf. Jaspers 1960: 64–76 for intuitive, aesthetic and rational attitudes, 181–182 for "Verabsolutierung".

thesis for conscious processes in his own way. The knowledge of and insights into consciousness in particular presuppose a peculiarly universal experience: the experience of great literature and great human beings. The ancient Greek tragic writers, Shakespeare, Goethe, but also and especially Blaise Pascal should be taken for granted as pillars of human universality. Their attraction is indeed such that neurobiologists too exploit their appeal in order to fill up their explanatory gaps. Gerald Edelman, for one, has used a quote from Pascal concerning the meaning of body and spirit and their interaction as the guiding perspective in his early neurobiological "reconsiderations".[26] Fallbacks on poetry, literary or literary-philosophical texts may be performed from all kinds of motives; they may be made, for instance, to demonstrate one's superior education. The point to be made here and throughout, however, is that a professional, whether scientist, scholar or so-called creative writer, who wants to be a good professional in a special field, must have a command of more than just his own professional discourse in order to play his professional role well.

To the tensions between universalism and particularism we must add matters of cultural relativity. Clearly, the whole cast of this book betrays a strong Western bias. This bias does not impinge on the phenomenology of consciousness. There is little reason to assume that the coming and going of ideas, that the fleeting quality of conscious events differs culturally in any significant way. Differences will crop up in the ways in which the dynamics of the inner life is transformed into products of thought. Such differences are related both to the peculiar built-up of the products as well as to their function within a culture. Thus Max Weber assumed strong ties between the economic system and the religious worldview of great cultures; he also thought that, depending on the drive of the economic system, the worldviews were exposed to peculiar pressures which either supported their stability or, for better or worse, tore them apart. Capitalism, Weber says, has existed for a long time almost everywhere. Nowhere has it exercised the same power of transforming social structures and the (originally religious) worldviews as in the European countries and areas of Calvinist economic activity.[27] At various other points, Eastern and Southern cultures experienced these pressures too. But Europe and the USA were the pioneers (also pio-

---

26 Johnson 1988: 28–29. For Emerson's essay on Swedenborg see Ahlstrom 2004: 1019. Fichte expounded his views on the fundamental role of the "Gelehrte" in various lectures between 1794 and 1811. For Jaspers, see Jaspers 1946: 261–262, 631, for Edelman see Edelman 1992: 65. In this book, Edelman uses quotes from all kinds of sources (newspapers, poetry, philosophy) as mottos for each chapter. But how are we supposed to understand them (as equivalents, illustrations, clarifications, variations, or alternatives)?
27 See Weber n. d.: 30–32.

neers of victimization) and pushed ahead with a – for some time – unique structural dynamics. That is also why their products of thought demonstrate the logic of development best. They came into being for specific historical and social reasons. But once the period of a relatively concrete anchoring in historical and social or religious grounds was over, their development followed primarily an inner structural logic. In the English eighteenth century, for instance, economic awareness infiltrates products of thought which, like Adam Smith's *The Wealth of Nations* and *The Theory of Moral Sentiments* could be described both as *Weltanschauung* or as theories. They display a comprehensiveness of analysis in psychological, moral, social and economic respects no longer really available to a contemporary author. Consequently, they were superseded by other specimens of its kind with a speed and in quantities not really warranted by the actual economic developments themselves. Ultimately, that type of product, having lost sight of standards of action long ago, came to be repeatedly overthrown by waves of severe economic crisis. Cultures, in which total conceptions of the world, including the place of human action in it, survived longer than in the West, do not, however, appear to have fared much better. The longer total or universal conceptions seemed to work, the more drastically they broke apart under the onslaught of competing or antagonistic Western models.

One comparative case will illustrate my general point sufficiently. I select Japan because most observers here have been struck by take-overs of (other Eastern and) Western thought and a stubborn, sometimes even enhanced (impression of) otherness which is often identified with the longevity of traditions. In Masao Maruyama's classical model of "thought in Japan" those traditions take on ambivalent features right away. In Japan, Maruyama has said, there is in fact no mental/spiritual/intellectual tradition which might function as a point of crystallization or coordinate axis relating and connecting the ideas of different periods. Thought and ideas are not accumulated as traditions; what is called traditional thought is hardly tangible and can re-enter the present in very unsystematic ways. Take-overs depend on the idiosyncrasies of the present or rather the person assuming that she or he adopts something for her or his purposes. This is especially true also for the extremely haphazard imports of Western set pieces of thought. Nor did any native religion, be it Shinto, Buddhism or Confucianism establish itself as a coordinate axis of thought. (By contrast, Confucianism, reduced to a catalogue of duties and virtues, was well able to regulate everyday behavior to a considerable extent.) Some have ventured to say that the imperial house – empty as far as ideas or an ideology are concerned, but capable of exercising an auratic binding power even today – provides the only possible axis of orientation. In any case, the European idea that the world was created by an absolute God following a certain plan, that the religious monotheistic doctrine was secularized and transformed into an elaborate system of law and bureaucracy, with further transformations following – all of that looks somewhat alien to the Japanese mind even if one can be sure to find the very same ideas somewhere in more isolated forms also in Japan.[28] This does not exclude, it rather encourages the regulation of everyday life. It should also explain to a large extent the situation, strange for Westerners, that a fetishization of institutions can coexist with the pretense of natural behavior, genuine feelings or simply human nature.

We dispose of various possibilities to lay out this picture in greater detail and differentiation. One is to see the lack of a coordinate axis of thought leading to an intensified emotional charge of specific places and times. Augustin Berque speaks of Japanese as a lococentric language. Japanese people, especially if abroad, therefore need a larger amount of information about their actual environment than Westerners would think they need for themselves. The assumption is that the information can be simply given and does not need interpretation in the mind of the person who needs it. The meaning of an action resides in the performance of the action. It is not hidden in some higher reason or theory. We are confronted, overarched by the iron contrast between monotheism and an ill-defined polytheism, not with a discursive, but with a "presentative" logic in which the structure of social ties (mostly according to Confucianism) and the functional-aesthetic complex of things enjoy priority. The presentative logic has been beautifully and convincingly related to the functional-aesthetic complex normally called a thing, whether natural or technological, and its cultural locus by Peter Pörtner. He holds that an overabundance of colors, materials, accessories, of breaks and shocks, of combinations normally seen as incompatible guides the local construction of reality. Consequently, Japanese culture never needed and did not develop anything like an *art-pour-l'art* movement. There is no very clear separation between the appearance of things and its supposed meaning. The enigmatic re-ontologization of things in Rilke moves back into suggested metaphysical dimensions too far. In sum, the lack of one or several coordinates of thought and the suggestions of thing-embodied materials do not demand products of thought like a theory always in danger of being superseded by another one in which such phenomena would be situated and interpreted.[29]

---

28 Maruyama 1988: 14, 23, 29, 31, 44, 45, 56, 65.
29 For the sources of these meandering remarks see Berque 1986: 25, 32, 36; Heise 1989: 79, 94; Pörtner 2000: 212, 217–220.

In periods of personal or historical-political stress, the lack of coordinates may lead to weird combinations of chaotic thought and catastrophic behavior. Both tendencies, marked by racism and other heavy 'ideologies' on the one, by savage aggression on the other hand, have asserted themselves in Japan *with relative ease* in the development towards the attack on Pearl Harbor, but also, in different, pseudo-idealistic orientations, after the defeat in World War II. Accordingly and understandably, the behavior and the way of argument of Japanese politicians have been denounced as an "utterly futile game of passing the buck", as "the idiocy of protecting one's own and institutional positions" having gone "much too far", or as dealings having "turned into a bigger farce, courage utterly and devastatingly missing."[30] The price paid for such a farce was high, much too high.

---

30 These are somewhat vague accusations, borne out, however, in minute detail in books like Hotta 2013: e.g. 195, 204 (quotes) and Dower 1999.

3 Patterns of Consciousness, Language, Discourse

The transitionality of consciousness on the one and the pulls and pressures of universalisms and diversity claims on the other hand will drive the following analyses in a continuous back and forth movement between different discourses trying to capture the dynamics and the momentum, both strong and elusive, of such elements. My argument will cautiously circle around the relative potentials of discursive forms in which the life of consciousness gains pregnant shapes and ultimately translates into larger-format products.

I use neurobiology in order to open up strong perspectives and texts mostly called literary in order to illustrate the dynamics, perhaps even a kind of logic of transitionality. Neurobiology does not lay down the law, but must be respected as a (perhaps the) paradigmatic modern science not to be ignored.

Consciousness does not present itself in any kind of unadulterated being. What is at stake, then, in the huge shifting mass of writing and of textual codes in which thought manifests itself is not so much representation but orientating power. Whatever can be written, for instance, can also be written in a different way. Any text is deficient, especially any text portraying consciousness, insofar as it points, however indirectly, to alternative versions. That does not mean that texts are equally valid illustrations of one another. Rather, they enter into relations of competition or necessary supplementarity. Hermann Lang, amongst other things the foremost German authority on Lacan, for instance, appears to take the words of Malcolm to Macduff in *Macbeth* for the best description of the psychotherapeutic process: "Give sorrow words; the grief, that does not speak, / Whispers the o'er-fraught heart, and bids it break" (4.3.209 f.). In similar fashion, Melvin Konner declared quite some time ago "that the 'humour' metaphor of the Elizabethans [was] intrinsically [!] closer to the truth as we understand it than was the 'drive' metaphor of the early twentieth century." In an even riskier vein he surmised that Burton's seventeenth century notion of melancholia might need "reviving".[31] But would these two authorities be similarly prepared to privilege, say, the poetic diction of the eighteenth century as a necessary supplement for science? Certainly also, the discursive power of one and the same text can vary tremendously, and so will its cogency and usefulness for other texts and purposes. I might cite for instance Tennyson's

---

31 Lang 2015: 125; Konner 1982: 103, 337. Konner's second edition (2003) maintains the humour thesis explicitly and the Burton thesis by implication.

https://doi.org/10.1515/9783110581836-005

In Memoriam with its many passages close to evolutionary theory, but also with its many falls into empty or sentimental rhetoric. One might appreciate the mixture of sobriety and latent despair in the language which Hume used in order to depict the delirium of pure thought. But should we accept or even prefer the interior monologues of Stephen Dedalus and Molly Bloom in Joyce's *Ulysses* as relevant representations of the ways of consciousness? A passage in Edelman concerning one "extraordinary phenomenal feature of conscious experience" would seem to endorse Joyce:

> Any experienced conscious moment simultaneously includes sensory input, consequences of motor activity, imagery, emotions, fleeting memories, bodily sensations, and a peripheral fringe [...] Yet, at the same time, one unitary scene flows and transform itself into another complex but also unitary scene. Alternatively, it can shift into diffuse reverie or into high focal attention by choice or under stress.[32]

This sounds very much like the famous descriptions of the "stream of thought" and its "irreducible pluralism" in William James' *The Principles of Psychology*: "[...] the mind is at every stage a theatre of simultaneous possibilities". Or, quoting Hume: "The mind is a kind of theatre where several perceptions successively make their appearance, pass, re-pass, glide away and mingle in an infinite variety of postures and situations. There is properly no *simplicity* in it at one time, nor *identity* in different."[33] In literary studies, the stream-of-consciousness technique in modern novels by Edouard Dujardin, Leo Tolstoy, James Joyce and beyond was frequently seen as an illustration or indeed application of James' characterization, as the most advanced and therefore perhaps the most adequate mode of representing consciousness. James, however, in passages immediately following the above quote, takes Hume to task for pouring out the baby with the bath, that is to say for overdoing the diversity and neglecting the mixture of diversity and unity in the conscious mind. Hume was indeed, at least for some time, an expert for the falls into delirium and chaos, their result being melancholy, which consciousness was prone to take if not hedged in by 'external' constraints and controls of some sort.

The stream of consciousness does not mirror the workings of consciousness; it does not provide us with *the* realistic or authentic picture of these workings as such. James himself clearly, if sometimes indirectly, assumes that his "stream of thought" is, to a large extent, the product of or related to modern subjectivity and

---

32 Edelman 2004: 61. One could glean similar characterizations from the writings of many neurobiologists.
33 James 2015: 137, 170, 209. I have altered the Hume quotation according to Hume 1978: 253.

its intensified, indeed compulsive forms of self-observation. As soon as the mind concentrates largely upon itself, none of the elements (thoughts, feelings etc) it brings forth can gain a stable identity – consciousness observing itself does not really observe identifiable elements, but rather elements slipping away: "A permanently existing 'idea' or 'Vorstellung' which makes its appearance at the footlights of consciousness at periodical intervals, is as mythological an entity as the Jack of Spades" (James 2015: 143). That is of course why the notion of a stream of thought makes sense. On the other hand, again criticizing Hume, James opts for the continuity of consciousness. We can make connections between thoughts entertained at different times, interrupted for instance by sleep (James 2015: 146 – 147). Again, one would assume, connections between clear thoughts, vague ideas, memories, feelings, will often aspire to something like a structure, will yield units or even unities.

Such formations of patterns of consciousness, eventually identifiable, analyzable by (scientific) discourses which they also challenge, will normally emerge under the pressure of evolutionary and cultural factors. We do not have to decide about the truth nor even the adequacy of the patterns under more or less specific circumstances. But we need to appreciate, as I said above, their orientating power and to assess their relevance with respect to human self-observation. The pluralism of patterns is thereby not abolished. But without efforts towards profile (my replacement for hierarchy) a chaos would loom large or be restored, in which "Nor *human* Spark is left, nor Glimpse *divine!*" (Alexander Pope, *The Dunciad*, IV.652). The transformation of thought into discourse would be blocked. Saying this, I do not at all intend to rekindle the old quarrel of whether there can be thought without language. From the outset, observational difficulties, compounded by conceptual oscillations and uncertainties, tend to undermine any effort to reach a reasonably undisputed decision. The distinction between thought and discourse, by contrast, appears to be called for. Discourses are fairly well-regulated and higher-order forms of language; thoughts being free, as the saying goes, may be influenced by, but need not follow discourse rules. On the other side, discourse bears the imprint of thought. That is why a concept like 'style of thought' makes sense, although it can refer, strictly speaking, only to the language before our eyes in which thought appears somehow to be couched. Discourse is (used as) an index to thought; we cannot help drawing conclusions from the one to the other. Within his 'genres', the poetic-dramatic discourses in Shakespeare, for instance, resemble each other quite a lot. But the resemblance hides and betrays enormous differences in styles of thought. Some of those demonstrate a perfect fusion of descriptive-metaphorical accuracy, suggestiveness and evocative power, others do not. Some of his characters, even among those ordinarily classified as great, are capable of little more than manic-depressive rant against a backdrop of confused or chaotic thought. In *2Henry IV,* West-moreland is perfectly justified in rebuking Mowbray's thought by rejecting his language: "You speak, Lord Mowbray, now you know not what" (4.1.128). The Archbishop of York applies the same procedure to himself: "Hear me more plainly" (4.1.65). Studies in Shakespeare's imagery have set up highly variable profiles in that respect.

We reach a further level of complexity if we go back to the questions of discursive competition and supplementarity introduced at the beginning of this chapter. To some extent, that complexity has been brought under control by older insights into the literary quality of (some) scientific texts and the scientific relevance of (some) literary texts, into the relations between 'literature' and especially scientific 'knowledge'. Also, my argument will exploit a built-in drive of discursive forms toward at least a semblance of autonomy, and it will profit from the almost universal presence of narrative and dramatic modes (even in science). I also follow Damasio in his distinction between mere poetic fancy and poetic accuracy, in his readiness to grant Proust or Bach special abilities in the building and rebuilding of powerful forms of autobiographical selves and thus to make up for the deficits of scientific language. All of this will help, but it will not help enough.[34]

In any case, general claims for any type of discourse, while being made all the time, will have to be managed with care. The sheer multiplicity of possible textual forms for shaping, catching or suggesting states of mind is simply bewildering, freedom of choice appears boundless. Also, the tension between prelinguistic and language levels in the construction of phenomenological self-experience will not go away. That tension, however, seems to make the choice and style of discourse more and not less important. Many forms chosen have disappeared or died out quickly. Consequently, if we admit, following for instance Edgar Morin (see chapter 5), that the complexity of brain activities amounts to a massive overproduction and culminates in an intense overinvestment of imaginative/imaginary materials, we must try to filter out forms of language and discourse which bring these materials into significant shape. I would like to illustrate my intentions, at this point, with a few remarks concerning Samuel Richardson's *Clarissa* (1757). This work has been repeatedly hailed as a masterpiece. Embedded in the characters' agitated minds, we encounter analytical passages concerning human affectivity in the context of morality in particular saturated with both intensity and investigative strength. In these respects, it is one of the greatest texts (texts! not primarily or even not at all novels) of perhaps not only the eigh-

---

34 See Damasio 2010: 36, 161, 211.

teenth century. These passages are frequently better, that is more sophisticated and more to the point than many so-called philosophical texts on the same topics. This applies, I maintain, to the analysis of emotions in Adam Smith's main works or even occasionally Hume's investigation of the 'passions'. The status of *Clarissa* as a conceptually complex and narratively dramatic (again: not primarily literary) text has been correctly and clearly described by Terry Eagleton:

> Richardson's novels, then, are not only or even primarily literary texts: they entwine with commerce, religion, theatre, ethical debate, the visual arts, public entertainment. They are both cogs in a culture industry and sacred scripture to be reverently conned. In short, they are organizing forces of what, after German political theory, we may term the bourgeois 'public sphere'.[35]

At the same time, the sheer length of this text (about 1500 pages) indicates that the descriptive-analytical problem Richardson had taken on could not be adequately handled within the official semantic framework of morality, family values, duties like honor, esteem, pride and the like. In *Clarissa*, Richardson presents consciousness in what appears as a series of fairly still well-ordered, but affectively highly-charged conceptual frames. The length of this text indicates that the conceptual ordering of emotions and/as social values could hardly be reconciled any more with normative biographical expectations. The semantic framework of morality, family values and duties, of love respecting honor and presupposing esteem is in constant danger of being undercut or overwhelmed by the incomparable dynamics of a consciousness occupied with adjusting accepted moral concepts to the unsavory violence of envy and its relatives like jealousy and resentment. In contrast to the seemingly manageable stability of the other terms, envy and its relatives are apt to wander and glue themselves to continuously changing objects and persons As a set of ideas (an 'ideology'), the framework of values can still be intelligibly quoted and referred to; as a control of consciousness and individual orientation it is turning progressively into a failure, because it cannot keep pace with the erosive mobility of money, work and social relations. In such a situation, the use of the term "pride" is symptomatic. Like many other concepts, it binds together shifting portions of personal emotion and social norm. But since situations, engineered by the inventive Lovelace, change all the time in unforeseeable ways, the meaning of pride, especially in its personal aspect, follows suit. It changes according to the situational challenges and provocations, in which the resilience of self-interpretations is tested. Clar-

---

35 Eagleton 1982: 6. For the following quotes from *Clarissa* see Richardson 2004: 560 – 561, 592, 695, 698, 868, 1301.

issa rejects for instance "a dirty low pride" which, as she sees it, has swallowed up Lovelace's "*true* pride", a pride capable of elevating him above his vanity. On the following page, she criticizes pride as such as a sign of weakness. Moreover, she interprets the generosity of Lovelace as a product of "his *pride* and his *vanity*"; her own attitudes and decisions, she claims by contrast, are derived from her principles. On the other side, she recognizes a "laudable pride (a pride worthy of his birth, of his family, and of his fortune". In his turn, Lovelace attributes a form of pride to Clarissa far surpassing his own. On other occasions he declares pride in women to be a surrogate emotion usurping the place of a feminine nature no longer available. Richardson breaks out of this conceptual dead end with the help of death as a narrative end: He shifts attention to the theatrical-emotional turmoil with which the death, unnecessary on almost all counts, of Clarissa is staged as a long-drawn out dying process. This turmoil has nothing to do with the hallmark of the text: its descriptive-analytical sophistication with respect to the dynamics of (self-)conscious affectivity in a clearly delineated, but no longer rigidly organized social space. In such ways, the early history of the British novel, that is narration as invented 'fiction', acquires liabilities for a fall into the fictitiousness of the problem represented itself. The very length of the text, threatening not so much to lose itself in the fictionality of the narrative but rather in the fictitiousness of represented problems cries out for 'counter-discourses' amply supplied in what literary terminology classifies as parody.

4 James, James and the Structure of Fluctuations

For an introduction to what is at stake here, there is an even more telling example. It is methodologically difficult, but still worth the risk, to compare the descriptions of consciousness and its workings in the works of William and Henry James. Both have a go at consciousness as process and at its products and therefore should supply us with paradigmatic models of transitionality. It has been frequently said that Henry wrote novels like a psychologist while William wrote psychology texts like a novelist. That opinion is neither to be taken literally nor lightly. William is more into the analysis of general mechanisms in consciousness, Henry into the representation of various concrete forms. But there are rapprochements. William defines one essential part of his enterprise, at the beginning of chapter 8 of his *The Principles of Psychology* (1890), as the "study of the mind from within". The two crucial features in this respect consist in the constant change of thought, but also, within each personal consciousness, in a "sensibly continuous" character of thought.

> Consciousness, then, does not appear to itself chopped up in bits. Such words as 'chain' or 'train' do not describe it fitly as it presents itself in the first instance. It is nothing jointed; it flows. A 'river' or a 'stream' are the metaphors by which it is most naturally described. *In talking of it hereafter, let us call it the stream of thought, of consciousness, or of subjective life.* But now there appears, even within the limits of the same self, and between thoughts all of which alike have this same sense of belonging together, a kind of jointing and separateness among the parts, of which this statement seems to take no account. I refer to the breaks that are produced by sudden *contrasts in the quality* of the successive segments of the stream of thought. (James 2015: 145)

While William is famous for the vivid style he brought to philosophy and science, he clearly experiences difficulties in his somewhat lame or overly poetic efforts to create convincing ('concrete') contours to the inside dynamics of the mind.

> We wonder how we ever could have opined as we did last month about a certain matter. We have outgrown the possibility of that state of mind, we know not how. From one year to another we see things in new lights. What was unreal has grown real, and what was exciting is insipid. The friends we used to care the world for are shrunken to shadows; the women, once so divine, the stars, the woods, and the waters, how now so dull and common; the young girls that brought an aura, of infinity, at present hardly distinguishable existences; the pictures so empty; and as for the books, what was there to find so mysteriously significant in Goethe, or in John Mill so full of weight? (James 2015: 141–142)

https://doi.org/10.1515/9783110581836-006

In crude ways, this may serve as an evocation of consciousness changing all the time. By contrast, William has a much harder time suggesting what the sensibly continuous nature of consciousness might consist in. His 'story' for instance about Peter and Paul sleeping in the same bed and connecting to their selves before sleep I find altogether too obvious, not to say banal (2015: 145). His conclusion smacks of scholastic tautology:

> Let us call the resting-places the 'substantive parts,' and the places of flight the 'transitive parts,' of the stream of thought. It then appears that the main end of our thinking is at all times the attainment of some other substantive part than the one from which we have just been dislodged. And we may say that the main use of the transitive parts is to lead us from one substantive conclusion to another. (James 2015: 146)

In an extended discussion of the fundamental cognitive role of relations and of the feelings it takes to perceive them, James, quoting de Cardaillac, appears to suggest implicitly where the most convincing of the interrelatedness of relations and feelings are to be found: "What is taste in the arts, in intellectual productions? What but the feeling of those relations among the parts which constitutes their merit?" (James 2015: 176)

Here, certainly the art and intellectual productions of Henry James come into play. In his texts, the unending arrangement and rearrangement of relations bathed in feelings gains manifold forms of provisional coherence. Kinds of selves (material, social, spiritual self, empirical me, pure ego) become apparent, but they do not acquire the somewhat substantialist quality with which William endowed them in chapter 10 of his *Principles* devoted to "The Consciousness of Self" – a slightly misleading title, because, as the terms for the types of self indicate, the emphasis is not so much on consciousness any more. William is aware that he is dealing with "a fluctuating material" (James 2015: 181). It now appears that psychology, or for that matter philosophy, cannot really elucidate the *structure of these fluctuations*. This would seem to be the job of Henry's texts. However, the task is a risky one because the structure depends especially on the substantive parts which enter into play. Depending on what they are, they may ultimately amount to rigid dogmas at the one, volatile imaginings at the other extreme. Henry's texts do indeed reveal to what extent those factors which create reality for an individual as meaningful relations have been reduced from values, norms or convictions (to say nothing of total conceptions or *Weltanschauungen*) to ('mere') feelings. I propose therefore to confront William's *Principles* (1890) with two well-known texts by Henry. *The Portrait of a Lady* (1881) and *The Golden Bowl* (1904) exert, as it were, cognitive pressure on the *Principles*. Conversely, William's psychology might have its own lessons for literature in store.

For my concerns, the very titles of Henry's texts are highly suggestive. What could it mean, for example, to call someone a lady (or a gentleman for that matter), especially if the person is not an aristocrat? In nineteenth-century England, the power and prestige of aristocratic behavioral orientations and therefore their imitation by others who can afford them is still very much in place.[36] The psychology of class sketched by Stein Ringen (see footnote 36) includes manners, that is to say a relative formalized conformity of behavior with respect to aristocratic as implicitly general social norms. More importantly, the interrelations between status and consciousness grant the freedom *not* to be coerced into the interminable debates which characterize the "reasoning public" and indeed the private lives of civil society, *not* to be forced into the confessional pressures which have penetrated that society ever more deeply since roughly the seventeenth century. Being a lady or a gentleman means, among other things, being able to refuse to be drawn into potentially embarrassing discussions, in a way to circumvent or outmaneuver the categorical imperative of communication and systems theory that you cannot *not* communicate, of relying instead on the regulatory strength of tact and tacit (pre)understanding. Within the framework of the famous international theme of Henry James, Isabel Archer is fully drawn, both interaction-wise and psychologically, into the British orbit ("England was a revelation to her, and she found herself as diverted as a child at a pantomime"). However: Whatever the possibly 'real' intricacies of the mind of a person like Isabel might have been, the narrator cannot pretend to reconstruct them. Apart from our ignorance about what is really going in any mind, more or less including our own, the pretense to represent would, in this case, neglect the predominance, both inside and outside, of what William James calls the social self. Representing consciousness can only amount to a sketch of conscious priorities which hopefully suggest the real priorities of feeling and thinking, but can do so only at a certain remove. Presenting materials of Isabel's consciousness, the narrator in fact starts out and fills young Isabel's "remarkably active" imagination ("a certain nobleness of imagination", "high spirit") with all kinds of theories beneficent to her "self-esteem", one of these erroneous theories, later reduced to "opinions", telling her that she was "fortunate in being independent".[37] Obviously, the fluctuation of consciousness takes place mainly on the

---

36 See above all Cannadine 1992: 557–558 (chapter 12, "The Reconstruction of Social Prestige") and Cannadine 2000: ix with the quote by Stein Ringen: "[W]hat is peculiar to Britain [and we can include the American Isabel Archer here] is not so much the reality of the class system and its continuing existence, but class psychology: the preoccupation with class, the belief in class, and the symbols of class in manners, dress and language".
37 James 1963: 49–55.

level of opinions and (something resembling) theories in the beginning. Most of these opinions turn out to be erroneous. Some are "delusions" to such an extent that the biographer shrinks from specifying them (James 1963: 50). Once these dubious and rather insubstantial early "substantive parts" of consciousness are destroyed, they must be replaced by others or, more often, by a transitory crisis of "transitive" parts. The novel presents a third possibility: It transforms consciousness into dialogue especially at those points where, without the dialogue, a crisis of consciousness would have to be depicted. The function of dialogue, then, consists in easing the burden of solitary consciousness and connecting the person with social interaction. Dialogue must also navigate and negotiate the perilous space between intrusive thematizing (violating the tacit standards of lady-like or gentlemanly behavior) and conventional banality ("small talk"). Thus, after Isabel has refused Lord Warburton's offer of marriage, she has a long talk with Ralph Touchett. Both, being also Americans, can take a few communicative liberties. Bodily reactions show, however, how quickly one can go too far (cf. also: "Isabel watched her cousin as to see how far he would go", 148): Isabel "coloured" (146), "suppressed a start" (147), responds "with a slightly nervous laugh" (147); both "exchanged a gaze that was full on either side, but especially on Ralph's, of utterances too vague for words" (150). Both finally seek refuge in metaphorical generalities about drinking the cup of experience, courage and the adventurous spirit (150 – 151). Though these must leave her disoriented, no state of mind is represented. The only suggestion, hard to interpret, is supplied by the body again: "Her silvery eyes shone a moment in the dusk" (151).

Once the dialogue is over, however, the narrative handling of disorientation cannot proceed without taking a closer look, especially as far as her possible future husband Osmond is concerned, at Isabel's mind again. Most people she knows "belonged to types already present to her mind. Her mind contained no class offering a natural place to Mr Osmond" (261). Her consciousness tries to cope with that riddle by transforming visual impressions into aesthetic values: "The peculiarity was physical [...], and it extended to impalpabilities. His dense, delicate hair, his overdrawn, retouched features, his clear complexion [...]" and so on (261), culminating in the "appearance of thinking that life was a matter of connoisseurship" (262). Osmond's fastidiousness (cf. 265), aesthetically grounded, carries moral overtones and thus facilitates his absorption into Isabel's mind: "her imagination supplied the human element which she was sure had not been wanting" (267). The mind does indeed move from substantive parts to transitive ones and back again, as William James would have it. But, as Henry's narrative suggests, the mind's imaginary overproduction which I have mentioned and will speak about again (p. 55–61), stands in dire need of a permanent control which even the social self cannot achieve. Marrying Osmond appears to her mind like entering "a dusky, uncertain tract which looked ambiguous and even slightly treacherous, like a moorland seen in the winter twilight. But she was to cross it yet" (313).

At this point, the marriage still lies one year ahead. In William's perspective, such a period of time, perhaps best called a moratorium, would be well spent by building up new substantive parts of consciousness, elements of the mind hopefully of a less delusive nature than those before. Henry James, however, does not use Isabel's draining the so-called cup of experience in order to illuminate the workings of her mind toward a new structure; he rather makes us somewhat painfully aware of the limitations of literature in that respect. The process of experience during the crucial moratorium is condensed into fairly non-descript phrases:

> She had ranged, she would have said, through space and surveyed much of mankind, and was therefore now, in her own eyes, a very different person from the frivolous young woman from Albany who had begun to take the measure of Europe on the lawn at Gardencourt a couple of years before. She flattered herself that she had harvested wisdom and learned a great deal more of life than this light-minded creature had even suspected. (319)

In this important case, Henry apparently does not think it necessary to devote narrative energy to the shaping of the quality contrasts so important for his brother. The conventional attitude of the narrator implying rather explicitly that he knows better does not help either. The potential of discourse to get at the drama of consciousness is also wasted in another dialogic confrontation between Ralph Touchett and Isabel. Touchett in particular breaks the norm of gentlemanly restraint by commenting aggressively on Osmond and finally confessing that his aggression is a form of jealousy – he is in love with Isabel himself (342–348).

Consequently, there is a tendency in this novel to reduce the complexity of consciousness by concentrating on its symbolically and socially stabilized, yet highly precarious "substantive parts", or on what, especially the idea of marriage, has remained of them. Henry is not really interested in what his brother calls "the potential social self", what William analyzes and describes at length, unfortunately mostly in medical as pathological terms, as "Mutations of the Self" (James 2015: 190, 219–246). Osmond is presented, perhaps semi-ironically, as "an admirable lover", "graceful and tender" (350). But it is abundantly clear, not only because of the opposition of others, that her great expectations will be crushed (cf. e.g. 401, 419–420.). If former changes in Isabel's consciousness were exacerbated into a crisis, she is now threatened by a catastrophe. James dutifully concentrates on an inside view of her consciousness which, however, has little more to offer than the melodramatically loaded notorious Jamesian "imagination of disaster".[38] A high-flown affectivity, painting everything in black, takes over ("her soul was haunted with terrors", "making everything wither", "mistrust", "gulf", "guilt", "dark narrow alley with a dead wall at the end", "depression", "distrust", "darkened the world", "malignantly", "impenetrably black", 424–425). The most pathetic summary of the domestic apocalypse follows four pages later: "It was the house of darkness, the house of dumbness, the house of suffocation" (429).

Ironically, or so it appears to me, Osmond is credited with wanting to lead "the aristocratic life" (431). Isabel – to say nothing of James himself – is anything but immune against its attractions. One might further ask whether Isabel (and again James too), striving for what appears as freedom pure and simple, does not mix up the rather different forms of an ultimately morally fed bourgeois individualistic liberalism and a rather stylistically oriented aristocratic mode. Interpretations of the novel have duly noted that, apart from keeping Osmond in the monster role (cf. for instance, 432–435), James, in roughly the last third of his text, shifts his narrative attention from the main protagonists to minor characters (Pansy, Rosier, Madame Merle, Lord Warburton, Countess Gemini, Henrietta Stackpole, Caspar Goodwood), suggesting, as it were, that he did not have much to say about the former anymore.

The Portrait of a Lady consequently could be seen as the case study of a consciousness which is largely directed by the substantive, but already fairly thinned-out parts of the social self. It is therefore a study which does not really meet the representational challenge springing from the thinning-out of symbolic and social binding power. However, Henry also indirectly goes beyond the conceptual boundaries of William because, in melodramatically overdoing the instability of the substantive, social and symbolic parts, he draws attention to their incipient decay. The question then is: What happens when and if that decay has fully set in, when, in other words, marriage and the rituals of interaction have become conventions demanding their social due but no longer libidinally engaging the characters? In the *Portrait*, the formalization of the relations between persons and social institutions has not only begun, but has already considerably advanced. Moral considerations can make up for that to some extent, especially if they can be merged with aesthetic preferences. Obviously, however, morality has turned already into merely a form of imagination. Ralph Touchett and Isabel are the main figures in which moral forms of life are still strongly im-

---

38 Osmond has been seen as the incarnation of evil in this novel at least since Ward 1961: 57. See James 1963: 424–425.

agined. In Ralph, illness and the concomitant loss of vitality, however, cast doubt on the moral motivation; in Isabel, likewise, a petty puritanism may have to carry a dubious motivational load. The imagination of disaster looms large anyway, ready to identify almost anything popping up as a threat to one's integrity.

In *The Golden Bowl* (1904), the binding power of social institutions has shrunk to a minimum. Colonel Assingham formulates the consequence, the absence of felt – to say nothing of practiced or normatively valid – moral dimensions as a matter of fact, most clearly:

> He knew everything that could be known about life, which he regarded, as for far the greater part, a matter of pecuniary arrangement. [...] The infirmities, the predicaments of men neither surprised nor shocked him, and indeed [...] scarce even amused.[39]

Much later, Adam Verver offers a self-description of his class which presents more or less the same diagnosis: "Well, we're tremendously moral for ourselves – that is for each other [...] there's something haunting [...] in such a consciousness of our general comfort and privilege [...] as if we were sitting about on divans, with pigtails, smoking opium and seeing visions" (James 1966: 362). This tremendous internal morality, self-ironically invoked and limited to the in-group anyway, consists mainly in a mutuality of respect for aesthetic preferences. Again, the title of the book is mapping out a basic orientation. Prince Amerigo asserts – or pretends – that the bowl has a crack which disqualifies it as a marriage gift. He admits that he knows that by instinct or superstition (108 – 109). Both his attitude and the mystifying sales talk of Charlotte with the Bloomsbury dealer (104 – 107) look like a desperate or playful effort not to save (aesthetic) appearances (which are safe, that is to be taken for granted anyway), but rather to maintain the possibility of staging and indulging in symbolic or quasi-moral interpretations in and of life. Much later in the novel, Mrs Assingham describes the bowl as a "brilliant, perfect surface", to which Maggie adds: "as it *was* to have been [...] The bowl with all happiness in it. The bowl without the crack" (445). And she goes on: "We alone know what's between us – we and you; and haven't you precisely been struck, since you've been here [...] with our making so good a show [...] To everyone" (445 – 446). The aesthetically perfect bowl provides the people "sitting on divans, with pigtails" (362) with occasions for keeping up the semblance of moral talk.

This continuous compulsion to keep a dimension of life in play which is not really available anymore produces a far-reaching consequence for the narrative

---

[39] James 1966: 72.

structure. Both dialogue and (re)presented consciousness cannot directly handle or focus upon this situation. In dialogue, the risk to injure somebody's sensibility is too great. Even when Maggie says that "we alone know what's between us", her interlocutor, Mrs. Assingham, certainly a fairly intelligent confidante in this novel, is at a loss as to what she is supposed to know. She asks question after question (446) until Maggie is forced to the conclusion: "Maggie had liked her to understand, so far as this was possible; but had not been slow to see afterwards how the possibility was limited, when one came to think, by mysteries she was not to sound" (447). It must remain doubtful whether these mysteries are not rather mystifications James spreads across a narrative which, without them, would simply collapse. Immediately following the last quote James invokes the even "duskier [...] recesses of her imagination", a technique of ominous but unresolved foreshadowing applied throughout the text.

Likewise, James has summarized quite conveniently what to expect and especially not to expect from the glances into consciousness which he deigns to grant the reader with. This is Prince Amerigo musing:

> These things, the motives of such people, were obscure – a little alarmingly so; they contributed to that element of the impenetrable which alone slightly qualified his sense of his good fortune [...] There were moments when he felt his own boat move upon some such mystery. The state of mind of his new friends, including Mrs Assingham herself, had resemblances to a great white curtain [...] When they were so disposed as to shelter surprises the surprises were apt to be shocks. (42)

But for Amerigo, even the vocabulary of surprise and shock, encouraging an attitude of readiness and openness, does not grow into a fixture ("substantive part") of his consciousness. He immediately goes on to replace it with an even more enigmatic phrase alluding to the "quantity of confidence reposed in him" (43). It is true that he tries occasionally to couch matters in moral terms. His speculations what that quantity of confidence might be end in a comparison of his worth with "some old embossed coin, of a purity of gold no longer used, stamped with glorious arms, medieval, wonderful" (43). This sounds like a moral, but is in fact more than just latently an aesthetic criterion. Similarly, the thought that he might ask Mrs Assingham "what *was*, morally speaking, behind their veil" prompts him into guessing what they expect him "to *be*" (43) – which in turn makes him imagine a scale, a "measure" not as an illumination, but as "the shrouded object" (44). The fact that such passages often, like here, come at the end of a chapter and are *not* taken up, to say nothing of elucidated in the following one, does not make it easier to understand what, if anything, is going on.

Certainly, the many conversations between Colonel and Mrs Assingham, with the couple as a kind of fusion of common sense and sensibility, function as a preinterpretation of what might be going on with the main characters. But the reader's assumption that they hit the nail on the head is unsafe at any time. The point is that, for consciousness, if not for life forms in general, aesthetic interests cannot simply take the place of moral ones because their possible objects are indefinitely manifold. The aesthetic consciousness becomes fleeting and elusive; it tends, using William's term, to consist in nothing but transitive parts. This is also because the aesthetic orientation materializes in a (normally anyway) rich leisure class; it cannot claim to be the result, as in Walter Pater's *Marius the Epicurean* and other writings, of systematic thought emerging as primary orientation after the relative merit of life forms has been evaluated. An intermediate figure in whom something like a new and partial return of consciousness toward substantive elements might happen is the millionaire collector Adam Verver, the father of Maggie. The role of the collector in the later nineteenth and twentieth centuries is culturally obvious. For financial reasons, the collector's consciousness is radically open, but must also be capable of substantial concentration on specific objects. In the *Portrait,* because of a lack of money, Osmond remains a poor candidate for that role, but a worthwhile object of literary study insofar as he tries to ennoble the financial side by moral and aesthetic self-stylizations.

Obviously, the preceding remarks are not intended as a criticism of crucial features in the writing(s) of Henry James. Before determining their own status, I should draw attention to a famous letter written by William to Henry on October 22, 1905, in which he does seem to criticize the narrative ways of *The Golden Bowl:*

> I read your Golden Bowl a month or more ago, and it put me, as most of your recenter long stories have put me, in a very puzzled state of mind. I don't enjoy the kind of "problem" (viz. the adulterous relation betw. Ch.[arlotte] & the P.[rince]), *and the method of narration by interminable elaboration of suggestive reference* (I don't know what to call it, but you know what I mean) goes agin [sic] the grain of all my impulses of writing; and yet in spite of it all there is a brilliancy and cleanness of effect and in this book particularly a high toned social atmosphere that are unique and extraordinary. Your methods & my ideals seem to be the reverse, the one of the other, and yet I have to admit your extreme success in this book.[40]

I am quoting this not because of the *criticism* the passage certainly spells out, but because the italicized words have given us the best conceivable *description*

---

40 James and James 1997: 463 (my italics).

of Henry's procedure. Moreover, if the criticism is honed to a slightly different perspective, it does indeed point out a problem of novel-writing and its implications for consciousness around the turn of the nineteenth and twentieth centuries. The thinning out of social and symbolic binding forces and the concomitant fleeting nature, volatility and loss of tangibility in consciousness corroborate William's diagnosis that novel-writing has in principle become endless. Endlessness, however, also implies or amounts to a dead end which ultimately blocked novel-writing of this kind and forced it into new adjustments of the substantive and the transitive parts of consciousness. I will come to that in due time especially in the second and third parts.

In his preface to *The Golden Bowl* in the New York edition, in any case, Henry appears to indirectly confirm his brother's opinion by curiously dodging the issues and shifting them onto different grounds. These grounds are not irrelevant. But they certainly were not the prime concern for this text. The first shift concerns the conspicuously careless handling of the question of illustrations. The relationship between and the relative merits of text and image did in fact become a problem at this time which saw the emergence of cinema and had to grapple also with intercultural discrepancies in that respect. Ignoring the problem that illustrations cannot literally be (mere) illustrations, for a text like *The Golden Bowl* illustrations are irrelevant, not to say counterproductive because they turn attention away from consciousness. After some pertinent remarks concerning the roles of the Prince and Princess in the first and second halves respectively, after a promising start in which James seems to denounce "grafting" or "growing" a picture "by another hand on my picture" [!] as a "lawless incident" (James 1966: 11), James loses himself in pleasant talk about "an amusing search" for adequate pictures in the shops of London (12–14).

In an entirely different vein, James takes on the "really interesting" and "admirably difficult" question as to the "effect of experience" and the "immense array of terms, perceptional and expressional" with which that effect is supposed to be articulated. This problem boils down "to the how and whence and the why these intenser lights come into being and insist on shining" (17–18). From there, the author's train of thought moves on to the original function of poetry in a broad sense, a function which prose seems unable to take over: "We may traverse acres of pretended exhibitory prose from which the touch that directly evokes and finely presents, the touch that operates for closeness and for charm, for conviction and illusion, for communication, in a word, is unsurpassably absent" (23–24). This is because it fails the "highest test of any literary form conceived in the light of 'poetry'" and does not "lend itself to *vivâ-voce* treatment".

Do we then have to assume that, for Henry James, texts like *The Golden Bowl* are to be seen, or rather heard and listened to, as a return to a poetic orality in which the *problematic relationship between processes and products of consciousness is submerged*, or pushed into irrelevance, by the *performative dynamics?* We do, if we follow for instance Irving Howe and his introduction to *The American Scene* (1906). (For *this* book, paradoxically, the use of pictures, possibly even called illustrations would be amply warranted. But this is unimportant here.) Howe's exposition merits a longer quote:

> He writes openly and with pride as a literary master, perhaps the only American who has ever succeeded to persuade us of his right to assume a role we associate with an older, a European tradition. James composes out of the security of his place and his achievement, and still more, his own measured sense of place and achievement [...] he composes out of the assurance of his eccentricities – that winding, circling, elaborate style which, if we only can *hear* it, comes to seem the essence and lucidity of high civilization.
>
> Let us not pretend that this late style of James comes easily to us or that a certain kind of training is not necessary before we can feel at ease with it. For all its baroque complications, it must be taken as a spoken style and, in a special way, as a style of oratory. Not the oratory of the public speaker, which is utterly alien to James; but the oratory of a formidable and acknowledged literary man addressing a group of friends in a drawing room, speaking with rounded intricacy so as to give pleasure [...] He stands there and he casts a spell.[41]

It is difficult to object to such beautiful phrases. Yet the very length of the texts raises skeptical questions about how long such a "syntax as performance" (Howe, in James 1967: viii) can be sustained; questions as to whether the performance can retrieve or simulate successfully the substantive parts, that is the resting-places of consciousness which have vanished from consciousness itself. John Locke had already pretended much earlier, in the "Epistle to the Reader" of his *Essay Concerning Human Understanding* (1689), that this book was addressed to "five or six Friends meeting at my Chamber and discoursing". In its calculated obscurities, the Epistle does not rule out that these friends took part in the composition as well. Where Locke's text follows this claim of primary orality and employs styles of speech, it produces masses of obscurity and redundancy. It appears at least empirically unlikely that communicative risks should have shrunk two hundred years later in cultures in which mass communication has been taken over by technologized media, in which sophisticated forms of communication, by contrast, seem to drown in contingencies of all kinds. The comparison between William and Henry James has yielded one result

---

41 Irving Howe, Introduction to James 1967: viii.

of which we may be fairly sure: Consciousness must regain *some* substantive parts *in some form*, yet neither the brothers nor anybody else have so far shown us the way. The transition from processes to products, while managing the selective procedures necessary to get from one to the other, is sorely deficient when it comes to the question concerning the uses of the products, their vital and even their survival value. James apparently feels compelled to leave their status and function in an aestheticized semi-darkness. His brother's comments on the *Golden Bowl* would suggest, in their turn, that not much can be done about that.

5 Neurobiology: Intricacies and Implications

The Jamesian situation certainly is of ongoing topicality. In both William and Henry, the plight of consciousness consists in processes of thought no longer absorbed and shaped attractively by available products. Henry in particular replaces them by aesthetic(izing) tendencies which, however, are undermined by the imagination of disaster as a form of the catastrophic. This situation poses problems for modern neurobiology which frequently creates the impression that, in the transition from processes to products, sociocultural norms and guidelines can be freed from their accumulated historical dross, brought scientifically up to date and reformulated in more objective terms on the basis of neurobiological findings.

We do indeed immediately find an encouraging suggestion in Damasio to this effect. In his book *The Feeling of what Happens* (1999), Damasio gives Shakespeare credit for having introduced the autobiographically and culturally crucial "extended consciousness" into Western culture. In contrast to the biologically central core consciousness, the extended form results from experience and culture, producing individualities capable of living in communities and sharing common ground. The thesis about Shakespeare having introduced that consciousness may strike us as an exaggeration. But it could be made palatable by saying that Shakespeare's complex and dramatic images of consciousness at work were the first to have created an irrefutable and irreversible awareness of the extended form.[42] If, however, we look further into neurobiology, the matter becomes much more complicated very quickly, not the least in Damasio himself. On a basic level it appears that the materiality thesis – the assumption that any conscious event must have some material grounding, an assumption absolutely essential for the neurobiological enterprise – must be accepted in principle. It is hard to imagine that free-floating mental entities can somehow come into existence by themselves. But here the intricacies begin. We must indeed grant a mental status, that is to say a certain mental independence or autonomy to conscious events, because we cannot insist on a one-to-one correspondence between material event and thought. The idea that such a correspondence is possible or even likely runs counter to the massive and solid evidence which brain research itself has accumulated. Given the inconceivable complexity of billions of neuronal and synaptic structures, including the multifunctionality of most brain units like brain stem, limbic system, neocortex, ganglia and so forth, it is well-nigh impossible to trace many mental events down to their material cause or to locate

---

42 Damasio 2000: 232. See 195–233 for a discussion of the extended consciousness.

https://doi.org/10.1515/9783110581836-007

them in any precise fashion. For any representation, there can be many underlying neural states and context-dependent signals (Edelman, see below). Within that complexity, the concept of a material cause or locus does not in fact make sense anymore.[43]

Neurobiology has tried to come to grips with these implications by constructing models of intermediate range in which the order of brain processes becomes neither rigid nor amorphous but rather both highly integrated and highly differentiated. Gerald Edelman's theory of neuronal group selection (TNGS) has enjoyed a certain notoriety. Edelman postulates a crucial evolutionary event: a new reciprocal connectivity which appeared in the thalamocortical system. The theory is optimized and operationalized by concepts like global mapping, that is the smallest structures in the brain capable of perceptual categorization, like functional clusters with their myriad of dynamic reentrant interactions, like genes, inheritance, individual history and experiential selection, like especially reentry, that is the "ongoing parallel and recursive signaling between separate brain maps along massively parallel anatomical connections".[44]

Models developed by Ramachandran and Damasio have singled out other, but, for present purposes, functionally equivalent aspects. Ramachandran has pushed the function of "mirror neurons" and their circuits to the foreground, thereby establishing, or so he claimed, a crucial link between brain structure and civilization. Important questions remain open: Why, for instance, was there a sudden explosion ("the great leap") in mental sophistication about sixty thousand years ago? For Mark Turner, the "staggering behavioral singularities that come with cognitively modern minds" (for him about fifty thousand years ago) present us "with the greatest scientific embarrassment, for they appear to indicate a mysterious and unexplained discontinuity between us and the entire rest of Life". The human brain, Ramachandran wonders, reached nearly its present size, and perhaps its intellectual capacity, about 300,000 years ago. What then was it doing during that long incubation period? Whatever it may have done, mirror neuron circuits help to understand and explain parts of human brain complexity, enabling us, as they do, to adopt the other's point of view, to see yourself as others see you (or at least, I would add, to imagine that you can do that), and to bring us closer to an understanding of the origins of language. Damasio, like Edelman, highlights the role of somatosensory pat-

---

43 I do not see that Gerhard Roth has really demonstrated *what* precisely we are meant to accept as "a very tight parallelism between brain processes and cognitive processes". See Roth 1996: 301, and, by contrast, Wolf Singer's remarks quoted in fn. 11. Roth is both a neurobiologist and a philosopher.

44 Edelman and Tononi 2000: 106. See 83–86, 95–96, 105, and Edelman 2004: 54, 61, 107.

ternings from which a conscious "core self" emerges "in pulse-like fashion". Edelman speaks of "interactions between sensory and motor systems" essential for global mappings. Edelman is impressed by the ever-increasing sophistication of the experiential qualia space. In parallel fashion, Damasio sees no end to the refinement of an "autobiographical self" built on the stabler constructions of proto- and core self. On the other hand: Both believe that the central problem of neurobiology consists in the "binding problem" (how does the brain succeed in identifying the identity of an object?). In that as well as other respects, they remain worried by "capacity limitation" and interference with the "integration and coherence" (Edelman) of that achievement. In Damasio, frictions in the binding process result from an evolutionary brain-stem–cortex mismatch which has "imposed limitations on the development of cognitive abilities in general and on our consciousness in particular". For Ramachandran, these limitations disturb particularly the relations between seeing and knowing. The achievement of object recognition remains "mysterious".[45]

We are entering here a central and sensitive area: the relations between the structures and functional ways of the brain and those of socio-cultural evolution. The extent to which one can reach results and make decisions here will determine the extent to which neurobiology can legitimately pass judgment on the crucial transitions from the processes of individual consciousness to its sociocultural relevant, compatible or normative products of thought. It will determine the extent to which neurobiology can say something about what I will call the drama of consciousness, that is to say the urge in the human mind to come to satisfactory terms with its own inner turmoil and with the demands to which the products of consciousness are exposed culturally. The dispute concerning free will and its impact on legal and moral matters, on notions of responsibility, guilt etc, has provided us with a rather unpleasant foretaste in that respect.[46] In the present case, a confrontation between neurobiology, supplying information about the functional mechanisms of the brain, and literary criticism, setting up typical forms of representing consciousness both as process and the products it brings forth, might seem to be the simplest characterization of what I intend to do. Unfortunately, things will be more complicated, because the two disciplines

---

45 Damasio 2010: 209 and chapter 9; Edelman 2004: 49, 72; Edelman and Tononi 2000: 26. See Ramachandran 2011: 118–119, 121, 128, 132; 120, 130–131 for language and chapter 2, especially 57, for the seeing-knowing problem. Cf. furthermore Turner (ed.) 2006: xiv.

46 It would appear that Germans, for reasons not altogether obscure but also not important here, have thrown themselves into this quarrel with particular zest. See for instance Geyer (ed.) 2004. See also chapter 15 on freedom of the will, determinism and autonomy in Roth 2003: 494–544.

do not go, not even in their limited ways, for what Turner describes as the correlations between a cognitively modern mind and a robust artfulness, as the "interplay, in the phenomena of artfulness, between biological dispositions, individual experience, and cultural history".[47]

In order to gauge the range of neurobiological relevance I propose to look at the logic of claims inherent in the development of neurobiology. We will find, to our pleasure or dismay, that neurobiology has not been able to extend its range of valid claims. Rather, the contrary has happened. Edelman for instance introduces his earlier book *Bright Air, Brilliant Fire* (1992) with the conviction that "what is now going on in neuroscience, may be looked at as a prelude to the largest possible scientific revolution, one with inevitable and important social consequences." Looking for that prelude, I can find only vague and disputed assumptions: The activities of two crucial brain systems, the limbic (concerned with value emotion and the like) and the thalamocortical (managing adaptation to increasingly complex environments) can "be matched". Edelman's and Tononi's *Universe of Consciousness* (2000) simply and certainly correctly states that "higher-order consciousness involves interaction", that communicating hominids must have used gestures and sounds to develop social interactions "which had some selective advantage in hunting and breeding", that, once higher-order consciousness begins to emerge along with language, "a self can be constructed from social and affective relationships." That is telling us something, but it is not telling us much. Edelman's *Wider than the Sky* (2004) denies that higher-order values are genetically specified. Rather, "such values will arise under the constraints of adaptive systems". There is a biological basis for values, but "it is only through historical encounter and social change as humans that we can build on such values to yield rights."[48] Again, this correct, but it is also begging the question of *how* to agree on those rights *in which contexts*.

Edelman, then, has progressively cut back on the revolutionary claims in *Bright Air, Brilliant Fire*. Damasio, by contrast, has progressively, if very carefully, widened the possible cultural reach of neurobiology. As mentioned in the beginning of this chapter, the earlier book called *The Feeling of what Happens* (2000) foregrounds an extended consciousness in and through which individual and social potentials are bundled together. Enter Shakespeare as its most impressive presenter. Damasio's later book *Self Comes to Mind* (2010) has to disentangle a much more complicated situation. Here now, consciousness has first to contend

---

47 Turner (ed.) 2006: xiv.
48 See Edelmann 1992: Preface and 118; Edelman and Tononi 2000: 194–195, 197; Edelman 2004: 138. Speaking about the improvement of an individual's taste for wine (2004: 72), Edelman presents an insight of a different caliber.

with an unconscious dimension called "the genomic unconscious", that is with a "colossal number of instructions that are contained in our genome and that guide the construction of the organism with the distinctive features of our phenotype [...] and that further assist with the operation of the organism" (2010: 278). Enter Shakespeare again, but this time with a different mission: The genomic unconscious contains instructions which have "something to say about the early shaping of the arts, from music and painting to poetry" (2010: 278–279). "It had a lot to contribute to the fundamental narratives of religion and to the time-honored plots of plays and novels, which revolve in no small part around the force of genomically inspired emotional programmes" (279), especially those concerning asymmetries between female and male sexuality, male mixtures of aggression and sexuality and the breaking of taboos (279). Othello, Iago, Oedipus, Achilles, Hector, Ulysses, down to their avatars in modern film, have assumed here a socially rather disruptive role.

This thesis sounds highly plausible. Human societies, one would suppose, need invented stories (including of course plays) about the violation of rules, in order to get used to both rules and violations, working them through cognitively as well as emotionally in their imagination at a distance from everyday conflicts, in order to get a better, one might say: a more realistic sense of order and its necessary instabilities. This function would be similar to the one for children, their anxieties and fairy tales, described and propagated in Bruno Bettelheim's *The Uses of Enchantment* (1976). But the unending quarrel about the stimulation of real violence through fictional images and stories in which they are equipped with a high degree of motivating intensity and attractiveness might raise doubts whether the thesis, instead of strengthening, rather weakens a later theory of Damasio's about the evolutionary and cultural role of the arts. That theory asserts that it is *"the homeostatic impulse"* which propels ahead cultural developments (292). The impulse responds to "the detection of imbalance in the life process". The imbalances are defined by social and cultural parameters and detected at "a high level of the conscious mind" in an overall process of *"cultural homeostasis"* (292).

For that process, storytelling comes in again. It makes all the wisdom "understandable, transmissible, persuasive, enforceable" which the human race, endowed with self-reflection, has accumulated. It makes that wisdom "stick" (Damasio 2010: 293). Damasio discovers the same homeostatic impulse behind the development of myths and religions and behind the emergence of the arts (294). The early arts probably provided information about threats and opportunities; later on, they acted more explicitly as "a privileged means to transact factual and emotional information deemed to be important for individuals and society" (295). Building up an ever-increasing variety of uses, they make it possible to "rehearse specific aspects of life and [...] to exercise moral judgment and moral action" (296). Damasio has reached the evolutionary dimension: "In brief, the arts prevailed in evolution because they had survival value and contributed to the development of the notion of well-being" (296).

Again, one hesitates to mar such a well-constructed picture. But I balk at the word 'wisdom'. Certainly, one would not deny that within the product range of the brain a lot of wisdom can be harvested. But given the immense, indeed inconceivable complexity of brain processes, the overproduction of imaginary elements cannot be reduced to a common denominator called wisdom. There is wisdom, there is knowledge, there are mixtures of knowledge and illusion, there are certainties, ideas, hunches, suspicions and many more. Damasio knows of course all of this. Very probably, he also knows that he might have bolstered his argument with collections of world wisdom like Aldous Huxley's *The Perennial Philosophy* (1944), supplemented today by huge efforts to put together encyclopedias of intercultural humanism.

Yet the question remains whether, in the very context of brain research and evolutionary theory, talk about human wisdom is advisable or warranted. The famous Austrian Nobel laureate Konrad Lorenz, looking at human evolution, was struck by the decline, the disintegration or even the dismantling of (what he considered to be) the human substance. Lorenz certainly overdid his role as a prophet of cultural doom. But it is difficult to say precisely how much he overplayed it. For him, the writing was on the wall because humanity had embarked on an unholy alliance with a new version of the eight deadly sins of civilization (overpopulation, destruction of natural life space, race of humanity with itself also through new technological possibilities, death of emotions, genetic decay, break with tradition, power of indoctrination, nuclear weapons). Some of these reappear in Lorenz' views on the dismantling of the human substance, others intensify the infernal threats especially in those cases where forms of behavior were once meaningful, but lost their function later on. Lorenz adduces overorganization, specialization, aggressive enthusiasm and political propaganda, scientism, loss of selection, pseudodemocratic doctrines.[49]

So far, then, the neurobiological description of processes of thought has not produced images of attractive products, images, that is, of an attractive transitionality of the mind. Somewhat surprisingly to my mind, however, Damasio has also confessed to sympathies for the controversial book *The Origin of Con-*

---

49 See Lorenz 1973 and 1983. The probably most important disciple of Lorenz, the Austrian Irenäus Eibl-Eibesfeldt, abstains from the often very shrill sounds of Lorenz, yet his assessment of the paths modern societies are taking goes into the same direction. Taken together, Lorenz and Eibl-Eibesfeldt are certainly the most powerful representatives of evolutionary ethology.

sciousness in the Breakdown of the Bicameral Mind (1976) by Julian Jaynes. For Jaynes, the *Iliad* and the *Odyssee*, close as they appear to stand together in terms of both topics, their continuity and development, and indeed culture in general, belong to two totally different times and mentalities. According to Jaynes, we have to describe the *Iliad* as being anchored in a period in which people still heard the gods talking to them. There was little or no symbolic space for a fusion of the gods with individual consciousness. Structurally, the bicameral mind is comparable to what is called schizophrenia today; Jaynes in fact sees it as a partial relapse to that archaic state. The world of the *Odyssee*, by contrast, is a world not necessarily of rationality, but rather of rationalizations which Shakespeare presented in their unpleasant modernity in *Troilus and Cressida*, for which Horkheimer and Adorno diagnosed the first emotional freezing in the relations between people and especially the beginning of an emotional calculus in the married couple – a less than flattering beginning of the European *Dialectic of Enlightenment*. Jaynes moreover quotes Alfred Russel Wallace, Darwin's partner and competitor in evolutionary theory, for whom human faculties could not have developed by means of the same laws which have determined the progressive development of the organic world.[50]

The importance of Lorenz, Eibl-Eibesfeldt and Jaynes for present purposes consists in the risk they are willing to take to describe human and/as civilized evolution at least as partly pathological, as being tinged by pathological tendencies. Jaynes in particular seems to insist that the transitions from processes (hearing the Gods talk) to products (like epic poems and their worldpicture) is full of tensions and conflicts. E. O. Wilson has presented us with a summary in which pathological trends of human cognitive evolution seem to be taken for granted.

> In my opinion the key to the emergence of civilization is *hypertrophy*, the extreme growth of pre-existing structures [...] the basic social responses of the hunter-gatherers have metamorphosed from relatively modest environmental adaptations into unexpectedly elaborate, even monstrous forms in more advanced societies [...] Even the beneficiaries of hypertrophy have found it difficult to cope with extreme social change, because they are sociobiologically only equipped for an earlier, simpler existence [...] I interpret contemporary human social behavior to comprise hypertrophic outgrowths of the simpler features of human nature joined together into an irregular mosaic. (Wilson 2004: 89, 92, 95)

---

50 Jaynes 2000: 9 (for Wallace), 407–431 (for comparisons with schizophrenia). With respect to the necessity for concepts of pathology one should see Jaynes together with Dodds 1962. See for instance chapter 3 with the nice title "The Blessings of Madness".

The "extreme growth of pre-existing structures" has provoked some French thinkers into even more radical models of thought. The work of André Leroi-Gourhan and Edgar Morin which I am exploiting here dates back to the sixties and seventies of the last century. Naturally, it does not incorporate recent research in paleontology and brain research. I do not see, however, that the age of their work interferes in any disadvantageous way with the validity, indeed the urgency of their questions. Leroi-Gourhan focused, among other things, upon the development of the size and shape of the skull. For him, the decisive event took place with the prefrontal unlocking of the skull. This refers to the enlargement of the forehead, a corresponding shrinking of supporting bone material, hardly any change in volume, instead a reshaping of the proportions of the different parts of the skull, and finally the upright gait. The combined effect of these changes unleashes, in the short or in the long term, challenges on all levels of human existence (country/city existence, writing, symbol and media systems, cultural memory, creativity and adaptation). The size of products flowing from an often unbridled mental creativity may clash, for instance, with the demands of a visceral and muscular sensibility, anchored in our somatosensory equipment, which we can neither get rid of nor satisfy any more in forms of behavior out of sync with civilized progress:

> In the following chapters, the good, the beautiful and the highest being will assume more and more intellectual values. Indeed, if you read a poem in full tranquillity, you may forget that any image triggered by the words is meaningful only to the extent that it refers to all the concrete experiences you have made, related to the bodily basis and the concrete experience.[51]

Audiovisual overproduction might similarly dry out human imagination. Societies which lose imaginative thought as the ability to create verbally based symbols will, in the long run, also lose their ability to act with the necessary flexibility (cf. Leroi-Gouhan 1988: 267). Put in drastically simplified terms: The productivity of the anatomically liberated brain, mainly the neocortex, is such that its products overtax its abilities of control and emotional contact based for instance in the older limbic system. Large parts of humanly created realities become 'abstract', disconnected from and more or less unmanageable for the individual person.[52] We do have a problem, then, since, as Damasio has also insist-

---

51 Leroi-Gourhan 1988: chap. XI, 358 (my translation from the German which was compared to the French original).
52 This is the point in Claessens 1980, a book which has not had the reception it deserves. It goes without saying that concrete and abstract are relative, but operationally very productive terms.

ed upon very emphatically, we cannot handle and know emotionally neutral objects. For Leroi-Gourhan, evolution has advanced on three levels. *Homo sapiens* of the twentieth century differs little from *homo sapiens* 300 centuries before our time ago (natural history); the basic structures of biological groups, however, do not harmonize well with the emerging social complexity (second level); technological evolution, the third level, grows at such speed and to such size that it outgrows human control (Leroi-Gourhan 1988: 216). Once the second and third level interact closely, the results may well be explosive, the explosion of cities being a prime example (230 – 233). The situation is made even more difficult because the human mind tends to privilege and overestimate its own symbolic (cognitive, imaginary) functions – 'literature' often provides impressive examples –in comparison to technology. Yet it is technology which pushes ahead all progress (235).

In Leroi-Gourhan's picture, then, the cognitive-affective consequences of massive brain development and upright gait are the causal result of evolutionary pressures (life in the savanna, hunting) which paradoxically *liberate* human beings from the immediate causal impact of further evolutionary pressures. The mind gains greater internal scope ('autonomy' would be probably going too far), but is now exposed to the multifarious, 'chaotic' dynamics of culture(s) for which the mind is also largely responsible itself. (In the philosophy of 'spirit' and of the humanities after Hegel this has understandably provoked terminological trouble: Nicolai Hartmann for instance felt compelled not only to admit an objective spirit in the great transpersonal traditions and institutions, but also, going beyond Hegel, an "objectified" spirit ["der objektivierte Geist"] especially of works of art which, produced by the living personal spirit, also depend on the latter for their continuing existence.[53]) Leroi-Gourhan has sketched an intricate, not to say contradictory situation. On the one hand, we would need an imagination, in analogy to Kant's *Einbildungskraft* bridging the gaps between pure and practical reason, capable of smoothing out the discrepancies within the chaos of culture. We would need also *media* of and for that imagination in and through which it can convincingly articulate itself. In this respect and in the West at least, linear writing systems, organized into well-regulated textual forms, were traditionally privileged in spite of their visual poverty, of the narrowing of images, the suppression of a halo of associated images, of the linearization of symbols and the connotational impoverishment coming with them (266). That is why, since the later twentieth century, audio-visual media have enjoyed so much progress. But the audiovisual in its turn favors and probably actively encourages imaginative impoverishment. It is managed by a minority of specialists who pro-

---

53 Hartmann 1949, especially the third part "Der objektivierte Geist".

duce pre-digested imagery for the masses (267). It is a pity that Leroi-Gourhan cannot comment on the social and humane commitments of the great technological leaders in Silicon Valley.

Reduced creativity in both writing systems and audiovisual media indicates, on the other hand, that the imagination has meanwhile split up into the fragmentary elements of the imaginary (T. S. Eliot's "heap of broken images", *The Waste Land*, line 22). The later twentieth century is the period of theories of the imaginary which, in spite of very respectable efforts, cannot be ordered into any coherent whole anymore.[54] The fragmented imaginary increases quantitatively to the same extent as its epistemological claims decrease.

This is where the problem is taken up by Edgar Morin who, like Leroi-Gourhan, was a member of the Groupe des Dix, a debating club of leading French intellectuals between 1969 and 1976. Morin has published (and is, now in his nineties, still publishing) a staggering number of books. It might appear illegitimate to concentrate on only two of them, both on the anthropological and even personal side. Apart from the fact that other Morin books are at least in the back of my mind (the one on cinema: *Le cinéma ou l'homme imaginaire*, 1956, with frequent reprints, the one on death: *L'homme et la mort*, 1970, and quite a few others like *Journal de Californie*, 1970 with its reflections on the relations, but also the distance between systems and system levels), I do refuse to handle (although I have read it) what many consider as his *opus maximum*, that is the series of six volumes with the overall title of *La Méthode* (1977–2004). Most of it not only lacks concreteness (that would be perfectly in order), but its abstraction is of a kind that I would call scholastic in the pejorative sense. Morin's interpenetrations of concreteness (like personal experience) and abstraction (theory) in the other books, by contrast, present a consummation devoutly to be wished.

In 1969, in *Le vif du sujet*, Morin puts forward, in mostly aphoristic form, his first strong version of the hysterical mind. Its genetic logic is the same as Leroi-Gourhan's imaginary: an evolutionary thrust which unhinges the mind from further evolution and propels it into (a partly self-created) culture. However, the term now injects a much more dramatic, not to say catastrophic quality into cultural processes. Morin denies that bourgeois existence possesses that peacefulness and tranquillity which it very often seems to exude. "Toutes ces vies sont rongées de l'intérieur." What is normally called reality turns out to be a treacherous middle ground ("bande moyenne") between forms of magic and of the undeniably real. One must grasp therefore where "ce sentiment de réalité" comes

---

54 Amongst these efforts, one would have probably to single out Durand 1969. See also Pfeiffer 2009.

from which seems to grant "substance, densité, vérité, authenticité" to whatever – a table, a country, a hallucination. Enter the imaginary: The imaginary is half-real, it follows that the real is half-imaginary. Or also: "Le réel est hystérique." The mind is operating on two levels: a structural, linguistic etc, logic and a psycho-affective magic one.[55] Freud's studies on hysteria launched psychoanalysis; anthropology must catch up with that. I would add that while hysteria is no longer used as a medical diagnostic term, one must not forget that it was the oldest of observed psychological disturbances. Furthermore, Morin presents a kind of formalized concept which allows him to see *hysterical tendencies*, a relative over-investment of cathectic or aggressive affective energies as a normal process in consciousness and of the normal version of extreme clinical cases. Such tendencies assert themselves at the crossroads of emotions and the body, of the imaginary and the real, of sentiment and magic, seriousness and play, of simulation and lived reality (Morin 1969: 144–145). In an interesting aside with important consequences as to the media Morin assumes that the writer, removed from so-called reality by a further step, must find a *modus vivendi* with phantasms more than the 'ordinary' person (306). This topic will creep up at crucial places of the argument later.

We might find Morin's position easier to justify if we confront it with the judgment of T. S. Eliot on the emotional (in)adequacy of reactions by Macbeth and Hamlet respectively. Eliot ascribes artistic "inevitability" to the words of Macbeth on hearing of his wife's death. He discovers a "complete adequacy of the external to the emotion; and this is precisely what is deficient in *Hamlet*. Hamlet (the man) is dominated by an emotion which is inexpressible, because it is in *excess* of the facts as they appear". [56] Many people will share Eliot's opinion; theoretically, it is totally untenable. We may agree in Macbeth's case, but only as far as the words "She should have died hereafter" go. The rest of the pathetic lament on the "sound and fury" and more like that is artistically impressive, to be sure, but certainly not artistically inevitable. We can find any number of utterances by Macbeth where we could find fault with the relation between situation and emotion; Macbeth's repeated loss of situational control is just one example. Conversely, it is possible (not necessary) to find sufficient reasons for Hamlet's pathos of inaction and his occasional aggression in word and deed.

Morin, in any case, does not find it difficult to supply a more explicit theory for the hysterical mind in his *Le paradigme perdu: La nature humaine* (1973). Combining the neurobiology, brain research and anthropology of his time into

---

55 Morin 1969: 27–28, 36, 38, 62.
56 Eliot 1977: 86.

a unified thrust, he reformulates the hysteria thesis as the "sapiens-demens"-dichotomy of the human being, that "animal doué de déraison".[57] Morin registers two sources of complexity: Complex sociocultural developments challenge the resources of the brain, the brain's innumerable activities, in their turn, function as an independent source of complexity of their own (93). We find what since Leroi-Gourhan could be called the usual suspects in the multidimensional wake of neurobiology and anthropology: the upright gait, the liberation of hand and forehead and their combinatorial potential (1973: 64–65), the appeal to huge numbers (a brain volume of 1500 cm³, 10 billion neurons, 10 to the power of 14 of synapses neurons – a modest estimate, Edelman in 2004: 15–16, opts for "at least" 30 billion neurons) – these alone would be sufficient to create "hypercomplexity" overtaxing the order capacities of consciousness (Morin 1973: 126, cf. 93). We can add a probably enforced shift of life from the forest into the savanna which demands a new calculus of reality with increased risks of incertitude and error (118), the early formation of especially younger competing groups granting an evolutionary and cultural special value to rebels, abnormal and rejected people, adventurers and "les *heimatlos*" (68). One must count in hunting with its impact on the division of labor between men and women and the emerging emotional closeness, sometimes producing binding socio-affective structures and bonds (72).

All of this is very plausible; none of this can be proved in any cogent way. Excepting the brain, described by Morin for instance as "la plaque tournante" (1973: 216) on which the organism, the genetic system, the sociocultural and the ecosystem somehow communicate with each other. The evolution of the brain has created an operational and consequently cultural logic which appears more or less irrefutable and uncontrollable into the bargain. Whatever its efficacy in its confrontations with objects, situations and persons, the brain is primarily committed to the imaginary. Morin starts out with the evidence of funerals. The belief in some kind of transformation argues strongly for the intrusion of the imaginary into what is taken, rightly or wrongly, as the real. Myths and the imaginary, from this point onwards, will become the co-producers and the products of human destiny (109). Death is not taken as the last word, but somehow distanced, not to say overcome by myth and magic (109–110). In a still more radical and speculative move, with the evidence of Eynan / Ain Mallaha about 9000 B. C. on the Levant in mind, Julian Jaynes assumes that a dead king, "propped up on his pillow of stones, was in the hallucinations of his people still giving forth his commands [...] The dead king is a living god. The king's tomb is the

---

57 Morin 1973: 107–126.

god's house, the beginning of the elaborate god-house or temple".[58] Early wall paintings, in their turn, do not prove the beginning of art. Biologically and anthropologically, a purely aesthetic phenomenon cannot be isolated. Aesthetically marked procedures are rather enmeshed in overall semiotic practices in which their signs take on message-like values: sexual, threatening, promising, seducing and so on. In late stages this does not prevent the development of the relative autonomy of a substantivized art, even of art for art's sake. But such movements remain fragile (Morin 1973: 116). It would be better to ascribe the potential of resonance with parts or all of the full human being to aesthetically conspicuous phenomena (117). Obviously, this direction of argument links Morin with Alfred Gell's *Art and Agency: An Anthropological Theory* (1998), but also, perhaps less obvious for many, with Oscar Wilde's "The Decay of Lying" and other writings. For sheer lack of competence with many of the art works discussed by Gell, it is impossible to even try to do him justice here. But his idea is that an enchantment with technology produces art as technologies of enchantment; he assumes that this idea, if taken seriously, would do away with both the conception of art as a carrier of ideology and as a pure object of disinterested contemplation. Likewise, Oscar Wilde does not plead for anything like art for art's sake, but rather for a respect for aesthetic procedures which can change the world only if they are not directly projected onto it. Morin strongly holds that the uncertainties and ambiguities in the relations of the mind with what it would like to see as realities must be negotiated through media in which their drama can be powerfully enacted. Waves of the imaginary take possession of everyday life; myth and magic flourish here, phantasms and phantoms strut around. *Homo sapiens sapiens* cannot take pride in a reduction of affectivity in favor of an independent intelligence but has to manage an eruption of psycho-affective energies (Morin 1973: 121–122). Efforts to eradicate or domesticate madness have evidently failed. Poets, "les moralistes", other writers and/or other media can adopt different techniques in order to give them scope and at the same time hedge them in (124, 144).

---

58 Jaynes 2000: 142–143.

6 Dramatic Narratives

These last remarks of Morin remind us forcefully that the search for and drive towards attractive products of thought in which the chaotic turbulence of processes of thought, in William James's terms, finds resting-places both gripping and peaceful, has by no means come to an end. This chapter takes first steps in the exploration of transitions from 'hysterical' turbulence to exciting drama or rather dramatic narratives.

It surely cannot be repeated often enough that "hysterical" and "schizophrenic" are not used as clinical or technical terms here. The terms suggest tendencies in the self-referential operations of consciousness. In conscious processes there seems to be inscribed an overinvestment of psycho-affective energies. At the same time, the products of these operations do have a hard time to cope with the complexities out there. Clearly, the levels of complexity in advancing social and technological evolution present challenges which neither the processes nor the products of thought can sufficiently control in conceptual, to say nothing of factual respects. In fact, this control has become more difficult also because the products, as we will see, have progressively lost large parts of their capacities for orientating action.

Former times, believing in the powers of the mind, might have used the term "imagination" for the epistemologically controlled forms of overinvestment. From the vantage-point of today, this is hardly possible anymore: "Imagination" looks like a treacherously optimistic metaphor simplifying the processes of consciousness in illegitimate ways. Consequently, we have come to talk of the imaginary instead. In contrast to many efforts in anthropology or psychoanalysis or even occasionally in philosophy, however, I do not believe that the imaginary, seen as the many directions conscious processes may take, can be brought into any kind of epistemologically relevant order. The catastrophic fate of the imagination, as Dietmar Kamper has said, should warn us. For Plotin and Neoplatonism the imagination opened ways of knowing true reality. Often, the arts were seen as the media through which the essence of nature and the principles of natural order could be recognized or 'imagined'. In various forms such claims were still raised, for instance, by Schelling, Shelley and Coleridge, with Schelling, for one, holding that the imaginative work of art presented the identity of the real and the ideal and therefore the 'blossoming' of the real as such.[59] Image-like ideas concerning heaven, the saints, hell and more offered orientation for a long time. Their power in this respect has been re-emphasized by Gernot

---

59 See Schelling 1979: 373; Kamper 1981: 12; Richards 1969: 27.

https://doi.org/10.1515/9783110581836-008

Böhme in his version, after Kant, of an *Anthropologie in pragmatischer Hinsicht.*[60] The image-ideas still are capable of ordering reality in significant ways, but their main function has come to consist in the "emotional organization of the subject" (Böhme 1985: 188). Böhme still speaks of the imagination. What he means by that, however, refers to what I call the imaginary here, that is to say to conscious processes somewhat but certainly not very thoroughly or intelligibly ordered.

A few remarks concerning Sartre as an instructive example will clear up this issue. In 1936, Sartre published a book with the title *L'imagination.* In 1940, this book was followed by another one called *L'imaginaire,* the subtitle however describing it as *Psychologie phénoménologique de l'imagination.* Clearly, "imagination" here had shrunk to a collective term for the multifarious movements of consciousness which are normally targeted by concepts like mental imagery. Above all, Sartre gave up the effort to find out about the cognitive potential of these terms. Small wonder, then, that Gilbert Durand, author of the classic work on the anthropology of the imaginary, castigated Sartre for his superficial descriptions of the 'content' of inner images.[61] With Durand, the imagination still occupies the throne of cognition in principle. He quotes André Breton, for whom the imagination is not just a cheap promise of happiness or an escapist pretense. Rather, for the individual, it offers the chance to do supreme justice to him- or herself, because it can lift the terrible ban which bourgeois society has imposed upon the notion of possibility. We can follow the imagination, Breton thinks, without fear of betrayal or deception. Durand uses these assertions as a kind of motto for the third edition of his great work. *Practically,* however, he concentrates on the material content of the great symbols, on their structural relationships and on the strength with which they take possession of the imagination (Durand 1969: 9–10, 29).

Following Durand, we can ascribe a certain general human validity to these symbols. We should not, in the manner of Freud, cut them down to mere indicators of repression (35–36). Durand does not want to follow Jung either; he is not willing to stylize the symbols into archetypes or mental material inherited in universal human history (36). Instead, he sees content and relations as results of the tensions between individual aspirations and natural, cosmic or social pressures which show up, in most cultures, in analogous forms (38).

We may grant analogies and even a certain universality to the great symbols. But the multifariousness of pressures in human life has led to an overload of the symbols with elusive and contradictory meanings. We do not live in one of

---

60 Böhme 1985: 187.
61 See Durand 1969: 28.

those earlier periods, in which J. G. Frazer for instance found dominant products of consciousness, guiding conscious processes, like forest kings, tree gods and other ideas efficiently embedded in magic practices. Frazer assumed with some justification that elements of these older worlds of consciousness had survived in the modern world in more or less intact shape. Certainly, treating someone as a scapegoat when things go wrong is a practice known at all times. Likewise, Roman saturnalia can be detected in today's Italian carnival.[62] But even if T. S. Eliot took inspirations for *The Waste Land* (which appeared, like the abbreviated version of Frazer's work in 1922) from Frazer's *Golden Bough*, the harvest for the modern world, the modern waste land, was restricted to the notorious "heap of broken images" mentioned by Eliot, in perhaps another ironic stab, in line 22 of his text.

In contrast to the tree gods, for instance, which appear time and again in analogical functions in *The Golden Bough* (Frazer includes Dionysos in his collection of tree gods), Durand acknowledges that images and symbols may mean more than one thing. A tree may symbolize the course of the seasons, it might mean an upward movement and more. The image of the snake may evoke ideas of being swallowed, but also of renewal and rejuvenation. Meaning overload leads to reversals of meaning ("renversements de sens", Durand 1969: 54) and logically, to a lack of meaning. Furthermore, it is not clear why we should believe in animal imagery as a primary source of conscious processes. Is it because, as Jung thought, they provide images and symbols of sexual libido (Durand 1969: 71–96, 74 concerning Jung)? Others like Ernst Topitsch and Dieter Claessens have maintained with at least equal justification that social and technological imagery must be treated as primary sources of conscious processes.[63] For them, interactive pressures and unintelligible natural phenomena like lightning and thunder count as central drives in the early development of inner images. Even Durand alludes to Leroi-Gourhan and the importance the latter ascribes to combinations of movements, gestures and tools (Durand 1969: 55).

The difficulties of elaborating such mental elements, in which the transition from processes to products becomes as it were tangible, are conspicuous in many examples in which Durand tries to prove the feasibility of his enterprise. There is for instance, he says, an Ophelia complex which, amongst others, Gaston Bachelard had also tried to tackle. With Ophelia floating dead in the water, her hair suggests an idea of "the irreducible femininity of water" (Durand 1969: 110). This, however, must be an extremely ambivalent femininity because water

---

62 Cf. Frazer 1967: 763–764. See Eliot 1974: 63, line 22.
63 See Topitsch 1969: 27, as well as other studies by this author; Claessens 1980: 131.

is also symbolically – indeed archetypically – connected with menstrual blood (107–110). Or, to take a very different example: When, for whom and how strongly do scepter and sword occupy conscious processes and determine the significance of some of their products? The information that we can find linguistic-etymological traces in almost all languages is not enough to help to prove that a "fantastique transcendentale" (438, following Novalis) is possible.

The present enterprise therefore has to redirect its ambition. The examples of Richardson, of William and Henry James show that consciousness gets couched very quickly in certain forms (here mostly narrative, often even in William James) and codes (here mostly moral or of an aesthetically marked quasi-moral kind). In most situations, the inner quality of these forms and codes, however, tends to be 'dramatic'. Thought, even if couched in the metaphor of stream, even if plunged into the reduced awareness of (day)dreaming, is propelled onwards by tensions and energies. It tends to be enacted in forms for which terms like drama and dramatic will, to say the least, come easily to mind. William James, leaving the deceptively plausible stream metaphor behind, has stressed the dramatic quality of conscious events repeatedly and emphatically, most conspicuously so in his chapter on the will: "The whole drama is a mental drama", especially for the heroic mind which it takes to stand this universe.[64] We certainly should not speak about origins and assume that the beginnings of consciousness took a definite dramatic form. But affinities there were. Bruno Snell, right in the introduction to his famous genesis and "discovery of mind" in ancient Greece, sees genesis and discoveries as "attacks" on, as interventions into human essence, surging up as "shaped [intense] experiences" ("gestaltete Erlebnisse"). The workings of consciousness appear to take on their most gripping shapes when they are produced by or are an index of "situational crises" (Jaynes). They break through with a passion which, because it is more than personal, cannot take any arbitrary form. Homer uses epic forms to tell his stories. But the events, mental or otherwise, are couched in terms of forces and (e)motions. Objects are seen (and indeed seeing itself is seen) not in their objective function, but in the place they take within an emotionally relevant dynamics. Early lyric poetry and tragedy, whatever their relation to or position between myth and 'reality' may be, give shape to the mental turmoil brought about by anxiety and need. In tragedy,

---

64 James 2015: vol. 2, 564. Cf. 578 as well as a host of similar assertions. My notion of drama certainly goes farther and is distinctly riskier than the concept of "energy landscape" with which Metzinger and Windt characterize the integrational work of consciousness. It certainly does not exclude, on the other hand, possibilities and periods of "inner quietude", a concept important for a theory of the open mind (Metzinger and Windt 2015: 9/28, 10–12/28).

in particular, chorus and characters perform a dramatic "thinking into the depths".[65]

I would like to extract and construct two models which ought to bolster the claim sufficiently that dramatic narrative offers the best dimensions in which the transitionality of consciousness gains its most relevant shapes. Both are founded on a generalization of what I have described as pathological tendencies in the workings of the mind. The first pursues Morin's 'hysterical' interpretation of imaginary investments. In analogous ways, the second handles the role of schizophrenia in Jaynes' theory of the bicameral mind and its vestiges in modern times. I am not using, to say that again, Morin and Jaynes in order to spread the diagnosis of mental illness all across civilized life. But we can hardly doubt that, whatever we identify as the reasons and causes of "civilization and its discontents" (Freud), this discontent translates into the discontent of the individual with him- or herself. Older as well as more recent typologies of the human personality (Hamlet as the melancholy man or malcontent), character studies, psychological descriptions, case studies like Erik H. Erikson's *Young Man Luther*, theories of alienation, Freud's model of the individual not being master in his or her own house, in our time Alain Ehrenberg's diagnosis of an uncertain and exhausted self in the context of another "société du malaise" – there is no end to the interpretation of personality as being on the road towards pathology. In situations of tension and stress, the ancient Greeks were inclined to impute their inner states and energies to the will of some god. Georges Devereux identifies Euripides as an excellent clinical observer, because he makes Medea switch from the assumption of an inner origin of her passions to the view that they are personified external entities, thus anticipating Devereux' own thesis that hallucinations, compulsive thoughts and intense drives can break into consciousness as realities appearing alien to the ego.[66] The end of the road, that is full-blown pathology, need not be reached, but it looms large on the horizon. This is why Morin can say that clinical hysteria is only the extreme case of a normal phenomenon which penetrates all our "expérience vécue" (1969: 145).

Lacking a master-model which would order his feelings and thoughts, Morin describes himself as "polyphile, polymorphe", as a particularly complex case of this basically dramatic structure, starting with his ethnic and family origins, as someone whose thought is continuously drawn into some "mimesis [...] gigantes-

---

65 Snell 2011: 11, 13–29 (the first chaper on "the notion of a human being" in Homer) and 102–103 for early poetry and tragedy. See Jaynes 2000: 407. Jaynes is referring here to schizophrenic patients, schizophrenia being, however, a vestige of the bicameral mind with a very strong general potential in postbicameral times. I will come back to that later in this chapter.
66 Dodds 1962: 6–8; Devereux 1998: 61.

que", exposed to a "flux imaginaire", pushed along by assimilation and a simulation "semi-hystérique" (1969: 356). We seem to be normally able to impose a structural, linguistically grounded 'Lévi-Straussian' logic on the workings of our minds. We use it as a kind of protection against "une ardeur affective", a dramatic second logic of 'hysterical' overinvestments which do not easily translate into communicative terms (62, 144). In Morin's case, the hysterical thrust may be tied up with a primary and inexorable manic-depressive rhythm (1969: 355).

In his *Paradigme perdu* Morin formulates the evolutionary momentum which underlies the drama of consciousness even once its original function does no longer matter. For him, hunting intensifies and 'complexifies' the dialectic between foot, hand and brain, changes human relations not only with the environment but with the various human groups (men, women, young and old) themselves. It pushes ahead ways of thinking in which the attention to mostly unclear signs, forms of tracking down and early identification, improvisation and caution, cunning and ingenuity and all their transformations will be condensed into dramas of clear awareness and blurred indirectness, of uncertainty and ambiguity (Morin 1973: 71–72, cf. 93, 118–119). Anxieties, with the fear of death at their basis, function as engines driving these dramas along; myth and magic develop as early coping techniques (110). The drama keeps going because we find ourselves constantly in the grip of these two very variable levels of consciousness: as simulating hysterics we transform into objective symptoms what emanates from our subjective "perturbation" (110). Sign and symbol systems like language cannot really channel these perturbations into stable patterns because the inner images tend to invade the outer world continuously (115). *Homo sapiens* is not defined by a reduction of affectivity for the benefit of intelligence, but rather by "une véritable éruption psycho-affective" (121–122).

Apart from dubious tasks of integration, Morin has comparatively little to say about culture which supposedly brings these eruptions under control (cf. 180–189). It takes a strong state or indeed Hobbes' Leviathan which can tolerate psycho-affective eruptions because, in a "nouvelle sociogenèse" (192), it can block their transformation into disruptive social action. Julian Jaynes has taken care of the survival of these eruptions under modern conditions in a more explicit, if also more difficult form. His theory of the bicameral mind and its breakdown as the origin of more modern forms of consciousness has been highly controversial. I do not assume that one has to literally accept the theory according to which people roughly from the tenth to the second millennium had auditory hallucinations they took for the voices of gods speaking directly to them. (I do think, however, that this may well have been possible.) Rather, I take Jaynes' theory as a speculative metaphor for a radical and dramatic otherness of conscious life, grounded in evolutionary anthropology, which has spawned quite an impressive series of survivors down to our present age. I derive this confidence from the fact that the historical evidence Jaynes offers above all with respect to the meanings of a crucial vocabulary and its development has been amply confirmed by prestigious classical philologists like Bruno Snell or Eric Havelock. We are talking here, both with respect to so-called mental and physical phenomena, about a language of oral performance in which the full richness and the dynamic complexities, the "mobility and liveliness" of overlapping physical and psychological response still obtains. This language survives in (not only Greek) drama whose "expressive dynamism" ("The city altogether bulges with incense-burnings" as against "The town is heavy with a mingled burden of sounds and smells") "offers no propositions, beliefs, or programmed doctrines in the style of a Dante (still more of a Milton)".[67] Certainly, an erosion of that fullness takes place, but it "extends over centuries of the European experience", and it is a partial erosion, "one which has left modern culture unevenly divided between oral and literate modes of expression, experience and living".[68]

Jaynes has collected an impressive list of what he calls "vestiges of the bicameral mind in the modern world" (Book III). I would single out possession, poetry and music, hypnosis, and schizophrenia as being particularly modern potent forms of Havelock's expressive dynamism. These phenomena obey Walter J. Ong's old principle according to which a new medium of communication does not only not wipe out the old, but actually reinforces the older medium or media. In doing so, of course, the new medium transforms the old so that the old is no longer what it used to be.[69]

Jaynes' list cuts across the domains normally called real life on the one and art on the other hand. A large part of modern literature, including drama, opera, poetry and all kinds of prose forms could in fact be located along the lines drawn by Jaynes' vestiges of the bicameral mind. We may assume that efforts to portray the workings of consciousness have found their most elaborate forms there. For a

---

67 See Havelock 1986: 90–95, 111 (concerning the origin of *theōria* and *theōrein* in viewing the written word rather than 'just' hearing it spoken); Havelock 1982: 261–303 on the slow erosion of orality in drama, but also its partial survival in Shakespeare. See also Snell 2011: chapters I, IX and XI on Homer, historical consciousness and the way from mythical to (so-called) logical thought; further Snell 1965: 26–27 (on *psyche*, *soma*, *noos* and especially *thymós* shaping what we have come to call emotions and affects but also setting physical movements in motion), 77 (on the split between inner and outer beauty), 101 (on the relation between new social forms and loneliness).

68 Havelock 1978: 4.

69 Ong 1977: 82–83. Ong has provided plenty of examples for his thesis which, it should be admitted, he has restricted to "verbal" media of communication. If Ong means purely and exclusively verbal media, then this restriction is a mistake.

fuller sense of their logic, a brief look at Jaynes' characterizations is however still imperative. Generally, Jaynes describes the active vestiges of the bicameral mind as a state of "diminished" or narrowing of consciousness. This is achieved by a formalized ritual procedure called "induction" embedded in a belief system or "collective cognitive imperative". The narrowing of consciousness may lead into a trance in which an "archaic authorization", usually by a god, but sometimes also a person, takes place (Jaynes 2000: 324). These are demanding criteria rarely fulfilled in the modern vestiges – for which, after all, they were formulated (cf. also 339) – of the bicameral mind. Yet the demands are softened anyway by allowing persons privileges of authorization (cf. 329). Thus, particularly in the case of idols, formerly effigies helping to hallucinate bicameral voices (332), status changes have occurred to a considerable extent. "Idolatry is still a socially cohesive force" (337). The statues of prestigious leaders are still on display in parks and gardens. Their political or social authority has been transferred, however, to a much more remarkable extent, into the cultural authority of present-day media and entertainment heroes and heroines. Jaynes' commentaries on music, in particular on song (364–370), would have to be extended considerably in order to do justice to this rearrangement of person and medium, particularly also because the hearing of voices (in combination with the 'sound' of music) plays such a crucial role here. It may well be that the transcendence achieved in the old and orthodox practices of the bicameral mind is replaced here by 'mere' self-transcendence. But this distinction is shaky anyway. Aldous Huxley, for one, has moved freely between the two terms, stretching the possible functions of music into both directions: "Music is as vast as human nature and has something to say to men and women on every level of their being, from the self-regardingly sentimental to the abstractly intellectual, from the merely visceral to the spiritual."[70]

Which elements must be present then for a non-ordinary communicative situation to count as a vestigial one of the (hypothetical) bicameral mind? If we rely on historical testimonies we might simply take the eighteenth century equation "One God, one Farinelli" as proof that the mystic voice can be replaced by the virtuoso voice without great difficulty.[71] Romantic myths may have privileged genius and the ingenious creation of works of art as the summit of human creativity. There is evidence, however, that the European nineteenth century placed the virtuoso, particularly the musical virtuoso like Liszt and Paganini or also great singers, on the throne of cultural achievement. (At that point the singers

---

70 Huxley 1986: 321–322 (Epilogue).
71 See Plate II of Hogarth's *The Rake's Progress* as well as numerous articles.

did not include the castrati anymore, because their very existence seemed to violate emerging humanitarian commitments. The last specimens, interestingly enough, sang in the Vatican up to the early twentieth century. There are recordings of the so-called last castrato, Alessandro Moreschi, 1858–1922. The last but one, Domenico Mustafà, 1829–1912, can be seen on a photograph together with Giuseppe Verdi at Montecatini.) The virtuosi could not normally claim creative genius. But their performative power was such that their version of the products of others, and not these *per se*, appeared to come from another world.[72] Roland Barthes tried a different, but related approach in order to rescue what I would call the cultural charisma of the singer's voice. In his seminal essay "The Grain of the Voice" he described elements of singing that can be put in the service of communication, representation, or (for instance emotional) expression. More importantly, however, there are others which concentrate in the grain of the voice, that is "the very materiality", indeed "the voluptuousness of its sound-signifiers." A cultural preference for the first levels will normally favor a sentimental clarity of and in singing. For Barthes, the German baritone Dietrich Fischer-Dieskau (1925–2012) is here the supreme example. That type fits an "average culture" which demands the expression of emotions and takes art to supply its most intense and sophisticated forms.[73] The other type, by contrast, enjoys the performative, virtuoso self-exploitation of the voice demonstrated for instance by Giacomo Lauri-Volpi (1892–1979).

The cultural virulence of this problem can be best appreciated by reading the debate on the relative importance of Racine's plays (that is to say the text as such) and the actress "la Berma" reciting them in Proust's *Recherche*. In the "Scène de la Déclaration" of *Phèdre* la Berma creates the strongest phenomena of an aesthetically marked liveliness and vitality; the scene gains a kind of "existence absolue" for Marcel. This does not invalidate Racine's verbal genius. But his words would fall flat if they did not materialize each moment in the voices and bodies of the actors. The distinction between work of art and performance does not break down. But the author's finished work turns into a material out of which la Berma creates her own masterpiece. By contrast, in virtuoso performance the distinction between Racine and a mere piece of fashion may disappear, because la Berma is magnificent in both.[74]

Jaynes, to be sure, might not go along with that extension of his approach. I do not see, though, how he could avoid it, given the fact that he defines the

---

72 I am drawing my own conclusions here from the instructive volume Brandstetter and Neumann (eds.) 2011.

73 Barthes 1984: 181–182, 185, 188.

74 Proust 1954: Vol. 2, 44–46.

speech of (modern) possessed prophets for instance as "articulated externally and heard by others. It occurs only in normally conscious men and is coincident with a loss of that consciousness" (342). Likewise, a widening of scope becomes unavoidable once one grants, as Jaynes does, that in the Middle Ages and in more modern times the majority of people possessed as well as most oracles and Sibyls were women whose brain is less selectively lateralized (Jaynes 2000: 350).

Ultimately, forms of possession appear to be crucially involved in most modern vestiges. At first, possession is listed as a phenomenon in its own right, although there is an early oracular form, "of the frenzied mouth and the contorted body after even more training and more elaborate inductions" (Jaynes 2000: 329). Strictly speaking, we are dealing with the domination of a person and his speech by the god-side which does not allow the person to remember what has happened afterwards (339). But then Jaynes nominates possession as the central element of poetry too (370–375). Poetry being a highly open-ended term in its turn, the number of candidates for the position of a modern vestige of the bicameral mind keeps increasing. Jaynes rehearses, starting with Plato and the divine madness of possessed poets, the commonplaces of poetic authority normally couched in verse and rhythms. Poetic authority preserves a supreme status throughout its range from divine knowledge (the first poets were gods) to the "sound and tenor of authorization. Poetry commanded where prose could only ask" (363, cf. 361–362). With the help of music, first the lyre, then the flute, poets maintain relations to the Muses identical with those which the oracles entertain with the gods (369–370, cf. 374).

To assert that there is an almost complete functional equivalence of poetry and states of being possessed or divinely inspired is a proposition difficult to sustain. Even if it were tenable, we would still have to ask questions about its suitability as a preferential pattern for conscious transitionality. In any case: Poetry shows up in many variegated forms. It may not lose "the sound and tenor of authorization" completely. But it cannot claim authority in any unified form. Nor does possession appear to be its precondition. In the next chapter, a theory of poetry developed by a both fictional and pretty much 'real' nineteenth-century poet in the novel *Possession* by A. S. Byatt will be adduced in order to show that poetic authority, emanating from the transitionality of consciousness (in this case towards a peculiar use of language), can be kept in the cultural game in less risky ways.

One of these, a central and also traditional one, consists in the coupling of possession (often called "enthusiasm") and cool calculus. Strangely enough, Jaynes omits or forgets the most impressive reaffirmation of poetic authority to be listened to in modern times: P. B. Shelley's *A Defence of Poetry* (1821), culminating in the final sentence: "Poets are the unacknowledged legislators of the world."[75] Shelley makes his claims for poetry much more explicit than Jaynes; he stretches them to such an extent that the weaknesses of both himself, but also of Jaynes become conspicuous. First, the supreme authority of poetry according to Shelley is not all derived from possession. Rather, his reference to a psychological state of poets as a precondition for poetry borders on the ridiculous: "Poetry is the record of the best and happiest moments of the best and happiest minds" (Shelley 1963: 133). More to the point: Poetry is the expression of the imagination as that faculty which perceives the value of the quantities enumerated by reason (102). It is "connate with the origin of man" (102). It both follows human development and expresses the "indestructible order" underlying it (103). For this double purpose poetry needs a special language, very often but not necessarily in verse. Any "mimetic" representation or performance must bring out the best in the object represented or performed; it must approximate its inner order (the ability to do so being called "taste" in modern times) in order to produce the highest possible delight in the audience. The real poet, in short, does not only invent his language, music, dance and architecture, statuary and painting. Real poets are also institutors of laws and founders of civil society, the inventors of the "arts of life" and the teachers of what will ultimately be called religion. They are respected as "prophets" not in the trivial sense of foretelling events, but of legislators (105–106).

With respect to such august commitments, the distinction between "measured and unmeasured language", between poetry and prose will not do (107). Plato and Francis Bacon were essentially poets because of their language: "the truth and splendour of his imagery, and the melody of his language" (Plato), the "sweet and majestic rhythm" of [Bacon's] language "which satisfies the sense, no less than the superhuman wisdom of his philosophy satisfies the intellect" (108). Conversely, Shakespeare, Dante, and Milton [...] are philosophers of the very loftiest power" (109). "The true poetry of Rome lived in its institutions, for whatever of beautiful, true, and majestic they contained, could have sprung only from the faculty which creates the order in which they consist". "These things", Shelley holds, "are not the less poetry *quia carent vate sacro*" (120–121). He is concerned, in other words, with the appearance of an order full of commanding power and beauty in and across history and media. That is why he credits drama as "being that form under which a greater number of modes of expression of poetry are susceptible of being combined than any other"

---

75 Shelley 1963: 138. For the many studies concerning the coupling of possession and calculus see, as one example, Gellhaus 1995.

(117). That assertion would strongly argue that peculiar uses of language must be included in the list of candidates for forms of conscious transitionality. On a different level, Christian and chivalric systems of manners and religion, for example, emerge after the fall of the Roman Empire. But they begin to manifest themselves as really powerful poetic paradigms only in the eleventh century (121–122). Dante's poetry, in its turn, is "the bridge thrown over the stream of time which unites the modern and ancient world" (125). Finally, Shelley works his way towards the supreme claim of his last sentence. Imagine, he says, whether the world would be a better place if philosophers (in the ordinary sense) like Locke, Hume, Gibbon, Voltaire, Rousseau (he essentially a poet though, 129, fn.) had never lived, if science had not expanded in the tremendous ways it can boast of. "A little more nonsense would have been talked for a century or two; and perhaps a few more men, women and children, burnt as heretics. We might not at this moment have been congratulating each other on the abolition of the Inquisition in Spain." But we cannot even imagine what the moral condition of the world would be if Dante, Petrarch, Boccaccio, Chaucer, Shakespeare, Calderon, Lord Bacon or Milton, Raphael and Michel Angelo had never existed, if Hebrew poetry had not been translated and the Greek revival never taken place. And, as to science: We have gathered more knowledge than we can wisely handle or reduce to reasonable practice (130).

The argument is suggestive, indeed seductive. It is of course not cogent. Even so, an intermediate climax like "Poetry is indeed something divine" (131) appears to be better prepared for than the same assertion in Jaynes. In the present context, Shelley's text looks like a dramatic tale about the subtle shifts in the fate of a special ('poetic') consciousness. Jaynes has underestimated the subtlety of these shifts. What, then, remains of the idea of the bicameral mind? Histories of mentalities, centering in what I would call a psychotheological dimension, could perhaps rescue the idea as a strong impulse in the domain of paradoxical, yet powerfully effective special communication. It is paradoxical and powerful because it combines, like mysticism, self- and other-reference. It intensifies and transcends self-reference or, *pace* skeptics, successfully creates that impression. Emerging from ordinary and especially modern textual and cultural complexities like Phoenix from the ashes, it does not present fascinated consciousness as an area of the unsayable, but portrays that experience as an ineluctably dramatic and insofar communicative form.[76] In Jaynes, contradicting implicitly

---

[76] I am taking inspiration here from Luhmann and Fuchs 1989: 83. Luhmann has several texts in which the availability of different 'media' for religious experience (like – similar to Jaynes – trance, prophecy) is discussed. See e.g. Luhmann 2000. For the continuing topicality of trance

his picture of an exclusive function of poetry within the history of the bicameral mind, even legal texts can occasionally shine in that function. In the Code of Hammurabi and similar texts, "the judgments of gods through their steward mediums began to be recorded" (Jaynes 2000: 198). Once cities expand beyond a certain size, the textual bicameral control of behavior becomes precarious. Yet if "divine authority" is weakened in writing (other than poetry), it is not wiped out (207–208, cf. 248 on Assyria). "Narratization" – a very complex set of patterning abilities with multiple ancestry – starts out as the codification of past events (218), crucial events, to be sure, for a community. The "*de facto* breakdown of the bicameral mind" in Mesopotamian texts does not automatically entail the disappearance of the analogues of a god who has forsaken his people (225). The association of writing, not only in its narrow rhythmicized and patterned poetic form, with "supernatural knowledge" (363) does not simply remain intact. But it can be produced ('staged') under specific circumstances. One of the situations in which the special knowledge of a fascinated consciousness can arise occurs in fact in a context described by Jaynes as schizophrenic hallucinations. He quotes the famous case of the German jurist Daniel Paul Schreber (whose father was the inventor of the notorious Schreber garden). That one heard voices which he identified, in the beginning, as divine ones. Later, they came from little men or also a woman, the men interpreted by Jaynes as the idols of earlier times, the woman by Freud as an index of repressed homosexuality (415). More importantly, however, the voices very often seem to anticipate what Schreber himself wanted or was going to say. The process of having one's thoughts anticipated and vocally expressed "is called in the clinical literature *Gedankenlautwerden* and is approaching closely the bicameral mind" (Jaynes 2000: 413). The process also represents one of those shifts just mentioned and foreshadows both the trivial forms of talking to oneself and of what will become the monologue or soliloquy in drama. This transition will be pursued later.

The combined impact of Leroi-Gourhan, Morin and Jaynes amounts to the assumption that conscious *processes* contain affective charges which, in the context of the relative opacity of the situations people normally find themselves in, tend to provoke overreactions both on mental and behavioral levels which resemble hysterical or schizophrenic patterns. It is true that socially defined situations can often absorb their energy quite well. It is also obvious, I think, that a large number of situations demand decisions not sufficiently controlled by common social rules. Therefore *products* of thought, especially of the older variety

---

and its media see Hahn and Schüttpelz 2009, especially the essay by Schüttpelz 2009 himself. A contemporary textual version will confront us in the following chapter.

called total conceptions here, will normally formulate norms of action which are derived from their images of (world, social and anthropological) order. The evidence collected here would suggest, however, that theories and models of thought, being committed to plurality, have more or less had to abandon that task and handed it over to systems or conceptions of ethics or to rules of procedure in their own narrow context. Many scientific theories and some in the social and human sciences (here for instance Marxist theory) contain such rules for application ("methods").[77] But in the social and human domain, such theories and their application are normally hotly contested. Moreover, in a context of plurality the relativity of ethical conceptions catches the eye immediately. Many thinkers – I will later quote Georges Devereux and Jacques Monod among others to that effect – have scourged the threatening, but often denied 'incoherence' of the so-called Western ideology. The second part of this book will take some closer looks at the dilemmas resulting from this situation. But it should be said right here that the overall structure of *Hopeful Monsters* (1990), perhaps Nicholas Mosley's best and most important novel, which I will use at the end as a kind of witness for my essential theses, mirrors this situation quite precisely: The first part is called "We know the predicament"; it highlights the contradictory and confusing propositions of the sciences, contradictions and confusion being exacerbated by the media for whom consensus has become boring and 'unsexy'. The second part, "So what do we do", gives no answers to this most crucial of all the questions asked in the book. Although the transitionality of the main characters' mind, by dint of their education early on, is strongly leaning towards the sciences, it is terms like "maze", catastrophe and chaos which dominate *all* spheres of action, whether private or public. For the latter, the Spanish Civil War offers one of the worst examples.

---

77 See the chapter on "Theory and Method" in Iser 2006: 10 – 11.

7 Transitionality and the Obsession with Form

The preceding chapter, in speaking only of *dramas* of consciousness, may be accused of *lacking distinctions*. Certainly, those dramas can take very different forms. Attractive and more explicit or elaborate varieties will be explored in this chapter. In his recent book on forms of consciousness ("Bewusstseinsformen") Gernot Böhme for instance distinguishes between the Socratic type, the model of Kierkegaard, the discovery of interiority in Christian confession literature, the suffering from consciousness (Kleist, Benn, Sartre) and others. It strikes me, however, that there is normally a dramatic core in almost all of them. With respect to Christian confession literature including Rousseau, Böhme holds that the inner human being, precisely because s/he is and must be hidden, is constantly on the move – St. Augustine looking for the sources of evil within himself, Rousseau justifying his behavior with his "pudenda" and so on. Böhme characterizes Benn with Kretschmer's concept of "schizothymia", a split in consciousness marked by hypersensitivity and indifference. And even the distanced flaneur, for whom reality shrinks into images, sees the "drama or poem" in these images. A distance without passion seems hardly possible. Likewise, the "consciousness of presence" is ultimately defined in dramatic terms – as an actualization, intensification of lived existence. It is possible to discipline consciousness, to bring it to rest in meditation (recommended by Böhme, with Thomas Fuchs, as an antidote against the "psychopathology of hyperreflexivity"). But these, like mysticism, are fairly rare states of mind, of consciousness taking a break from its ordinary functions. Moreover, such moments may contain their own dramatic elements and forms (see the following chapter on Dorothy Richardson).[78]

The transitionality of consciousness demands and enforces the speedy transformation of its primary elements like thoughts (in Luhmann's sense) into formally stable(r) units like words, syntagmas, sentences and more. We must ask whether it is worth our while to try and filter out a rough logic of such transitions into form. Before tackling total conceptions, *Weltanschauungen*, theories, models of thought, that is to say larger products of thought in which "the rage for order" (Wallace Stevens, see below) reigns supreme (if also largely unsuccessfully), it will be best to turn to smaller, but well-worked out forms embedded for instance in so-called literary texts, in which ordering activities and dramatic transgressions compete with each other all the time. For that purpose, Jaynes' model

---

78 Böhme 2017: 54, 59, 61, 102–105, 169, 177–178. In passing, it may be said that the name of Chandler's detective is Philip Marlowe, not Christopher Marlow (35, 36).

https://doi.org/10.1515/9783110581836-009

can still be used as a speculative, but inspiring point of departure, to be followed up later by the limited extension into biographical forms and from there into larger and, in terms of catastrophic potential, much riskier conceptions in part II. It is, I think, self-evident that the kinds of poetry which Jaynes identifies as "the dialect of the gods" (or even "those things" which Shelley describes as the highest poetry although they must create their effects without the sacred seer, see above) do not only occur in those genres which we call poetry in the ordinary, that is the conventional sense. They are certainly present in drama and in many combinations of ritual and formalized language. Poets, in contrast to the priests and priestesses of the great oracles, did not "simply cease their rhapsodic practices". The "continuance of poetry, its change from a divine given to a human craft is part of that nostalgia for the absolute" (Jaynes 2000: 375). We may assume, for instance, that the chorus in ancient Greek tragedy preserves parts of its original ritual function in the Dionysian festivals, in which it maintained contact with the god by dancing and singing around the altar. The chorus, in due course, becomes separated from the action, but uses that separation for solemn reflections which yield, in quite a few cases, at least the semblance of auratic objectivity.

The parallel development of the monologue produces a somewhat more complicated situation. First of all, we must accept, or so it appears, that talking to oneself under emotionally charged conditions should count as 'psychologically' normal. Talking to oneself can be seen then as one of the first, perhaps the first product of the transitionality of consciousness, a product which embarks, in its own turn, very quickly on transitions especially into literary forms of the monologue. Friedrich Leo has argued convincingly that if one does not go along with the first assumption, namely that there is "the real and natural talk of the lonely person with solitude", the ubiquity of monologues in *all* ancient Greek discourse types becomes incomprehensible. In Homer, the monologue is activated in situations of affective stress and laborious thought. The forms it takes do not appear readymade, but look like an "original movement" alien to stereotype.[79] We cannot identify monologues as the direct offspring

---

[79] See Leo 1908: 1–3, 114–115, 117; Schadewaldt 1926: 1–35 (discussion of Leo). Schadewaldt by and large follows Leo, but in a different framework of argument: For him, there is a scarcity of real monologic situations in tragedy. Instead, the soliloquy presents the self-revelation of a person in a dialogic framework. Also, the Greek vision of human beings had to sink into oblivion before the monologic core in important parts of dramatic speech could be appreciated. Schadewaldt's theses do not, however, affect the present argument. In more recent times, Heinz Mathias Meltzer has summed up the discussion in his PhD dissertation Meltzer 1974: 16–42. For

and embodiment of the bicameral mind. But in many cases they carry some special weight of authority, intensity and aura because they carry over that weight from their original function in drama not as monologue, but as speech to the chorus by the actor of early tragedy. Since, for a while, there was only one actor, it was or became easy to perceive his utterance as a monologue. That type of speech develops into a full-blown monologue or soliloquy and is accepted as such, as soon as the role and relevance of the individual person takes on major significance in the 'world picture' of a drama either as an active given or a problematic absence. This does not mean that dialogue is unfit to do justice to that task. But monologic presence is at least a strong index for the virulence of the problem, strengthened even further by the fact that *de facto* monologues can occur in a formally dialogic situation. We could take for instance only Shakespeare's *Richard III*, *Richard II*, *Hamlet*, *Macbeth*, *Othello*, and *King Lear* and, by analyzing the extent and directions of significance of monologues and monologue-like situations, start to redraw the cognitive map of the Shakespearean mental cosmos from there. Likewise, it is legitimate to treat the famous speech of Racine's Phèdre (1.3.269–305), formally addressed to her confidante Oenone, as a "quasi monologue" in which Phèdre seeks to come to verbal terms with a feeling normally called love which has overpowered her mind.[80]

The elusiveness *and* intensity of consciousness drives people, especially in the shapes they take as literary characters, into an obsession with forms in which both elusiveness and intensity are transformed into irrefutable conciseness. Monologues are documents confirming the urgency of this transformation. Many prose texts focus upon the potential of drama and begin their exploration of a wider range of obsessions from there. In A. S. Byatt's novel *The Virgin in the Garden* (1978), for instance, the transformation of obsessions into form is called "the awful balance of the ineluctable". The need for balancing forms creates a crucial and powerful complex of episodes in this text. Racine's Phèdre provides a paradigmatic example again. Frederica Potter, one of two daughters of a school teacher, must grapple with Racine at school. She wonders how one would describe the differences between Racine and Shakespeare. One could compare and contrast, for instance, Phèdre and Cleopatra "as portrayals of passionate women".[81] Finally, it dawns upon her that the difference must have to do with

---

a review of contemporary positions on "the voices within" see Kaulen 2017 (accessed May 11, 2017).

80 See for instance Corinne Godmer, http://www.eclairement.com/spip.php?page=imprimer&id_article=3579 (accessed May 5, 2016).

81 Byatt 1981: 348, 202. The analysis here targets mainly the two final lines "Ce n'est plus une ardeur dans mes veines cachée, / C'est Vénus toute entière à sa proie attachée".

the difference in verse. Verses are specifically transformed "thought processes". Shakespeare's blank verse produces fluent images. By contrast, in the Alexandrine of Racine, the images look comparatively "argued" (202). That is why, I take it, they convey the ineluctability of thought explicitly, as long as the impression of cogent emotional argument does not look like 'mere' rhetoric. In a later episode, the teacher and dramatist Alexander Wedderburn quotes (correctly or incorrectly) Pound and Wordsworth in order to illustrate and enlarge upon Frederica's "awful balance of the ineluctable". Pound is quoted as saying that "poetry was a sort of inspired mathematics, which gives one equations not for abstract triangles and spheres but for human emotions"; Wordsworth asserted that sex and metre were all functions of the flow of the blood and of "the grand elementary principle of pleasure in which we live and move and have our being."[82] Pound's claim as such is surely exaggerated. But the formal rigor of Racine's Alexandrine serves to illustrate the plausible intentions behind it. This is the point at which another contribution of brain research to aesthetic matters may corroborate and illustrate the Alexandrine thesis and its general implications. Ernst Pöppel has drawn attention to what he calls three-seconds units or packages in the brain. Any conscious content has a survival chance of three seconds, and within these three seconds only one content finds conscious space. These units are the biggest and possibly also the most pleasurable packages the brain will normally handle. Shorter ones are possible, longer ones will in most cases be split up in shorter ones. This basic pattern has a strong impact on the way we speak, planning on a break after three seconds. And it is equally visible in the verses of poetry. Where verses, as they do in the Alexandrine and others, go beyond the three seconds, the verse will normally be spoken with a break within the line[83].

In Byatt's novel, the problem is also treated with respect to the chances of poetic or verse drama in the twentieth century. The discussion reminds us of course of the debate concerning verse drama associated particularly with T. S. El-

---

82 Byatt 1981: 349. The Wordsworth quote does not seem to be quite precise. Like the equation of sex and metre, however, it does not misrepresent Wordsworth's argument in the preface to the *Lyrical Ballads*. Anthony Storr (1992) seems to endorse the Wordsworthian position. See his chapter II on "Music, Brain and Body", 25 on arousal (including "sexual excitement") and 31 Stravinsky's feelings (immediately physical and causing bodily illness) about "sounds electronically spayed for overtone removal" as a "castration threat". A different but related approach to the topic of an emotional mathematics is unfolded in Klein and Kuttler 2011.

83 Pöppel 2000: 72, 75, 85–90. With respect to my remarks on the Camerata following below, the application of the three-seconds thesis to music seems highly controversial (Pöppel, 91–92). This could mean that music is much more strongly capable of structuring its own rhythms.

iot. Moving away from the always conventionalized realities of the socio-economic sphere and from a misleadingly so-called "psychological realism" (359), verse drama had to explore the almost paradoxical nature of sophisticated and yet also elemental, but not conventional emotional realities. The problem here is easier to understand if we remember the debates of the Florentine Camerata at the turn of the sixteenth and seventeenth centuries. For the members of the Camerata, even the language of Dante did no longer convey the precision and the intensity of emotions which had been habitually associated with and found in Dante. Different experiments to find contemporary equivalents finally brought about the 'invention' of opera. The calculated construction of verbal-musical units appeared capable of engendering an exact emotional code. The idea was plausible, even if, strictly speaking, it turned out that it was a mistaken conviction. Instead of an emotional *code*, we get emotional *intensity*. It is also possible to look upon musical rhythms as the more elementary and powerful version of Wordsworth's poetic flow of blood and to what he calls "the sexual appetite" in the *Lyrical Ballads* preface.

This is the background to what, in Byatt's text as well as quite a few others of her writings, is deployed as an obsession with the forms which thought assumes when it is oriented towards what the mind perceives and construes as elemental realities. Wedderburn's verse play *Astraea*, written both to celebrate the first Elizabeth and the accession of the second, occupies a kind of middle ground, with openings into all directions. In the director's production the drive toward elemental realities is indeed elementary. "And Lodge [the director] had worked steadily away from this fleshed complexity to the bare bones of primitive obsession: sex, dancing, death; death, dancing, sex [...] What they had made was not immortals stalking under Hesperidean boughs but sex in sundresses, sandwiches in gilded papier-mâché helmets" (315–316). The staging contrasts strongly with the original intentions of the dramatist. He had aimed at a "renaissance of language, florid and rich and muscular", working "towards complexity and solid incarnation, all the incorporated stuff of fact" (314–315). It can be doubted that the chances for such effects were very good, since Wedderburn himself leaned almost exclusively towards the merely imaginary side of things, a leaning amply borne out in his dealings (or the lack thereof) with women (343, cf. 44–45). Yet this leaning contains the possibility that words hit upon the urgency of a conscious state in such a way that they become real because – this might well be the basic form of transitionality – they take complete hold of the person: "He saw with a kind of haggard horror that those were, now, true, that he had made them true" (333).

Others, like the actor and psychologist (!) Edmund Wilkie go Shakespearean, opting for what they take to be Shakespeare's denial of love, honor and suchlike

(326), but also having "to do Ralegh, that man of many parts, climber, poet, mountebank, scientist, atheist, soldier, sailor, historian, prisoner", thus carrying a lot of the play's weight (131). Stephanie, the older Potter daughter, tries out, on her pupils, whether Keats' language in the "Ode on a Grecian Urn" or "Ode to a Nightingale" can actually make them *see* (78 – an ambition more directly tackled in the preface to Joseph Conrad's *The Nigger of the Narcissus*). Finally, there is the curate Daniel Orton who tries to draw a direct line between the vague but inexorable urgings of consciousness and form by pushing behavior to extremes ("Extremes *exist*", 83, cf. 85).

In all these cases, the tension or drive inherent in transitionality finds a transitory form in that it meets with an uncertain, sometimes also rewarding fate. In their fumbling and stumbling dealings with each other, Stephanie Potter and Daniel Orton become aware that behind "the cliché was something old and fierce and absolute, a primeval passion of taste, Biblical honey" (175). It is especially in the night of the dress rehearsal of the play, where the interplay between so-called ordinary behavior and so-called acting is still possible, that drive and form can merge for a while whatever judgment or classification a scene might plausibly provoke (comic, archetypal, dramatic in the double sense, pathetic, ironic, parodistic). There is also evidence, however, that the search for form misfires if it relies on models either too abstract or too concrete. This is the case with the theories of Lucas Simmonds, a biology teacher, his relationship with Marcus Potter, the youngest Potter child, and the use of the youngster as a medium. In the terminology of William James: As resting-places of consciousness, Simmonds' theories are too static; his use of Marcus as the medium through which, with the help of photisms (experiences of "floods of light and glory which frequently accompany moments of revelation", 125), a transcendent(al) order (cf. especially 128, 228 and chapter 14, "Cosmogony") might be transferred to earth, remains ambivalent, to say the least, because it is overshadowed by the ever-present suspicion of a cover-up for homosexuality. Thus, a sentence like "We have lost whatever primitive techniques we once had for communicating with the consciousness that Informs us" (64) reads like a dogmatic, conservative and one-sided version of Jaynes. In between, however, Simmonds also propounds middle-to short-range theories with which he can demonstrate the practice of theory as an activity for finding dynamic forms. These have to do, for instance, with the relative and relatively wrong relation between and function of religion and science in and since the Renaissance (127) or with the intelligible reasons the Puritan "anti-theatrical prejudice" (Jonas Barish) must be credited with, having to do less with morality than with the anxieties which a radical human transformation in and through acting (60 – 61) may plausibly call forth. He ends up, however, having obviously gone mad, sitting naked in a pond and singing religious songs (397–398).

The Virgin in the Garden could be seen as Byatt's opening gambit in a game of uses and abuses of media (mainly language, media in the current trivial sense and rituals or ritual analogies) which we need for structuring the dramas of consciousness into at least a semblance of plausibility. Both the two novellas of *Angels & Insects* (1992) as well as *Possession* (1990) work out the enormous amounts of energy it costs to keep going our "Blessed rage for order", an order which always appears to be co-produced by the mind and by the objects imposing themselves on consciousness. In his poem "The Idea of Order at Key West" Wallace Stevens portrays the tensions, the "ghostlier demarcations" between the *eigenwert* of objects and their (de)formation in the mind as a serious drama. In *Possession* as well as *Angels & Insects* Byatt strongly suggests that this drama is best seen as both serious and as a parody of its own pretensions. Both texts strike a precarious balance between the unavoidability of (ideas of) order and the labyrinths in which the mind loses itself, saved only if it does not take its own workings too seriously.

A general remark in between. The contemporary novel must suggest, if it wants to claim some culturally still important function, senses of feeling alive, however naïve, problematic, illusionary, brutal or perverse these may appear, amid the stifling burden of codes and images (a burden to which novels and the reading of them certainly contribute) and the constraints, rules and regulations of organized societies. For that purpose, in *Possession*, Byatt first explores what being a poet might have amounted to in the nineteenth century. That certainly also means what being a woman poet might have amounted to in that time. The picture does not seem to be an optimistic one. Christabel LaMotte is granted narrative and poetic space. With the poet Randolph Henry Ash, however, Byatt presents a nineteenth century writer of greater, if traditional centrality. As a combination of Tennyson and Browning, the poetic experiments of Ash culminate in what has come to be called the dramatic monologue. This 'genre', that is to say an exemplary poetic form of the drama of consciousness, had to face a lot of resistance from the reading public for whom the turns that drama frequently took seemed to be closer to madness than anything else. It was, however, a crucial effort to show interiority at work and to contain consciousness in complex but well-ordered language, in other words to reconcile consciousness and/with language. The ambition was not to paraphrase the topics a mind was thinking about, but to present a structured form of consciousness itself.

One of the challenging areas for the nineteenth century for that purpose consisted in the workings of the scientific mind. In this respect, we get a 'self-portrait' of Jan Swammerdam (1637–1680), the pioneer Dutch biologist and microscopist.[84] Shortly before his death, he finds himself in a monk's cell. His thoughts do not take stock of his life or sum up its meaning. The directions they take do however indicate where some overall meaning might emerge. There is, on the one hand, the discovery of smallness, hitherto ignored: "I am a small man, closed in a small space, / Expert in smallness, in the smallest things, / The inconsiderable and overlooked, / The curious and ephemeral" (203). But the significance of smallness might be tremendous: "I sought to know the origins of life. / I thought it lawful knowledge", a knowledge of a radically new kind, "of dizzying order and complexity" (206).

Swammerdam's achievements with the microscope provide a powerful variation on the compelling nature of seeing as a means to bring the search of consciousness for a trustworthy "resting-place" (W. James) to a provisional end. The microscope reveals "the Many", "images of Truth", "elegant Visions of life", to be sure. It does not betray the secrets of "the One", "Prima Materia", "Nature's shifting shape / Still constant in her metamorphoses" (206–208). For consciousness, science thus turns into a metaphorical potential which may – but more often than not does not – offer the desirable shortcut between thought and object.

For Ash, there is, however, one metaphorical source in science which functions as a yardstick against which all other possible transitional spaces for consciousness must be measured. There is repeated talk about the "kick galvanic", the stunning blow emitted by some electrical impulse in a liquid medium, comparable to the blow the Moray eel deals out to unsuspecting marine explorers. The metaphor is applied to the early and very careful, partly unintentional touches between Ronald Michell and Maud Bailey (147). Ash tries to figure out poetically whether love is more than the kick galvanic or the thundering roar of volcanic 'ash' (273). The kick galvanic may hit consciousness so unexpectedly and powerfully that its workings are stopped momentarily. Or it may denote the powerful reality underlying and orchestrating surface shyness (197, Christabel La-Motte's version). Adopting and adapting Dennett's distinction quoted in the beginning, the kick galvanic may be described as a combined state of reduced consciousness and heightened awareness. At the same time, it is also communication, tacit mostly, using a silent language in Edward T. Hall's sense which connects easily both with ordinary language and mute, but conscious feeling. The kick galvanic is not or should not be an obsession. Clearly, however, its efficiency is hard to verify. For Ronald and Maud, it takes more than half the book to reach something like a fulfilment of the early promises (147 and 507). For both of them,

---

84 Byatt 1991: 202–209.

the image of "a clean empty bed in a clean empty room" puts consciousness on the track of a connotational nothingness, "where nothing is asked or to be asked" (267). This image appears to them much more attractive than a modern culture, including the nineteenth century, which "has gone on piling up speculation and observations until truths that might have been graspable in the bright Dayspring of human morning [...] are now obscured by palimpsest upon palimpsest" (164). Ash and LaMotte in their turn are forced spend quite a lot of epistolary efforts to convince themselves of the exquisiteness of their Yorkshire stay.

For two versions of personal relationship, the kick galvanic produces a trembling cogency of awareness in which consciousness takes on an irrefutable but undefined clarity. For both poets and scholars, trained with and depending on words, such a situation cannot last long. But they also feel under the obligation not to lose that quality in and through words. Quite on the contrary: Nobody wants to embody Schiller's dictum that where the soul *speaks*, the *soul* speaks no more (*Xenien und Votivtafeln* 1797). Consciousness, once coupled inseparably with language, must be redirected and guided towards a more elastic conception of language. Small wonder that Ash in particular charges himself with that task. In an analogy to Shelley Ash develops the theory of a language which is motivationally deep-seated and can be deployed in different 'genres' of discourse. Ash's description looks like an intensified version of ordinary consciousness. He does not claim a "Lyric Impulse" as the allegedly most deeply motivated authority of poetry. Rather, his poems spring from "something restless and myriad-minded and partial and observing and analytic and *curious*, which is more like the mind of the prose-master, Balzac". What makes Ash a poet, and not a novelist, has to do with the singing of language, with its life, that is with a transition of consciousness into a language in which the vital concerns of consciousness are preserved or touched upon and not subordinated to other, perhaps even humanitarian purposes (132). In a later passage Ash speaks of "the driving force of the lines" – lines of verse, but also lines of life "which run indifferently through us". In such moments, no longer confined to its conventional formal or genre characteristics, poetry happens (182).

This may sound like a faded Romantic ideal or, worse, like another form of nineteenth century sentimentality. Its empirical chances are slim, its advent adventitious – Ash presents this conception as a vision occurring to him during a ride in Richmond Park. One might indeed see Ash's conception as being basically indebted to Shelley. But Byatt tremendously extends Shelley's willingness to grant a poetic potential also to architecture for instance. The whole novel looks like the sounding of activities and media with respect to analogies in a poetic potential capable of mobilizing and engaging consciousness. Scholarship, in its best moments, whether in the form of biography or textual interpretation of some kind, moves into the direction of detective work (237, 483), that is to say into instances of "narrative greed" (335, cf. 176). It tries to nail down the "power of necessity in tales" (155, 79), inventing alienating theories and codes all the time as exercises in multifariousness and relativity, yet using them mainly as shortcuts in the quest for a "plot of a Romance [...] as the expectations of Romance control almost everyone in the Western world" (425).

It does in fact appear that "primary pleasures" (eating, drinking, sex) and activities depend on "the power and delight of words" (470), on a relatively elaborate use of texts written or spoken in order to gain the mixed status of being real and imaginary at the same time, to unfold something like poetic fascination. In the world of Western textuality, Shakespeare pushed the power and delight of words as enhancements of experience to a first climax, intimating at the same time the possibility of their self-sustaining potential. G. C. Lichtenberg was perhaps the first to provide a theory of mutual enhancement: By treating drugs with words and words with drugs, words may turn into the better drugs. (Lichtenberg should have included music; images are a different case whose potential he demonstrated, however, in his Hogarth interpretations.)[85] This is certainly not true in any indiscriminate way. Byatt has composed a lot of nineteenth century-like texts in which the effort to fascinate consciousness and its reading activities by laborious detours into myth and legend surely take precedence over contemporary topical problems.

This may work, as we know from similar efforts in the twentieth century. Due to the many restrictions imposed on the "Female Pen" in the nineteenth century, women writers of that period like Christabel LaMotte in particular often try to dodge the restrictions by escaping into this heavily encoded domain – and paying the price of obscure reference and symbolism. On the other hand: In spite of the instability of the kick galvanic, the simple and merely practical pursuit of obsessions and states of being possessed will hardly attain more than surrogate status. This pursuit relies on a certain violence with respect to the enforced and conventional role of language, the crude use of images and the more or less equally crude practice of social ritual which must make up for the trembling cogency of awareness in the kick galvanic situation. This is why in the two Byatt texts a parodistic trend asserts itself frequently. There is an ironic hint concerning Professor Mortimer Cropper, a leading US expert on Ash, and his use of pornography as "his own ways of sublimation" (Byatt 1991: 111), there are the more than ironic comments on Cropper's turning of biography into fetishism, disturbing and digging up the ashes of Ash in order to find out what was buried with

---

85 For more details see Pfeiffer 2002: 44–50.

him (492–496). There are in particular spiritualist séances staged as shortcuts between mind and object but liable to break down at any time, susceptible to disturbance, disruption, exposed to sheer contempt or destroyed by laughter. Ash receives some notoriety for his "Gaza exploit" when he "wreaks damage" on a séance held by the medium Mrs. Lees in the house of a friend (393–394). He immediately warns Christabel about what he takes as indubitable "trickery" (391), made possible by our "infinite capacity to be deceived by desire" (390) – shortly after she expatiated on her ability to see spirits and creatures (388). He writes the satirical dramatic monologue "Mummy Possest" (405–412, unfinished) with the special intention of unmasking the pretension that through "the Medium [...] the sublimest Souls / Make themselves known to those who sit and wait" and of destroying the claim that this alleged relationship between medium and sublime soul can be understood as a parallel to the relation between poet and language or as the one between the medium of paint and the ideal form of the Eternal Mother (409).

The devastating perspective on séances is foreshadowed in the lines from Robert Browning's dramatic monologue "Mr Sludge, 'the Medium'" directly in front of the first chapter. And it is cemented by the comic treatment séances receive in the second novella "The Conjugial Angel" in *Angels & Insects* (1992). Here, the denial that séances can vitally engage consciousness strikes home with particular force because the theory of spirits and angels and their order is pushed into transcendental Swedenborgian heights. These are constantly and comically undercut by the 'comments' of a raven and the noises of a dog "occasionally snoring, or emitting other wet, explosive animal noises at the most sensitive moments".[86] Even the presumed appearance of John Keats (251) does not save the spiritual events. On the other hand, the historical allurement of séances as a promise of direct spiritual or at least valuable communicative contact for a period experiencing massive thrusts in the medialization and the circumstantiality of communication should not be underestimated. In the second novella, Tennyson, for one, tries to find a personal way outside the group ritual of communicating with his dead father. Less than a week after his father's death, he sleeps "with some ceremony in his father's own bed", desirous, he says, "of seeing his ghost" (185). This is understandable since "art", that is to say his habit of "diffusing" everything quickly into poetry, of "singing away like the Nightingale", comes to him very easily (226, 269). Consequently and plausibly, he lives in the fear of overvaluing art (268–269), of getting "in an awful mess if he tried to

---

86 See Byatt 1992: 172.

elaborate on that kind of oracularity" (264) which characterizes especially his later poetry.

Byatt does not directly highlight the tensions and the mutual support of trance media and new media like photography which present-day research has recently come to emphasize. But even her Swedenborgians are aware that, to whatever heights of spirituality they may aspire or indeed ascend, the problem of the materialization of the spirits they communicate with must be faced (277).[87] However, the last séance in particular, apart from the contrast program offered by raven and dog, is marred by suspicions of obscenity (286 – the preceding one is compared to a "parlour game", 202); Tennyson's own experiment ends in hallucination and breakdown (272). It appears that, technically, the séance has turned into a counterproductive self-referential form of consciousness. Consciousness cannot thrive on a spirituality under suspicion. Nor can it feed upon the unconscious ("an evil spirit") where obscenity seems to be on the prowl. That is why Mrs Jesse, the sister of Tennyson, says: "*Something* is playing games with much that is sacred to me, and it is not myself, Mrs Papagay, but can be no one else, and I find I do not wish to know more" (286).

With Mrs Jesse, Mrs Papagay and their husbands, both sea captains, the second novella embarks on a conceptual compromise in which consciousness, in the form of a desirable double transition, finds an object which propels it back into an attractive form of self-reference. That form is suggested by terms like "being alive", connotationally surrounded by "life", "alive", "vital" (238) and "vitality" (289). For the captains, who mainly advocate that vocabulary, the situation is relatively simple. Their dangerous profession enforces an absolute concentration on objects and situations at hand. Conscious self-reference as the feeling of mastery – even in what is normally called failure (Arturo Papagay was twice shipwrecked and once cast away, 289) – is its own reward. With Papagay, the conceptual compromise is re-imported into the first novella ("Morpho Eugenia") in the form of a conceptual test. Papagay is the captain who takes William Adamson and Mathilda Crompton to Rio de Janeiro from where they want to travel into the Amazon region and the "further reaches of the Rio Negro" (158). He presents Adamson with a butterfly whose most important epithet is (the thrice repeated) "alive" (160). The Rio Negro area will be "in many ways an *Inferno*", yet they want to "live that life" (157). But going into the Amazon area, to be sure, does not simply mean that one will be alive because one

---

87 See Schüttpelz 2009: 278, 280, and 294–295 for the relation between materialization and photography. Schüttpelz is particularly concerned with Great Britain and, more specifically, with Edward Tylor, the ‚founder‘ of academic cultural anthropology whose famous *Primitive Culture* had come out in 1871.

lives a certain kind of life. Adamson and Crompton are also challenged or rather challenge themselves to practice genuine science there. Science, especially under such conditions is another activity which might occupy consciousness intensely and ought to drive the mind into a vital willingness for supreme achievement. The auspices for science, however, are not very good. Shortly before the end of the first novella, Mathilda demonstrates to the insect biologist Adamson in an anagrammatic game that "insect" and "incest" are almost interchangeable (153). This comes just after Adamson discovers the incest between his wife and her brother which had been going on for years on end. Its most provoking or revolting feature in Eugenia's confession consists in a playful beginning which grew "little by little, out of perfectly innocent, natural, *playful* things" into "something perfectly *natural*" (150–151, 158–159). We do not get any further explanation where that attraction might ultimately spring from. But for all the unpleasant qualities which Edgar, the brother, continuously displays, there seems to be a vital inevitability at work which science cannot claim. Harald Alabaster replaces a scientifically controlled feeling for living beings with dead collections and static theory. William, asked for comments, must admit: "It is, as you most eloquently say, a matter of *feeling*. And I cannot feel these things to be so" (89, cf. 73). But William's own work on social insects, culminating in a book on a woodland society of ants which he finishes with the help of Matty Crompton, seems to pay for its liveliness with anthropomorphic tendencies scientifically hardly warranted (cf. 108–109). Crompton herself points out these tendencies (104). The fact that he finds an enthusiastic publisher who thinks that such a book, with its "facts in abundance, useful reflections, drama, humour, and fun", is just the kind of book "of which the world of letters, at present, cannot have enough" (144), nourishes the suspicion that William himself has fallen victim to nineteenth-century sentimentalism. Moreover, the anthropomorphic tendencies concerning the ants find themselves in stark contrast with the zoological interpretation, by a Belgian naturalist and friend, of advanced human societies and the "terrestrial Paradises towards which the social designers of human cities and communes are working so hopefully" (115, cf. 114–115). The debate, also conducted in a framework of both biological and social theories of evolution (Darwin, Wallace, Robert Owen, Réaumur, Michelet), remains, to say the least, ambivalent (109–116).

Moreover and more importantly, shifting to such debates means approaching science too much on its own terms. Scientific debates are an epiphenomenon of either fascination or frustration with scientific work. But where do these stem from? "Morpho Eugenia" targets an activity and a discourse which must make themselves felt in science in order for science to become an absorbing form of consciousness. Established for a while on the Alabaster estate, William goes on "nature rambles". There he is able to "feel his old self again, scanning everything with a minute attention that in the forests had been the attention of a primitive hunter as well as a modern naturalist" (29). We must remember here Morin's assessment of hunting which intensifies and 'complexifies' the dialectics between foot, hand and brain, changes human relations not only with the environment but with the various human groups (men, women, young and old) themselves. It pushes ahead ways of thinking in which the attention to mostly unclear signs, forms of tracking down and early identification, improvisation and caution, cunning and ingenuity and all their transformations will be condensed into dramas of clear awareness and blurred indirectness, of uncertainty and ambiguity. The discourse science must partake of is poetry. Discussions on the (non-)relations between science and poetry have perhaps grown somewhat stale. Byatt has selected an aspect which bears at least a reminder or repetition. During his early ten-year first Amazon stay William carries with him an anthology *Choice Beauties of Our Elder Poets* in which, at some point, he is intrigued by a poem of Ben Jonson which takes on "a new urgency": "Have you seen but a bright lily grow? [...]" (12–13). Jonson tries to come to terms with the phenomenological and functional intensity of perception. If we could make sense of what we perceive we would not need scientific explanation. The latter is a detour not really solving, but at least appearing to come close to the riddle of perception. Arnold Gehlen was probably right in describing one of Schopenhauer's ultimate concerns as precisely both the irresistible temptation and the inability to come to terms with the intensity of appearance. Schopenhauer is profoundly moved by "the intuition of the living organic form, the physical, silent being of what has been given shape. Whoever was gripped, in looking at an animal, a leaf, by the perplexed wonderment that something like this exists, has understood one of Schopenhauer's prime experiences."[88]

---

[88] Cf. Chapter 4 ("Appearances") in Pfeiffer 2002: 119 for the Gehlen quote with endnote 21. The quote is from the early philosophical writings of Gehlen. There are anecdotes about Schopenhauer 'being lost in thought' in such situations of perception.

8 Existential Impressionism and Cultural Status: Dorothy Richardson (1873–1957)

Dorothy Richardson, a writer whose importance is rarely acknowledged, takes on symptomatic relevance in the context so far discussed. She demonstrates the far-reaching consequences produced not by new orientations and norms pursued by consciousness or adopted in action. She rather dismantles a dominant form of transitionality by disconnecting processes of thought from ruling standards of consistency to which the processes are mostly subjected for the sake of communication. But Richardson should also be seen as a problematic preparation for the second part of this book: Concerned almost exclusively with the flexible re-organization of situationally attractive perception, she gets disconnected from the dangerous amalgamations between the processes of consciousness in the framework of biographical patterns and the products of thought in the framework of 'history'. In these amalgamations, however, the fascinating transformation of the quasi-hysterical obsession with form(s) is more or less pushed aside by the catastrophic potential looming large in the decay of products (especially *Weltanschauungen* and theories) and the risks of history.

In Byatt's "Morpho Eugenia" it is easy to underestimate Matty (Mathilda) Crompton. It is difficult, however, to decide what her significance might consist in. With the story "Things Are Not What They Seem" (Byatt 1992: 119–140) she appears, for instance, as a writer in her own right. The story reads like a fairy-tale, haunted, despite her disclaimer ("a fabulous Tale, not an allegory", 141), by allegorical shadows. These might concentrate in a kind of self-interpretation according to which names weave the world together and make sure of its constant transformation. Metaphor, "carrying one idea into another", drives forward metamorphosis (132), producing "parables" which are projected onto other stories turning parables.[89] As a theoretical idea defining a form of transitionality,

---

[89] I am using here, certainly somewhat simplistically, Mark Turner's terminology in Turner 1996: 4–5, a book on the origins of thought and language. My impression is that the use of parable as "the root of the human mind – of thinking, knowing, acting, creating and plausibly even of speaking" (Preface, vi) is a bit too general. I would prefer, as Turner occasionally tends to do himself (cf. 42, 63, 88), to reserve metaphor and metaphoric projection and sequences for processes in the mind (possibly also unconscious ones), and parable as narrative imagining, story and their projection onto one another for their products. I fully agree with Turner that "the literary mind is not a separate kind of mind", but the fundamental human mind which produces image schemas, conceptual blendings, (metaphoric and) parabolic projections all the time (vi, cf. 4–5, 7, 10–11).

https://doi.org/10.1515/9783110581836-010

this does not sound very exciting. Transformed into biographical stories, however, it may harbor surprises. One of these surprises comes along as the metamorphosis of Crompton from a neutral, restrained and guarded human being of indefinite age into an attractive young woman, full of initiative, in her late twenties.

Such ingredients do not make the text into a suitable candidate for a feminist interpretation. But it is possible, indeed I think likely that certain "energy landscapes" (Metzinger and Windt, cf. fn. 64) of consciousness will, depending also on time, show up in a gendered form. The connection between metaphor and metamorphosis, the first dynamizing the mind, the second thoroughly reworking biographical patterns, looks like a preferred feminine domain in the early twentieth century. A crude comparison might suggest the direction of this argument. The multidimensionality of Joyce's *Ulysses* is primarily the product of a sophisticated aesthetic calculus and a very self-conscious artistic endeavor. Beckett quotes Joyce as admitting that he may have "oversystematized" this text. That tendency results from the ambition to be in complete control of enormous masses of language materials coming along with the double origin of the English language, its richness of associations and allusions, its potential for wordplay and, in comparison with French for instance, a relative mildness of language control.[90]

It would of course be naïve to assume that Dorothy Richardson did not keep a tight control over her materials. In important respects, however, she continues the work of her eighteenth century namesake: The specific intricacies of consciousness and its modes of transitionality are not determined by, but also not simply separable from the peculiarities of biographical curves. In *Clarissa*, Samuel Richardson presents consciousness in a series of fairly well-ordered, but affectively highly-charged conceptual frames. The length of this text indicates that the conceptual ordering of emotions and/as social values could hardly be reconciled any more with normative biographical expectations. The semantic framework of morality, family values, duties like honor, esteem, pride and the like was in constant danger of being undercut by the incomparable dynamics of a consciousness occupied with finding acceptable conceptual forms for the unsavory violence of envy and its relatives like jealousy and resentment. As an ideology, the semantic framework is still rigidly quoted; as a control of consciousness and individual orientation it is turning progressively into a failure, because it cannot keep pace with the erosive mobility of money, work and social

---

90 For the Joyce-Beckett relation see Knowlson 1996: 102, 105, 353, 357. Beckett was of course acutely aware of the debt he owed Joyce.

relations. Richardson breaks out of this dead end with the help of death as an end: He shifts attention to the theatrical-emotional turmoil with which the death, unnecessary on almost all counts, of Clarissa is staged as a long-drawn out dying process. This turmoil has nothing to do with the hallmark of the text: its descriptive-analytical sophistication with respect to the dynamics of (self-)conscious affectivity in a clearly delineated, but no longer rigidly organized social space.

In Dorothy Richardson, normative biographical expectations have largely vanished. In terms of family life (mother's suicide and father's bankruptcy), personal relations (miscarriage following the affair with H. G. Wells), job needs and time (especially World War I), however, we have to reckon with considerable biographical pressures. In contrast to the eighteenth century, these pressures do not strengthen, but rather dilute the binding power of social institutions. Their loss of symbolic attraction opens up spaces for personal profiles of experience. In Dorothy Richardson, this amounts to an influx of orientations which, for want of a better term, could be called feminine, though (as far as I am concerned) not feminist.[91] There are certainly quite a few passages which must be called feminist, criticizing male behavior and thought as insufficiently elastic and overly one-dimensional (cf. e. g. vol. 2, 27: "Any interest in generalities, any argument

---

91 Richardson criticism has it of course both ways. See for instance Kaplan 1975 *vs.* Hanscombe 1982/83. Hanscombe's summary of her position in her introduction to the Virago edition here used is, however, fully acceptable. See introduction (to each volume) to Richardson 1979: 4–10, 8 (in the first volume the introduction is differently placed, the passage in question is on p. 5): "[...] she affirms, implicitly and explicitly, the value of her own perceptions and judgments [...] The particular virtues concomitant to such a feminism are the deliberate rejection of female role-playing, an insistence on personal honesty, a passionate independence and a pilgrimage towards self-awareness"). I would also agree to "the qualities of intelligence Richardson most prized": "the ability to perceive relationships between phenomena and the effort to synthesize feeling and reflection" (9). I do not feel competent to comment on Joanne Winning's study (Winning 2000) which regards Richardson, mainly on the evidence in *Dawn's Left Hand* of 1931 (the relation with Amabel) as part of a larger group of lesbian writers (*Dawn's Left Hand*, to mention that too, also has the only sexual relation with a man, Hypo Wilson [= H. G. Wells]). Closer to my concerns is the thesis that Richardson was interested in finding a third space beyond masculinity and femininity. I hesitate to call *Pilgrimage* a mystical novel in the way of Blake 1960. One can find elements of the mystic way. But as a general (co-)editor of four volumes on the topic of mysticism and modernity, I do not see an overarching perspective there. See e. g. Vondung and Pfeiffer (eds.) 2006. Still interesting is Gregory 1967. In more recent times, there is the (English translation of a German) study by Bronfen 1999, an important and controversial book which raises the crucial question to what extent corporeal and cultural "enspacements" can restructure or even rehierarchize dimensions of the real to such an extent that the notion of (personal) identity must be recuperated.

or criticism or opposition would turn him into a towering bully. All men were more or less like that"; 220 – 222 the criticism of Jesus Christ as taking on only "*male* humanity"; vol. 3, 257: "*Men* can't get on together"; vol. 3, 297 the male combination of cleverness and utter stupidity; vol. 4, 92–93: the illusions of male *mechanical* schemes). In most cases, however, that criticism is anything but original. It is one-directional in its own way. More importantly, it resembles prejudice because it does not entertain any relation with or follow from Richardson's own constructive orientations. More about these orientations will be said later. Suffice it to say at this point that they start out as a distancing of social demands, then turn into an exploration of their remaining potential and of what is possibly beyond. In such processes, hierarchization must be avoided as long as possible. The distancing is not the result of explicit criticism. It rather emerges within a readiness to adjust perception and consciousness to the changes brought about by a moderate – certainly not a radical – attitude of openness, responsiveness and acceptance of stimuli. The consequences of distancing might explain why the *Pilgrimage* texts taken as a whole are even longer than *Clarissa* (about 2000 as compared to 1500 pages). It might also explain that the overall title of *Pilgrimage* is not downright misleading, but certainly cannot be used as an allegorical key unlocking the mystery of experience contained in the 13 mostly shorter texts. Their series rather undermines the status of the work as a unified whole, as a picture or symbol of cultural achievement or challenge; Dorothy Richardson's texts are neither committed to the telling of a story or stories, nor to the subversion of all traditional narrative patterns which we get in Joyce. At a first glance, the advice that readers should focus instead on the consciousness of the main character Miriam Henderson might not work very well either since, as a common criticism of Richardson has it, that mind is not interesting enough to carry the narrative load through all the volumes. Richardson, so the story goes, introduced the stream of consciousness novel (she preferred to speak of interior monologue) to England and was forgotten, because she did not artistically control it.

The texts were mostly written and published between 1914/15 and 1938 (the last text, *March Moonlight* was published posthumously in 1967). They are concerned, if I may say so, mainly with the life of the main character Miriam Henderson from roughly 1890 (when she is 17) to 1915. That life appears, on the surface of it, heavily trivial. Miriam works as a teacher in different positions, as a secretary and receptionist in a dentist's office, she goes in for political and religious experiments (socialism, Quakers) during the years after the end of the nineteenth century until the beginning of World War I. That time frame remains however rather vague. Efforts to put the texts into focus may yield, for quite a while, a kind of negative diagnosis. The texts oscillate between an infinite registering of the apparent trivialities of everyday life and the sudden eruptions of more emphatic, sometimes feminist passages which, however, vanish as quickly as they appear. A general feature of the texts, then, consists in a lack of connection, relation between different situations of speech and action, whether private or professional. Situations are hard to define. In spite of a certain "enspacement" (Elisabeth Bronfen's term), for instance a cultural one, they appear to be somewhat decontextualized. This would hold true even for situations of relative intensity in which something like a transfiguration of the commonplace (to quote the title of Arthur C. Danto's well-known book) takes place. In the second volume (*The Tunnel*, 1919: 48–54), for instance, Miriam and her boss, the dentist, are looking at pictures and sculptures in the dentist's office. The 'art objects' are mainly Japanese so that, implicitly, an intercultural problem concerning the 'place' of art in culture enters the scene. Miriam and the dentist are thinking about how to hang or place the objects, how their decisions will affect perception in the context of the room, itself part of the dentist's practice. All of this, however, is discursively barely touched upon. Perceptions, sensations and thoughts move quickly from one picture or detail of the room (for instance copies of the magazine *Studio* lying around or the "flushed forehead of the dentist", *The Tunnel*, 1919: 49–50). The dentist tries to place Oriental pottery between two pictures of Devonshire where it "looks somehow too big or too small or something" (50). Then a place near the corner cupboard is tested, with the result that the cupboard itself would have to be moved. The decision is postponed, instead we get: "Miriam's perceptions happily raced along. How had he known that she cared for things? She was not sure that she did ... not in the way he did ... How did he know that she had noticed any of his things?" (51). They then talk about the years it takes Japanese artists to learn how to produce "simple effects" (52). This leads to the problem whether "single specimens of Japanese art, the last results of centuries of an artistic discipline, that was it, that had grown from the life of a secluded people living isolated in a particular spot under certain social and natural conditions" can be used for purposes of "English household decoration" (52) at all. Again, no decision is reached, instead talk moves on to Lafcadio Hearn (53).

Apparently it is not so much the perception of art objects which is at stake; the objects rather function as formally well-defined and therefore strong appeals to let perception – which of course proceeds from the subject – sink back into the subject again. The question, then, is to what extent *perception* can be consciously *felt as a fusion* for which the distinction between 'subjective' and 'objective' plays a very subordinate role only. In that respect, the Japanese objects are particularly 'pregnant'. For Westerners, their aesthetic-sensuous appeal is very strong. Their semantic-intellectual appeal, their 'significant' or symbolic side, is however rather elusive. The fusion between perception and consciousness as felt form differs considerably from Western romantic fusion which normally occurs in the name of some higher value or state of being. Romantic fusion, for instance in Wordsworth, bears a close resemblance to mysticism. In Richardson, the social framework, which remains intact, would in itself prevent such an ontological leap. The framework merely gains an elasticity in which, under the influence of special objects, the dynamization and rearrangement of perception, feeling and thought gets under way. The scope for a different perceptual-mental give and take between person and 'aesthetic' object is enlarged. Latently or openly, this active receptiveness illustrates Morin's notion of the 'hysterical' drive of consciousness. The simple question concerning a possible obligation (date, appointment, engagement of some sort) provokes the following reaction:

> She answered, stammering, in amazed consciousness of what was to follow and accepted the invitation in a flood of embarrassment. Her delight and horror and astonishment seemed to flow all over the table. Desperately she tried to gather in all her emotions behind an easy appreciative smile. She felt dismay and astonishment coming out of her hair [...] (*The Tunnel*, 1919: 168).

In different situations, for instance those defined more strongly in 'aesthetic' and less in 'social' terms, the perceptual-mental give and take is similar to Hegel's characterization of what is triggered by the best portraits like those by Dürer or Titian and their perception: "The longer one looks at such a picture, the more deeply one immerses oneself in it, all the more does one see emerging from it." These portraits "meet us so individually and they give us a conception of spiritual vitality unlike what a face actually confronting us gives". Such a portrait is "more like the individual than the actual individual himself".[92] What we call reality and its ordinary objects, can and should also invite and stimulate perception, but does not absorb and redirect consciousness to the same extent. Soon after the "decoration" scene, another fairly 'personal' meeting between Miriam and the dentist takes place. She feels her mind to be "alight with the sense of her many beckoning interests, aglow with the fullness of life." Yet the meeting, although atmospherically pleasant, is far less engaging (72–73). In all cases, however, a latent process is going on behind the socially conventional situation. In the process, the reality status of parts of the environment is undogmatically and often tacitly changed.

---

92 Hegel 1988: vol. II, 866–867. The preceding quote from *The Tunnel* also shows that the important aspect about the representation of consciousness is not the frequently used narrative technique of stream of consciousness or interior monologue, but techniques of drawing attention to the functional processes and mechanisms in meeting the and constructing a world.

In the texts collected in the first of four volumes (*Pointed Roofs, Backwater, Honeycomb,* 1915–1917) the lack of contextualization and relatability is most clearly worked out. Miriam finds herself in Germany as a very young tutor of English. In its best function, the *intercultural* situation serves to keep perception fluid and thought pleasantly stimulated. It does not, or need not, sharpen or provoke questions about personal or cultural identity and difference. Perceptual and mental shifts are jotted down in short passages, but not extended into commentary or interpretation. The shifts in perception seem significant, but they do not provoke, they rather block questions for significance. Richardson attempts the feat to simultaneously reduce a culturally predetermined selectivity of narration (many things may, but need not be important) and yet to suggest some profile of experience. A typical example might be worth quoting:

> Whenever she found herself alone she began to sing, softly. When she was with others a head drooped or lifted, the movement of a hand, the light falling along the detail of a profile could fill her with happiness.
> It made companionship a perpetual question. At rare moments there would come a tingling from head to foot, a faint buzzing at her lips and at the tip of each finger. At these moments she could raise her eyes calmly to those about her and drink in the fact of their presence, see them all with perfect distinctness, but without distinguishing one from the other. She wanted to say, 'Isn't it extraordinary? Do you realize?' She felt that if only she could make her meaning clear all difficulties must vanish. (*Pointed Roofs*, 1915: 158)

Likewise, looking into "a thin volume of German poetry" alters the status of the German girls around her. They are *reduced and enhanced* into "beautiful forms" which "rose and moved around her". Music – warblings of the birds, songs and piano – reinforce that effect which, however, remains fragile. The words of the songs impose themselves because they establish dimensions of misleading (cliché-like, sentimental and similar) definiteness (*Pointed Roofs*, 1915: 142–143). The rhythm of reduced enhancement and misleading definiteness becomes even more hectic a bit later. Culture, society and religion demand recognition. But at the same time, in their fragmentary totality, they shrink to a collection of headlines and book titles, transforming consciousness into a feverish chaos for which distinctions between information, relevance on the one, redundancy and information overload on the other hand can hardly be drawn (168–173). In analogous ways, the distinction or opposition, culturally and psychologically mostly taken for granted, between genuine and feigned feelings *may* play a role for Miriam. But on the whole she is more interested in situations where that distinction – and the one between reality and fiction into the bargain – is superfluous. These are situations where the stimulus of the environment (which may consist mainly in another person) and the atmosphere in which consciousness feels itself couched can engage in some transitory symbiosis. For that, another passage deserves quotation as one paradigmatic mode of transitionality:

> The dust of the school was still upon her; the skin of her face felt strained and tired, her hands were tired and hot, her blouse dim with a week of school wear, and her black skirt oppressed her with its invisible burden of grime. But she was staring up at a clean blue sky fringed with tree-tops. She stretched herself out more luxuriously upon her cushions [...] The soft fingers of the air caressed her temples and moved along the outlines of her face and neck. Forty—two days ... like this. Tomorrow she would wake up a new person [...] The gently lifting water seemed to come nearer; the invading air closed in on her. She gave herself ecstatically to its touch [...]. (*Backwater*, 1916: 294)

Clearly, an existential dimension is involved; clearly also it is not downright existentialism or mysticism. The prerequisite for that seems to consist 'only' in a kind of elementary trust in and patience for perception, the willingness of consciousness to be itself an agent in the impact of the outside world. This existential drive does not preclude occasional social criticism; but it permits that only in a very unsystematic form (cf. *Backwater*, 1916: 336–338 'against' English education, 386–387 against worldly life in general).

Richardson's writing is not without a polemical thrust. But it does not operate in the service of feminism or some other concern in any consistent way. It is rather intended to undermine the logical-cultural-psychological forms of consistency-building so deeply entrenched in Western culture. "Consistency is the something of something minds" (*Interim*, 1919: 414). Lawrence Durrell has followed suit with an analogous formulation: "No, there's nothing wrong with cogito or with sum; it's poor bloody ergo that's been such a curse."[93] Likewise, it is easy to find the timeframe in which the stories in *Pilgrimage* take place. But that surface historicity does not allow us to detect any far-reaching shaping power of history. Historical contexts which, for ordinary, including ordinary historical thinking might offer themselves as explanatory devices for events and character, are negatively evoked in short polemical attacks against images of European history: the Greeks, the first to evolve universal ideals, passed on through Roman Law and the Christian Church, the Hellenization of Europe, the rebirth of the Greeks in the shape of the sedentary French, the materialism of modern Germany – these and other historico-cultural notions are petrified stereotypes (*Revolving Lights*, 1923: 375–376).

In an analogous move, the cognitive validity (better known as truth claims) of thought systems is not rejected, but downplayed and downgraded. This hap-

---

93 Durrell 1968: 13.

pens above all in the part fittingly called *Deadlock* (vol. 3, 1921), where many talks with the Russian-Jewish intellectual Michael Shatov take place. A self-relativizing tendency in the dynamics or "progress of philosophy" comes to the forefront: "A system [...] very generally corrects the fallacy of the preceding system, and leans perhaps in the opposite direction [...] Thus the movements of philosophic thought may be compared to the efforts of a drunken man to reach his home" (157). Or, perhaps of greater relevance if one is still interested in the contents of thought: "Descartes should have said, 'I am aware that there *is* something, therefore I am" (171).

There is then no unified direction to transitionality in Richardson. By and large, she adheres to common ways of seeing (or feeling) reality. But that adherence certainly is reduced – which means that the cost of changing the energy landscape of consciousness is reduced in the perception of a situation. On the basis of what I have called the openness, receptiveness or readiness of an attentive consciousness very much aware of its own state and alert with respect to what is there or going on in its environment, small changes in perceptual arrangement can bring forth massive environmental transformations. These transformations, in whichever domain, never reach revolutionary degrees. But they suffice to alter Miriam's self-relationship by making her refer to herself sometimes in the first, sometimes in the third person, and with that step regroup also the references to and the relevance of the forms of the other. They are also capable of relativizing self-ascribed Western cultural achievements in comic or aggressive ways.

In spite of my reservations concerning the presence and power of historical saturation in Richardson, situating her work in a framework of broad intellectual trends is still called for. Max Weber has described the direction of Western cognitive behavior (in religion, philosophy, science in particular) as the disenchantment of the world. For Georg Lukács, a "disanthropomorphization" of life has been going on since the beginnings of science with the ancient Greeks. According to Arbogast Schmitt, Plato and Aristotle propounded an unsurpassed model of rationality as a philosophy of discrimination, as the 'art' of identifying both things, objects and more 'abstract' matters *adequately through continuous and comparative conceptual work*, culminating in the concrete, definite and conceptually consensual content of any act of knowledge. The more the sciences extended their domain, the more curiosity brought about an expansiveness of the real at the same time enjoyable and frightening, the more a certain relativity of truth claims asserted itself as well. Both science and the Platonic-Aristotelian model then had to defend themselves against the suspicion of not embodying only *rationality*, but also adopting variable strategies of *rationalization*. Moreover, it does not seem so difficult to reach a conceptual agreement about what is perceived as a point, line and circle. But it *is* difficult to agree, for instance, on what constitutes individual happiness within the complexities and conflicts of a state, on the relations between economy and ethics, on rational self-realization as a condition for the merging of personal advantage and the social whole, to say nothing of a culture of emotions and its aesthetic, ethical and political meaning.[94]

It seems to me that this is the epistemological situation which drives the activities of consciousness in *Pilgrimage*. Both rationality and rationalizations were intended to open up the secrets of nature. The *multiplicity of rationalizations* has, however, mainly increased the possibilities of distinguishing provisionally between reality and fiction. It follows that for Richardson the distinction between autobiography and fiction (texts like novels) is not really significant and necessary only for those who expect an autobiography to stick as much as possible to a simple concept of factual truth. Generally, the costs of the distinction between reality and fiction have been too high, because the distinction has decreased our access to *certainty* and the undisturbed development of *senses of the real*. To some extent, a criticism of men's role in science and culture is in place here. In science, Richardson's Miriam thinks at one point, women show up only in the reductive forms of gynecology and a superimposed idealizing morality (*The Tunnel*, 1919: 220). In culture, men must take the greater part of the blame for the transformation of experience, more particularly so-called aesthetic experience, into object-like works of art and their elevation into "humanity's highest achievement". But women have followed suit: "At present they [men] are surrounded, out in the world, by women who are trying to be as much like them as possible". The past, with Italian women leading "men by the nose in the old way", was probably not so different either (*Oberland*, 1927: 93, *The Tunnel*, 1919: 219). The general diagnosis, merging epistemology and culture, remains therefore in force:

> Out in the world life was ceasing all the time [...] Young men died in advance; it was visible in their faces, when they took degrees and sat down to tasks that made time begin to move [...] But why is the world which produces them so fresh and real and free, and then seizes and makes them dead old leaves whirled along by time, so different from people alone in themselves when time is not moving? People in themselves want nothing but reality. *Why*

---

94 I have assembled here, not quite at random, but also not very systematically a few salient positions. See Weber 1922: 1–12; Lukács 1972: vol. 1, 55–114 (especially also on the contradictory upswing of disanthropomorphization in early modernity); Kofler 1976: 41, 43, 78; Schmitt 2012: 28, 78, 235–236, 341–380, 421–423, 433–434, 442–443, 506–507. For both Lukács and Kofler the shift fom rationality to rationalizations of all kinds is intimatelly linke to the rise of capitalism.

> *can't reality exist in the world?* All the things that happen produce friction because they dis-
> tract people from the reality they are unconsciously looking for. (*Deadlock*, 1921: 188, my
> italics)

At this point, psychoculturally crucial functions of writing assert themselves. Writing is essential for a consciousness both open for the impact of the external world and actively seeking that impact. Writing must reinforce, shape and stabilize transitions of consciousness which, because of their conspicuous double character, occur with new intensity. Writing is the most important 'medium' of and a kind of relay for these transitions because it keeps contact with both processes and products of consciousness. It shapes processes into momentary definiteness, granting them the appearance of a finished product, without destroying their processual dynamics:

> While I write, everything vanishes but what I contemplate. The whole of what is called 'the
> past' is with me, seen anew, vividly. No, Schiller, the past does not stand 'being still'. It
> moves, growing with one's growth. Contemplation is adventure into discovery; reality.
> (*March Moonlight*, 1967: 657)

For all that is known and said we need language. But in language meaning changes. Merely through language we do not know "for certain. Everything depends on the way a thing is put, and that is a question of some particular civilization". Culture then comes through literature which, as a collection of texts, "is only a half-truth". The Bible is not true, it is a culture, and religion is wrong "in making word-dogmas out of it". "It clings to words which get more and more wrong" (*The Tunnel*, 1919: 99). Writing, then, is a difficult matter. It is something "one had always wanted to do, that everyone probably secretly wanted to do". But it is also an activity where the fall into mediocrity looms large. (*The Tunnel*, 1919: 165 – 166)

Given the criticism of consistency in *Pilgrimage* already mentioned, we might expect that such reflections are not to be tested for clear consistency. In a later passage, the fragmented visual layout of the printed page suggests difficulties of sense-making even before reading begins. The passage presents a list of book titles and brief thought commentaries. If I am not sorely mistaken, Miriam focuses upon a book called *Critique de la Pensée moderne*. Opening it, she picks up a series of words which, in their turn, provoke a series of questions. Her attention finally settles on the sentence "There is a dangerous looseness in the fabric of our minds". Imagining the writing process, letting that sentence sink into her mind and the words unfold directions of meaning, she finally sees the imagination, or the imaginative mind, of the author at work in the production of that sentence. Writing then in its non-mediocre form appears to tap the potentials of an imagination which in its turn is "based upon reality" (i.e. senses of the real). In that way writing opens paths into metaphysics. This is metaphysics not as a system or closed text, but as a transcending movement into various directions. Writing shapes experience and preempts its contamination with its conventional forms. Near the very end of the whole sequence, Richardson reflects on the necessity of being alone, since only "when I am with others does my sense of isolation return" (*March Moonlight*, 1967: 656). This diagnosis moves on to a unique "cheap restaurant" most of whose "customers don't seem to be fully present", but where she also encounters people "in meditation, breathing out now and then [...their] Buddhistic O–m" (657).

We are now in a position to determine Richardson's approach more precisely. She does not condemn systematic thought as such. But writing for her means writing against those forms of system building in which processes are hardened into 'objects' or objectifications. With the concepts of reification and fetishism many forms of philosophy and ordinary psychoanalysis have developed both milder and more rigid parallels to objectification. Thus Hegel sees objectification as a basic and basically normal process ending in products (that is material and materialized mental products like systems of thought, political systems, historical periods). This is why Hegel would talk about Christianity, and not about Jesus who might have embodied, in a transitory historical form, an important type of human experience perhaps to be saved in various, but not dogmatic ways for later times. Thus the Bible is read as a collection of dogmas and not as a heterogeneous collection of case studies of early forms – and more than just early forms – of intense human experience. (*The Tunnel*, 1919: 99)

9 An Interlude, Or, From Richardson to Richardson

It may be time for a brief summarizing and comparative interlude. Looking first at Samuel Richardson and his *Clarissa*, a few perhaps slightly critical remarks seem to impose themselves. Richardson did not, as he (or rather Lovelace in Letter 224) claims, "write to the moment". Nor did he practice an "instantaneous description" (Preface). Both terms refer merely to the speed of responding to an event, but not to something like the immediacy or intimacy of consciousness. It is true, of course, that the letter form nourishes such an illusion. But it shows rather that, whatever consciousness is or may be, it is beset, from the outset, by conceptual priorities which translate any so-called movement of the heart into the social significance of the event. The intricacy of the social and financial calculus infiltrating the text implies that the social structure, based on status and property, does no longer conclusively define social situations. The Harlowe family provides one instance. Certainly, such situations can always change and offer surprises. In *Clarissa*, however, these changes, whether in action or merely in thought, appear to have become interminable. Events, in their turn, have become unforeseeable to at least some extent. This is shown by any detailed summary of the plot – starting with the initial fact that Lovelace visits the Harlowes to court the older sister Arabella and falls for Clarissa instead. One could even say that Lovelace, not only as far as the rape is concerned, is the first personal prototype for the manufacture of the unforeseeable, sometimes, as in the impact of Clarissa's virtuousness, even for himself. Lovelace and Clarissa are aware of the conceptual priorities mostly in the forms of normative categories which they can bend in such a way that their dignity as a person appears to serve the dignity of their families. But if the dynamism of change in situations and events disturbs the coordination of emotion and situation, the priorities can be handled best as a conceptual game.

In a privileged position, one can play that game with gusto. This is more or less the case with Lovelace. He can afford to have his correspondence, apart from the letters to Clarissa, practically monopolized by the exchange with his friend and later critic John Belford. Moreover, taking the initiative, he enjoys a definitional advantage. Clarissa, however, must play that game defensively on too many fronts (above all and parallel to Belford in the case of Lovelace her confidante Anna Howe, her extended family and a host of other persons). It gets deadly serious once the psychological impact of conceptual control is too heavy.

For Henry James and even more so for Dorothy Richardson the 'psychological' vocabulary for conscious processes can no longer be embedded, however

https://doi.org/10.1515/9783110581836-011

dynamically, into social categories. Nor can the products of the characters' minds, much as it would appear necessary, be consistently related to what imposes itself as 'reality' out there. The lack of control for processes points to the 'unconscious', the lack of relatability in the products to 'history', both of them urgent and inaccessible at the same time. In the nineteenth century, this situation is foreshadowed in the cooperation, both in life and literature, between George Eliot and George Henry Lewes. With capitalism no longer merely incipient but in full and especially uncomfortable swing, the illumination of what might be going on in consciousness cannot be left to the limited resources of people. A direct, as it were natural access is out even more than before. Scientific investigation, with its increasing prestige, poses as its controlled replacement. In *Middlemarch*, the representation of consciousness is therefore not only conceptual, but theoretical. I do not want to commit George Eliot to the positions of Lewes. But his analyses of both the necessity and the insufficiency of introspection in his *Problems of Life and Mind*, especially on "Problem the First. The Study of Psychology. Its Object, Scope, and Method"[95], certainly provide a guiding framework with which she was familiar. "Introspection is defective", Lewes holds,

> in that while its disclosures are absolutely *certain* they are never *exact*, and are always individual, never general. They do not admit of being measured by sharply defined standards of comparison; they may be discriminated, named, and classified; they cannot be numbered, measured, compared. They have no common measure, only a common nature. (95)

For Eliot, the comparative aspect – comparing the states of mind of Dorothea and Casaubon – is of crucial importance. In fact, Dorothea's mind illustrates a confusion of theory and pathos ("theoretic" vs. "lofty"). Casaubon's, in its turn, is flooded, satisfied with and lost in historical knowledge. The drawback of this shift into a theoretical structuring of consciousness is the neglect of what Lewes, in spite of his criticism, accepted as the limited validity of introspection. As we have seen at the end of chapter one, its results, in *Middlemarch*, are admitted only in the form of vague metaphors which, in another turn of the screw, are used as material for a general theory of consciousness. The "play of minute causes producing what may be called thought and speech vortices" (1961: vol. 1, 48) is named, but not represented. Instead, metaphorization is proclaimed as *the* law of consciousness: "for we all of us, grave or light, get our thoughts entangled in metaphors, and act fatally on the strength of them" (vol. 1, 71). Or also: "We are all of us imaginative in some way or other, for images are the brood of desire" (vol. 1, 284). Similarly, the famous pier-glass parable

---

95 Lewes 1879, chapters V and VI on the introspective method and its limits.

(vol. 1, 232) by an "eminent philosopher", lifting everything "into the serene light of science", lays down the law concerning the relationship between events and (the "egoism" of) our consciousness which arranges events ("scratches") into well-ordered shapes.

Eliot, then, is more interested in the functional mechanisms of consciousness than in what is going on there (its 'phenomenology'). Consequently, the representation of consciousness in Eliot normally moves on a level from which her characters are barred. Another arbitrary example: "All Dorothea's passion was transfused through a mind struggling towards an ideal life; the radiance of her transfigured girlhood [!] fell on the first object that came within its level" (vol. 1, 34). Eliot knows that character formation is a "subtle [...] process of [...] gradual change" (vol. 1, 125). But she does not represent that subtlety. Even in the case of Lydgate, the doctor who has a mind informed by theory, that theoretical awareness is restricted to medicine. He does not really understand what is happening to him in other areas; he falls in love with an actress in Paris, but is not aware of the source of attraction ("a sweet matronliness even in youth", vol. 1, 131). Rosamund Vincy, clever as she is, does not see through the "preconceived romance" she is embarking upon with Lydgate. We have to wait only for a few lines to get the corresponding theory: "Our passions do not live apart in locked chambers, but, dressed in their wardrobe of notions, bring their provisions to a common table and mess together, feeding out of the common store according to their appetite" (vol. 1, 145; cf. 221 on the theoretical dimensions of Caleb Garth's religious feelings, and vol. 2, 240, on Bulstrode's "images and conjectures, which were a language to his hopes and fears").

Eliot's is a risky strategy, because, as Lewes for instance was well aware of, the theoretical control of consciousness at the time would have to take into account the subconscious and, still more removed from conscious awareness, even the unconscious. Lewes does not follow Carus who affirmed that "the key to unlock all the problems of Consciousness is to be sought in the Unconscious". But he is confident that the paradox loses its strangeness "if we extricate it from the contradictoriness of its terms, and translate it into the expression of the constant and definite relation between function and organ, between mental and bodily states." Then the formula will run somewhat in these terms: "The key to unlock all the problems of mental activity is to be sought by studying each strand of observation, organic facts and mental experience, the Mechanism and its History"[96]. In spite of his chapter on the limitations of introspection, Lewes seems more impressed by what introspection can achieve, especially since he

---

96 Lewes 1879: 91.

cannot convincingly establish a concept and practice of observation and inference which could compete with the role of observation in chemistry or physics. The unconscious, inaccessible to introspection, could of course be pushed into the domain of functional mechanisms. But the burning question of what it contains, how unconscious content relates to conscious content, cannot be pushed aside any more. The situation does not improve very much with the tentative proposal of replacing the concept of consciousness by the one of experience. Experience supposedly transcends the fact of individual feeling and includes the experience of the race. With experience, observation and inference enjoy the help of "that sympathetic inner movement which may be called mental contagion" (1879: 92). Moreover: "In Literature and Art there are expressed the thoughts and feelings which I can interpret by my own" (98). Lewes then, after seemingly moving into the opposite direction (introspection), ends up with a notion of consciousness and its accessibility which supports and tacitly calls for the methods of George Eliot. If we emphasize consciousness, readers of *Middlemarch* do not get "mental experience" (Lewes 1879: 91). But they might indeed find a theoretically informed representation of experience which is able to bring about the mental contagion Lewes speaks of. Eliot's range of represented people and their 'experience' is fairly comprehensive (race), also because her methods resemble those of science (theory, observation and inference).

Given Lewes' awareness of the growing emphasis on the unconscious in his time (he knows Eduard von Hartmann for instance), it would have been surprising if he or George Eliot, with their methods, could really have kept a lid on this pushy topic and sprawling domain. Henry James shifts representation therefore towards a phenomenology of consciousness, including suggestions pertaining to the unconscious. It is triggered especially in situations of biographical crisis and cultural clash. The transformation and the expanding historical horizons of the nineteenth century, however, take on such power and take place to such an extent that the need for forms of control makes itself imperiously felt. We meet historical forms of control in typical media of memory and self-observation like archives, libraries, museums, encyclopaedias, world exhibitions, statistics, news (papers), photography, but also in descriptions and analyses of all kinds like social reportage and its scientific (sociology) and artistic (the novel) counterparts. In various degrees, all [!] of them are committed to the combination of factual investigation and categorical order.[97] To a limited extent, James apparently assumed he could still afford older forms of narrative authorial-omniscient control.

---

97 See the monumental work of Osterhammel 2013: 46, generally 25 – 83. For the combination of factual investigation and categorical order see also the parallel analyses in Pfeiffer 2015.

James "the old intruder", as the relics of this practice have been dubbed, tries to resuscitate a lost cause: Sentences like "It may be affirmed without delay that Isabel was probably very liable to the sin of self-esteem" (James 1963: 50, cf. 139: "I say he did nothing, and I maintain the phrase in the face of the fact that he thought at these moments of Isabel", or 312: "The working of this young lady's spirit was strange, and I can only give it to you as I see it [...]") offer a contradictory mixture of primitive omniscience and a pretence of ignorance. It does not help to grant, in some cases, an ironic attitude to James (1963: 457: "It is our privilege to look over her shoulder [...]"). On the other side, William James' descriptions of conscious complexity will have prevented, one would suppose, Henry from adopting the stance of theoretical superiority which George Eliot had cultivated. Therefore, in order to represent consciousness, Henry James typically goes for a semi-theoretical *and at the same time* semi-phenomenological style which blurs ascriptive clarity. We cannot then decide whether conscious processes are seen predominantly from the narrator's or more from the character's point of view. Nor can we be sure whether to call the procedure an interpretation or 'merely' a stylization:

> It will probably not surprise the reflective reader that Ralph Touchett should have seen less of his cousin since her marriage than he had done before that event – an event of which he took such a view as could hardly prove a confirmation of intimacy. He had uttered his thought, as we know, and after this had held his peace, Isabel not having invited him to resume a discussion which marked an era in their relations. (1963: 388)

In *The Portrait of a Lady*, the blurring of language and perspective ascription remains fairly intelligible, because the narrator-cum-characters amalgamation, especially of course in Isabel's case, focuses upon a series of problems. In *The Golden Bowl*, however, problems as filters of intelligibility have largely vanished or are treated as almost non-existent, because they would disturb and damage the self-image of an affluent leisure class. The crucial facts – the relationship of Prince Amerigo and Charlotte Stant before their marriages to Adam and Maggie Verver and the ('adulterous') renewal of that relationship after their marriages – are mentioned twice by Maggie in chapters 33 and 34 (James 1966: 409, 429), but played down by her interlocutors. Depending on how one interprets the 'crisis' chapters 33 (between Maggie and Mrs Assingham who smashes the bowl) and 34 (between the couple Maggie and Amerigo), it is doubtful to what extent even the crack in the golden bowl can be treated as a real problem or must be left alone in its multiple but on the whole obvious symbolic meanings. Under such conditions, the double style, mixing narrator and character perspective and largely deprived of problem referents, tends to produce obscurities. Sometimes a comic effect results from the simple explanation which the narrator provides for the verbal enigmas produced before. I quote at length and without omissions:

> An impulse eminently natural had stirred within the Prince; his life, as for some time es-
> tablished, was deliciously dull, and thereby, on the whole, what he liked best; but a
> small gust of yearning had swept over him, and Maggie repeated to her father, with infinite
> admiration, the pretty terms in which, after it had lasted a little, he had described to her
> this experience. He called it a 'serenade', a low music that, outside one of the windows
> of the sleeping house, disturbed his rest at night. Timid as it was, and plaintive, he yet
> couldn't close his eyes for it, and when finally, rising on tiptoe, he had looked out, he
> had recognized in the figure below with a mandolin, all duskily draped in her grace, the
> raised appealing eyes and the one irresistible voice of the ever-to-be-loved Italy. Sooner
> or later, that way, one had to listen; it was a hovering, haunting ghost, as of a creature
> to whom one had done a wrong, a dim, pathetic shade crying out to be comforted. For
> this there was obviously but one way – as these were doubtless also many words for the
> simple fact that so prime a Roman had a fancy for again seeing Rome. (James 1966: 161)

Using the terminology of the brother one could say: The last sentence provides a resting place for consciousness with a vengeance. Even so, we cannot say for sure whether it gives a reliable summary of the 'poetic' passages before.

This is a tendency in *The Golden Bowl*. It is a tendency, however, which is not suited to deal with the hard facts in the intimate relationships of the two main couples. As I said, these facts are mostly played down in the dialogue. To a large extent, they are also faded out of consciousness. After the crisis chapters, the characters seem to opt for a *pax Britannica*, "quite as if everyone were, by the multiplication of human objects in the scene, by the creation, by the confusion, of fictive issues, hopeful of escaping somebody else's notice" (James 1966: 440). "They learned", we learn later, "fairly to live in the perfunctory". It "took on fi-nally the likeness of some spacious central chamber in a haunted house, a great overarched and overglazed rotunda, where gaiety might reign, but the doors of which opened into sinister circular passages" (494, cf. 498). "A consensus of lan-guor, which might almost have been taken for a community of dread, ruled the scene" (500).

The massive disparity between such perfunctory or even fictive modes and the pressure of the facts overtaxes the resilience of the mind, at least as far as Maggie and Charlotte are concerned; it provokes what might be called either a breakdown or an explosion of behavior. Charlotte forces Maggie to admit that she cannot be reproached for anything and to kiss her, completing "the coldness of their conscious perjury" (469) in the sight of their party guests. And, leaving with her husband, the father of Maggie, for the United States, she brings about "the definite break" (513) between the couples and possibly between father and daughter too (cf. 511–514). The resilience of the mind, then, which James suggests in a semi-theoretical, semi-phenomenological style apparently presupposes social limits of behavior, including rules of politeness, without which the precarious balance of consciousness between control (intelligibility, also for the persons themselves) and explorative complexity with respect to the outside world would not work.

Up to this point indeed, the examples so far characterized seem to indicate that Morin's assumption of emotional overinvestments, triggered by a central *evolutionary* shift, of the 'hysterical' mind, is compounded by *cultural* amplifiers. There appears to be a chronic belatedness of minds not in control but in pursuit of the situations which they have partly created themselves. Material and financial affluence may go some way to advance a certain shock-absorbing elasticity to the mind, but it also creates its own twilight zones. In such a perspective, psychiatric and psychotherapeutic endeavors do not deal with illnesses as the pathological opposite of mental health; rather, they must try and cushion developments going a bit far on the ordinary road.

In Western European literature, Dorothy Richardson is probably the first to break up that pattern. Her Miriam Henderson is the counterexample to Samuel Richardson's Clarissa Harlowe. Speaking of a counterexample does not mean to see her in opposition to Clarissa. Changes in character conception are moderate. But their impact on consciousness, its products and their grip on history out there is far-reaching. First, Miriam finds herself often in social contexts which, in the pettiness of their norms and conventions, do not differ that much from those which hedge in Clarissa. Much more than Clarissa she knows that the normative power of a situation also depends on a limited openness of mind which, in accepting a basic situational value, is also ready to change it unobtrusively. In some cases, in what one could call the 'feminist' passages, this may end up in a new closure, situational and ideological. In my view, this is not the characteristic feature of *Pilgrimage*. Nor, on the other side, does Richardson conform to the model of Virginia Woolf, that is to say to those famous passages in her essay "Modern Fiction" on the "myriad impressions", the "incessant shower of innumerable atoms" which the mind receives, shaping themselves into the life of Monday or Tuesday, composing finally life itself. For Miriam, such a version of experience would be too passive, the pattern of life emerging from it would amount, in spite of the impressionistic shower, to a simplification of the world, and to a withdrawal from life into art. I am aware, of course, that this is one type of conventional criticism addressed to Woolf early on: the consciousness of her characters as an ocean of words and phrases which do not evoke the fullness and immediacy of concrete experience.[98]

Richardson, as already mentioned, was ill at ease with the term autobiography for her work; she was even more ill at ease with the terms fiction or novel. Instead, on one occasion, she suggested "an investigation of reality" to an inquiring reader. It would be more than easy to reject such an expression on the grounds of epistemological and other naiveté. But the techniques of that investigation are anything but naive. They sometimes resemble a calculated refutation of other, failed efforts in that respect, especially those belonging to either the realist or the idealist variety. In each case, an assertion like "Yes, this is my reality" follows from the bold, but controlled interaction of openness and activity in perception and thought set in motion by the stimulation of the environment. In such situations, consciousness does not simply produce images which are then transformed and partly conceptualized as metaphors. "What she had just set down, he [Michael Shatov] would take for metaphor. Up in the clouds. Seventh heaven" (*Clear Horizon*, 1935: 281). This reads as if directly pointed at George Eliot's notion of images as "broods of desire" (see above). The suspicion that Miriam thinks herself in seventh heaven does loom large – she has just passed on the information that she is pregnant. The ordinary ("male"?) interpretation would be that "the prospect of having a child had given her a great emotional moment, very much to her credit as showing her to be a properly constituted female, to be followed in due course by a return to the hard world of fact". But for Miriam "it was the world of hard fact she had just visited. Feeling there, in the very midst of joy and wonder, not surprise but an everyday steadiness and clarity beyond anything she had yet experienced" (*Clear Horizon*, 1935: 282). The experience refers to her "adventure in the sky" (282) when, in the context of what appears as "this instant of serene and powerful realization of the being of spring" (278), both she and the sky were moving (279). Variations on this openness and initiative, this give and take of perception and thought occur repeatedly within very few pages (including a deprecatory shot at 'French' rationalism and logic 278). They happen, to be sure, also in environments like London or the Swiss Alps, but sometimes also in one utterly trivial. While it is difficult to find a concept which would cover that kind of experience (it is not mysticism, since no claim to an experience and cognition of some ground of being or higher being is made), it is easier to stick a label like nervous breakdown or neurasthenia on

---

98 See for instance Moody 1963: 29, 64.

Miriam once her experience (here the miscarriage), while structurally similar, goes into the opposite direction. (*Clear Horizon*, e. g. 377–378, 391)[99]

The "world of hard fact" and of history is mentioned. But it does not gain any real and intelligible presence in the perceptual situations Miriam finds herself in and tries to cultivate. What is clear, however, is that the notion of *resilience (of the mind)*, so much touted these days, looks both overly optimistic and simple when one compares it to the pictures of the varieties of consciousness at work presented so far. The consciousness of most people depicted in the texts here operates at the limits of its resources: The processes of consciousness are pushed towards an – inaccessible – unconscious; its products are exposed to the wear and tear of an equally inaccessible complexity of 'history' out there from which they consequently shy away too. The individuals whose minds we get acquainted with may acquire superior abilities in the handing of challenges of all kinds. But no one among them, not even Miriam Henderson, gains that mental distance, serenity, composure and flexibility of mind (the "alacrity of spirit" which Richard III, according to his own diagnosis, is losing towards the end in V.3 of Shakespeare's play) which would turn them into superior players in the (*pace* Clarissa Harlowe) non-lethal games in which they participate. They do not, apart perhaps from Lovelace whom, however, we are supposed to see very critically, develop sufficient abilities to change the rules of the game. That these rules can be changed is no novelty. Shakespeare offers plenty of examples, indeed a whole range from the allegorical kind (Richard III), *via* variations in Machiavellistic sophistication (Richard II, Henry IV, Henry V, Julius Caesar), *via* a self-ascribed nobleness of life (Antony, perhaps even Cleopatra) down to comic and criminal careers (for the latter see Macbeth).

There is a final important feature. Even in changing the rules, Shakespearean characters are still perfectly capable of connecting their thought, their conscious processes with the total conception of the world and human life which has frequently gone by the name of "Elizabethan world picture". Processes and products of consciousness merge into a unifying, if perhaps not always unified rhetoric. Similarly, a text like Pope's *Essay on Man* can present at least the semblance of a general, indeed a universal conception of the world and human beings.

In the novels treated so far, processes of thought have expanded tremendously. In Henry James and Dorothy Richardson especially, references to prod-

---

99 But see already *Interim*, 1919: 315–316, and *The Trap*, 1925: 505–509. The area of psychosomatic medicine and its 'application' to women has been treated with circumspection in the PhD dissertation of Fox 2008.

ucts have been drastically cut down, although, for the eighteenth century at least, a certain vitality of the "great chain of being"-conception can still be taken for granted. But even the debates of Thwackum and Square in Fielding's *Tom Jones* on human nature and the moral order of the world are obviously *not* meant to inform us about Tom's structure of experience or even his character. They rather insinuate a certain *pointlessness* and irrelevance of general and unified conceptions. Similarly and understandably, the Christian "intrepidity" of Clarissa Harlowe in the face of approaching death has little to do with reasoned convictions. It rather consists in emotionally high-pitched *moralizations* couched in ready-made formulas or, as Richardson himself puts it in a note: "High as her Christian spirit soars in that letter [Richardson 2004: letter 510.4, 1425], the reader has seen [...] that that exalted spirit carried her to still more divine elevations as she drew nearer to her end" (1425 note, see 1304, 1362, 1375, 1427). In spite of the sociocultural *pervasiveness of aristocratic ambitions*, the shift to a *bourgeois mentality* in combination with the changing psychological impact of Church teachings would seem to be responsible here.[100] For the daily bourgeois mastery of life general conceptions of the world and human nature become useless and are replaced by moral interpretations of action. In an increasingly capitalist economy, these become quickly useless, too. But they are maintained far beyond their expiry date, since somewhere appearances must be saved. What people really believe is harbored in the non-thematic underground domains of *fides implicita*.

However: In these as in other respects, sociological distinctions are anything but clear-cut. Being a member of the high aristocracy does not automatically protect self-confidence against the inroads of doubt, against the extension of a pressing inner world looking for a language. In Lord Peter Wimsey, the private detective used by Dorothy L. Sayers, we meet a late, but instructive example of the *failure of emotional self-immunization* normally characteristic of the high aristocracy. Lord Peter, the younger brother of a duke, must live through traumatizing experiences which change his emotional make-up drastically. But even in the Freudian early twentieth century, Sayers does not include this directly in her story. We learn about it in a postscript letter by an uncle. The aristocratic way of life, like bourgeois morality, is mainly a *code of behavior*.

---

100 The analyses of Levin L. Schücking are still pertinent here. See Schücking 1964: 9, with the thesis that the religious-moral core largely relevant for the moral and spiritual development of all of "Anglo-Saxonism" was to be found in the Puritan family, that, moreover, Puritan and Anglican moral teachings were largely identical anyway. For France see the classic analyses by Groethuysen 1978. For the more or less extensive transformation of faith into *fides implicita* with moral-psychological effects see vol. 1, 81–92.

It follows that the expansion of the inner life and its relation to products of thought has become radically open to negotiation.[101] Once the *psychological path* has been opened, the claim (Clarissa's prototypical claim for instance) that it enacts the individual implementation of the higher moral life gradually loses its persuasive force: Hegel has described, in the *Phenomenology of Spirit*, the decline of the "law of the heart" into the "madness of subjective arrogance" (chapter V.B.b.) and, in the *Philosophy of Law*, the perversion of opinions into "soft" elements in which anything can be imagined (Preface). The "beautiful soul", again prototypically embodied by Clarissa, worrying about the purity of heart and the splendor of the inner life, does not have the strength to endure "being". The beautiful soul fades away, dissolving into thin air (Hegel, *Phenomenology*, chapter VI.C.c., *Law*, § 140). At some point, therefore, the *confrontation* between processes and products of thought, especially the larger ones embodying the "rage for order" very openly – with their range of validity questioned and their status challenged – will be on the agenda again.

---

101 See Sayers 1970: 441–446 and 436 for the code of behavior.

Part II **Consciousness and History: Biographical 'Novels' and their 'Liberal' Extensions**

1 Biography on the Rebound

So far, I have been concerned with the transitionality of an intensely charged human mind, whether called hysterical, schizophrenic or by terms suggesting analogies thereof, which creates or finds forms in which the threat of pathology is transformed into the fascinating dramas we have so far mainly encountered in 'literature'. Concentrated and core forms of such 'dramas' are often enacted in poetry. Drama in its ordinary sense of theatrical performances transforms the turbulence of consciousness into languages of action. From the eighteenth century onwards, however, it is mostly novels which must take care of combinations and interpenetrations of the dramas of consciousness and the riskiness of products of thought which must make some kind of sense of increased complexities of life and, what with the catastrophes (in the ordinary sense) of the twentieth century, of history. Consequently, many novels take on an explicitly biographical form capable of absorbing both processes and products of consciousness and the empirical 'backgrounds' to which they are intimately related in experiences of (mostly) conflict and (far more rarely) unison with the world. Longer texts like biographically structured novels and their cognitive elasticity are also needed because, in the transition from total conceptions to models of thought, the satisfaction of a crucial human need has encountered increased difficulties. Michel Houellebecq may have exaggerated the urgency of that need, but he certainly has a strong point. In his *Particules élémentaires* a scientist argues that Western societies in particular, with Eastern ones having followed suit for a long time, have become ready to sacrifice everything to a desire for rational certainty: "Aucune puissance économique, politique, sociale et religieuse n'est capable de tenir face à l'évidence de la certitude rationnelle." And also: "À ce besoin de certitude rationnelle, l'Occident finalement aura tout sacrifié: sa religion, son bonheur, ses espoirs, et en definitive sa vie".[102] The thesis of total sacrifice strikes me as overdone. But "le besoin de certitude rationnelle" certainly extends to the unprecedented events which have marked 'history' in the twentieth century. This is not just an abstract scientific ideal or an ideal which can materialize only in 'objective' scientific language. The crucial word is "certitude" (certainty) which targets a powerful individual feeling of conviction. To satisfy such a feeling, we need flexible languages (and/or other media) in which the appeals of 'fact' and 'feeling' can merge. Biographical novels are prime embodiment of such languages.

---

102 This is the argument, put forward and belabored at some length by Desplechin, the retiring boss of a cutting-edge modern laboratory, in Houellebecq 1998: third part, chapter 1.

https://doi.org/10.1515/9783110581836-012

Intimate links between biography, history and novels begin to show up in the eighteenth century, that is to say in the period when replacements for the failing total conceptions of the world and of life must be found. Biographical dimensions, patterns and curves, whether openly or indirectly, have therefore turned into a hallmark of texts broadly called novels. Indeed, one could say, linking the last chapter with the turn of argument here, that the exemplary or merely interesting, the typical or unusual course and shape of a life have come to occupy the functional slot left empty by receding and retreating general conceptions. This is true, and continues to be true, also in the face of the shrinkage of biographical patterns into fragments of life without an overall significance. Reasons for this shrinkage are not too difficult to find: Since – at the latest – the early eighteenth century, especially its English variety, patterns of life are no longer really predictable. They are not sufficiently controlled by, or to be extracted from, social status (rank), religious, philosophical and general anthropological assumptions or common wisdom concerning human destiny. I have already alluded to the eighteenth century as the period of the "great transformation" (Karl Polanyi) and the "age of revolutions" (E. J. Hobsbawm). In that transformation, human life must try to assert itself as a meaningful series of moral choices squeezed between an obsolescent general conception (the great chain of being) and the calculus of neutral probabilities developed by insurance companies. The novel handles contingencies from shipwreck to the risks of marriage by treating them as psychologically or symbolically valuable elements in the formation of a personality. Insurance companies, taking care of real financial risks and thereby relieving the basic strain of life, provide the scope of freedom in which psychological or symbolic constructions of personality, however fragmentary, can be attempted at all.[103] The huge number of competing patterns of biographical meaningfulness, however, cuts down on the range of their validity. In the end, one day may have to suffice to suggest remnants of meaningfulness (Joyce's *Ulysses*). In an even more radical reduction or in a series of reductive steps as in Beckett, meaningfulness may turn into a purely imaginary affair.

But even if there is no real protection against the intrinsic risks of capitalist societies, biographical contours in novels hold their ground. Nineteenth-century Western capitalism, going through serious crises ("depressions") and turning "nasty" ("ungemütlich", Dieter and Karin Claessens), drives many forms of art,

---

103 See Polanyi 1957, Hobsbawm 1962. The parallel development of narrative and conceptual fictions of probability has been cogently analyzed in Esposito 2007. Probably the oldest life insurance company still existing today is the Equitable Life Assurance Society founded in 1762. In 1810, S. T. Coleridge, Sir Walter Scott and William Wilberforce, the important politician and fighter against the slave trade, were notable policyholders.

including important forms of the novel, into adopting attitudes of autonomy. Consequently, this is the period in which the novel is at last received into the realm of 'true' art and no longer discriminated against as the "half-brother of poetry" (Schiller, as against Henry James, "The Art of Fiction"). At the same time, however, counteracting the seeming escape into pure fiction, the novel takes on its most explicit biographical form. It does so to such an extent that a theorist like Lucien Goldmann defines the novel as being "nécessairement à la fois une biographie et une chronique sociale". And even Georg Lukács, in his pre-Marxist period of *The Theory of the Novel*, held that the external form of the novel was "essentially" biographical; that the novel produced the appearance of an "organic biographical form"; that its "central shape" was the biographical one.[104] The biographical invention comes to flourish precisely at a time in which the real apparatus of capitalism and industrialization threatens to suck up the power of personality and to cut it down to a *residuum personale*. At the same time, the growing importance of science, often with conflicts concerning religion drawn out into the open, will henceforth undermine the role of *fides implicita* and compel narrators and/or characters to bring their processes of thought into some form of alignment – or open conflict – with products of thought. These, in their turn, do not exist in uncontested self-sufficiency. We are rather witnessing the gradual transition from *Weltanschauungen* to *theories*, whether in geology, biology or physics or even theology, largely indifferent to the claims of human biographical significance. Science fiction reinforces that trend.

Yet the depletion of human significance is never complete. Novels still thrive on biographical suggestiveness and establish themselves, one might say, as (one of the) guardians of anthropomorphic impulses and commitments. Surely, as the conceptual and historical work of Michael Lackey has shown, Goldmann, Lukács and others were liable to use the terms 'biography' and 'biographical' in a loose way. For the moment, we must ignore that because the loose usage can help us to understand an apparent decline of the biographical novel form in the twentieth century *and its rebound*. Novelists and apologists of the novel tried to unhinge the criticism of the use of fictions, so common in and since the eighteenth century, by ennobling the novel into a full member of high art. Pathetic talk about the "sacred office of the novelist" tended to run wild.[105] Sober voices like Trol-

---

104 See Goldmann 1964: 75–76. Lukács 1965. These books have remained extremely interesting and relevant, although somewhat superseded, as far as the precision and differentiation of the term 'biographical' is concerned, by the work of Michael Lackey. See e. g. Lackey 2016 as well as Lackey (ed.) 2014.

105 Richard Stang has collected that talk on more than 80 pages. See Stang 1959: 3–88. See, by contrast, Trollope 1950: viii, 52–53, 271–272, 329, 346.

lope's in his autobiography, chronicling the more than just personal transition, clearly foreshadowed already in the eighteenth century, from an industrious writer to writing as an industrial activity, had a hard time making themselves heard – Trollope himself held the publication of his autobiography back until after his death. It seems symptomatic that Gissing's *New Grub Street* (1891), appearing eight years after Trollope's autobiography (1883) and also concerned with the fate of writers and writing, by and large still adopted the pathetic mode, an overcompensation, that is to say, of the threats against inescapable anthropomorphic commitments.

The anthropomorphic urge to use the narrative medium of the novel as the main vehicle for inquiries into possible senses of identity, for meaningful patterns of biography in an 'alienating' but historically somehow intelligible society, collided directly not only with the above-mentioned prestige of the sciences, but also and not at all paradoxically with a generalized awareness of fiction, that is to say the fictitiousness of all constructions of the real. The driving forces behind that awareness have been detailed very often. There is above all the internal development of philosophy, culminating in Nietzsche and Hans Vaihinger's monumental collection of fictions in his *Philosophy of As If*, spreading out the awareness of fiction in the sciences, law (a problem at least since the eighteenth century) and social life. The awareness of fictitiousness goes hand in hand with the growing explicitness of second-order observation since the eighteenth century. It is due probably both to a certain autonomy of conscious and unconscious operations of the mind as well as an increasing external (e.g. structural) complexity. The result is, to say the least, an extension of polyperspectivism across and for most fields of life. For Vaihinger, the fictitiousness of literature (later called fictionality and assigned a special cultural place) was just a weak avatar of the pervasive and deep-reaching fictitiousness of concepts and language in these other areas. Its impact can be summarized with two quotes, one as it were ontological, the other epistemological: "Illusion is whatever is fixed or definable, and reality is best understood as its negation: whatever reality is, it's not *that*." And: "No, there's nothing wrong with cogito or with sum; it's poor blood ergo that's been such a curse."[106]

To a large extent, modern(ist) and also postmodern texts, especially novels, *did* in fact largely turn into illustrations, explorations, and problematizations of the potential inherent in that awareness of fiction. Overlooking this field, we run therefore into a huge mass of built-in redundancies, interrupted and partly push-

---

106 Frye 1968: 169–170; Durrell 1968: 13. Durrell has also the ontological variety: "Reality is what is most conspicuous by its absence" (1968: 11).

ed back only by rare authors like Proust, Musil, Beckett, Claude Simon amongst others. Two world wars and the horrors, the wholesale destruction which they inflicted upon the world did not of course bring reality and history back. But they made the question unavoidable which patterns of experience, shapes of biography, and interactions between biographically marked 'actors' might have contributed, over and above the usual suspects of the social, historical and economic kind, towards the worst man-made catastrophes of history. Thus Musil, in chapter four of the first part of his *Man without Qualities*, appears to plead for the development of a sense of possibilities ("Möglichkeitssinn") which does not shy away from reality but treats it as a task and invention. But if such a sense can be developed, a sense of reality ("Wirklichkeitssinn") for Musil also has the right to exist. Christopher Clark, to take another relevant example, in his recent bestselling history of World War I, is very much interested in the "exchanges between key actors", in the how of history more than in the why. The why-question "invites us to go in search of remote and categorical causes: imperialism, nationalism, armaments, alliances and finance". The how-question "invites us to look closely at the sequences of interactions that produced certain outcomes". Therefore, Clark's book is saturated, he thinks, with "agency". Agency implies biography, however non-subjectivist it might be conceived. For the nineteenth century already, Osterhammel has sketched the double perspectives of individual agency and observation and larger movements.[107]

History, consequently, has returned in(to) many textual genres. But it could not return in its older well-ordered pictures like the "grand narratives" (of cyclical repetition, salvation, progress, decadence, socially symbolic reconciliations and so on) which, according not only to Jean-François Lyotard, had lost their credibility. History, in its enigmas, horrors, triumphs and treacherous normalcies, has rather returned into the heads of actors and/or observers, that is to say as an unstoppable impetus and inner drive for an extension and intensification of the work of consciousness. As an intimate part of consciousness and biography, however, history could not be stylized any more into the product of key attitudes of great historical actors behaving, as Hegel's philosophy of history still assumed, as the managing directors ("Geschäftsführer") of the world spirit. There had to be new amalgamations of history and biography.

It is striking, for instance, how shifts in what one would call historical constellations exert pressure on the minds of the persons involved; it is striking to what extent the constellations are only accessible through and take shape in the mind of the actors concerned. In this sense, the 'historical' novels of Hilary

---

107 Clark 2013: xxvii; Osterhammel 2013: 25–27, 45–47.

Mantel, plunging into English history in the time of Henry VIII or into the French Revolution, are tilting towards biographical novels, presenting for instance the life of Thomas Cromwell and more particularly his consciousness in crucial situations, without falling prey to "heroes, hero worship and the heroic in history" which had fascinated Carlyle so much more than a century earlier. In crucial situations, the method of narration changes from the frequent use of the historical present to an insistence on thought work. The change of style does not aim at a mimetic representation of the mind but rather at the suggestion of the intensity of problematic awareness, the level of excitation as it were, in which it finds itself. Thus, for instance, with the downfall of Cardinal Wolsey approaching, Cromwell's life, with his position in the power structure of and around Henry VIII at its center, will undergo significant changes too. Mantel tries to convey that by a repetition of "he thinks" or "he remembers". This repetition might appear simple and mechanical, but functions rather as an index of obsession. Related effects are achieved by a transfer of excitation into images for instance of Christmas rituals, or by having Cromwell imagine, with an intensity verging on hallucination ("ghostly places"), both class tensions and power distribution. By contrast, with history and power taken away from him, the engine of Wolsey's mind, deprived of solid food for thought and action, is left idling.[108]

In *Bring Up the Bodies* Cromwell has come into power as chief minister ("Master Secretary") of the King. This advance into official history does not reduce the burden of consciousness. Its resilience is rather challenged in increasingly varied ways which demand a variation of narrative methods to cope with it. The title refers to the order to bring defendants imprisoned in the Tower up for trial. It sounds programmatic because it nails down the point at which the coupling of the mind and the course of events splits asunder. The mind of Cromwell is accordingly mainly opened in situations where he has to perform a difficult weighing of evidence crucial for further action. The diversity of, in fact the discrepancies between the patterns of consciousness evolving in such situations tacitly emphasize the high probability that the mind and what is broadly called history are not normally well coordinated, that, in other words, causal relations between consciousness and history, in any direction from one to the other, should not be assumed. The first important passage, called an "inner vision"

---

108 See Mantel 2009: 71 (Wolsey's mind drying out with his power declining), 92 (Cromwell's new intensity of thought and memory given the imminent change of his position, reaching a climax 133 with especially the repetition of "think"), 109 (flexibility of Cromwell's ideas and their 'Italian') source, 155 (imagery), 187 and 196 (with the awareness of class tensions and the hallucinatory imagination of the power structure). I am grateful to Ingo Berensmeyer for drawing my attention to Mantel.

in the text, in such respects, is energized by Cromwell's own unclear personal situation after the death of his wife on the background of the queen's, Anne Boleyn's, position becoming slowly precarious. A second passage, composed of memories and dreams, combines attitudes of the Church towards Anne, the sting of the Fall of Man and the yearning, never openly admitted, for a new paradisiacal stability. The third, resembling an interior monologue in well-ordered form, unfolds the implications of the position of Master Secretary tied to the question of whether that position is compatible with the office of Lord Chancellor offered to him by the King. The fourth, a daydream to all intents and purposes, is also a demonstration to what extent writing, more precisely the elaboration of options and possibilities in writing, can both inspire and stabilize consciousness. The fifth finally looks like a traditional thought report. It does not, however, present a successfully ordered mind. Rather, it suggests a dynamics of thought ("He does not sleep. His thoughts race") with which writing cannot catch up.[109]

Mantel's texts are not exactly biographical novels in the sense in which above all Michael Lackey has defined them, although they "are based on the lives of actual historical figures" (Lackey 2016: 5). It is true that historical materials or facts might be less important than symbolic values emerging in complex and vague forms from the intricate narrative. That would bring them close to an important feature of biographical novels (Lackey 2016: 13, cf. 20, 25). Structurally and in terms of narrative emphasis, however, they do not sufficiently maintain a unified perspective on one or very few actors. Historical materials rather branch out into the sprawling multifariousness of what might count as coming close to historical situations or even facts. But they belong to the intellectual and historical configuration which accounts for the "rise and legitimization" (cf. Lackey 2016: title of chapter 1) of (not only) the American biographical novel. That legitimization, for Lackey, is owed to the transition from a declining "deductive imagination" to "the emergence of the inductive imagination, which converts a historically significant event into a literary symbol" (Lackey 2016: 27). It is driven by the distrust of grand narratives (metanarratives) which I spoke about above (cf. also Lackey 2016: 27), but also by the urge to empower the inductive imagination for more than just the production of literary fictions. As I said before, this does not signal a return to definable realities. But the inductive imagination is on the prowl for possible and probable biographical patterns within larger (historical) contexts.

---

109 Mantel 2013: 432 (explaining the title), 28–30, 110–111, 168–169, 229–233, 333–335 (for the five passages).

In Mantel, this imagination does not take a shortcut back into history as the formation and reception camp of an otherwise irresponsible and free-floating subjectivity. It explores consciousness in order to find evidence for the closeness or distance between biographical and historical dimensions. In Cromwell, the complexity of power structures and hierarchies especially in the political domain proper, challenges his intelligence and his energies much more than the ordinary range of cultural experience. Tacitly, Cromwell is getting close to thinking the unthinkable, that is to say the instability of the hierarchies supposedly ordering the world and human life. He repeatedly sees the king in situations of physical or psychological weakness (Mantel 2013: 216–217). That challenge, however, remains latent; the king and the aristocracy especially are able to believe or pretend successfully that they take the hierarchical order for granted, that they serve the compact made with the people: to "maintain the stability of the realm" (219). These parts of the general conception and the conception itself are hardly focused upon explicitly and thereby protected against subversive thoughts to some extent. Only very secretly, Cromwell sets up an inventory and calculus of possible power conflicts between king and ancient families (229–231, cf. 258–260). Cromwell knows that you "can be merry with the king, you can share a joke with him. But as Thomas More used to say, it's like sporting with a tamed lion. You tousle its mane and pull its ears, but all the time you're thinking, those claws, those claws, those claws" (249). And, of course, Cromwell must navigate with extreme caution in the field of tensions between his king and other monarchs or rather their ambassadors whose intelligence he appreciates and values (273–275). Cromwell may be "master of phantoms" (title of the last but one chapter 289) only. Some of these phantoms, like the handling of the king's marriage (marriage being certainly a central element of the general conception) and the desire for divorce from Anne Boleyn may have degenerated into cruel jokes (422–428). But up to the end of the second part of the Cromwell trilogy, these phantoms are still very much alive and real. The execution of Anne Boleyn can even be performed by a French executioner. I assume that the third part of the Cromwell trilogy (*The Mirror and the Light*, not yet published at the time of writing), however, will probably show an unmanageable accumulation of contingencies leading to Cromwell's execution. It would be appropriate if the effective reasons for his death remained mysterious (as they have been for many historians). This would characterize a situation encountered rather frequently: Cromwell's thought, fed by intercultural experience, reaches far beyond the boundaries of the ruling total conception (later called the "Elizabethan world picture"). And yet he acts as the chief instrument for the preservation of this conception, managing its gaps and shortcomings in his talks with foreign ambassadors in particular, because the management of deficiencies is more enjoyable than the pursuit of perfection.

History, whether in the shape of events and/or structural change, whether narrated or analyzed, *does not however present itself normally in unified modes, in identical units and packages.* Tudor history, it is true, centering in Henry VIII on the one, Cromwell on the other side, dominated by problems of marriage and religion, does appear to come as an identifiable package even if spread out in various minds. The *French Revolution* is of an entirely different caliber. The number of people involved in some way or other is immense; interpretations of 'causes' and driving forces vary widely. In this respect, the long list of historical actors (about 150) of small, big or vague importance making up the characters in Mantel's earlier monumental text devoted to the French Revolution (*A Place of Greater Safety*, 1992), looks like a test program exploring the interplay of consciousness, products of consciousness and history. In her introduction she draws additional attention to the interpenetration of biography and history or the lack thereof: Mantel has left out Jean-Paul Marat, because, being 20 years older than the other main actors, his "long and interesting pre-revolutionary career" is hard to connect intimately with revolutionary events. In their famous standard history of the French Revolution Furet and Richet describe that pre-revolutionary career as a series of failures. The son of an Italian priest in the principality of Neuchâtel converts to Calvinism and is driven from one place and activity to the next until he can stay in London for about ten years and achieves some status and affluence there. His return to Paris triggers nothing but disasters as the physician of the Duke's of Artois body guard, as a traveler and as a writer. For his accumulated intellectual capital, the Revolution seems to offer unlimited possibilities of investment.[110] But this investment remains a fairly abstract one, similar to the well-meant, but idealistic title of his paper *L'Ami du Peuple*. He is in fact popular as a friend of the people, but also not taken seriously: Marat, Levasseur has written, never had the slightest influence in the convent, his follies, while symbolically representing a democratic maximum, were never dangerous.

This is just an aside, but a significant one, since it points back to a central problem of the novel. The huge number of characters, most of them entering in some relation with a large number of others, requires a shift of narrative attention towards dialogue and the report of events. Even almost 900 pages, however, are far from enough for the development of structured relations between minds, dialogues and events. Instead of suggesting historical realities both complex and

---

110 Mantel 2010: ix. See xi–xviii for the "cast of characters", but also Furet and Richet 1968: 280–281.

concrete, revolutionary situations tend to appear amorphous. The space remaining for the delineation of consciousness involved in and struggling with what is going on is even smaller. We do not really see consciousness working through historical situations or establishing some meaningful profile, however unreliable and provisional such a profile must necessarily be. That is why it might be rather difficult for readers to get a 'feeling' for what happens.[111] Rather, a typical chapter like "A New Profession (1788)" (2010: 130–159), concerned mainly with Robespierre, is marked (and I think marred) by decontextualized narrative leaps: Fabre d'Eglantine suggests to Camille Desmoulins, for no obviously good reason, that they should "collaborate on some project" (139). Desmoulins responds to that vague proposal with the coarsely concrete, but ill-motivated intention "to collaborate on a violent and bloody revolution. Something that would give offence to my father" (140). Later, we suddenly find ourselves in May 1788, when the king announces that he will abolish the Parlements (142). The narrative falls back into the private domain. Ten pages later, however, the disconnected political situation is taken up again: On August 8, the king fixes a date for the meeting of the Estates (152). With a discussion of whether Necker should get back in office to handle the national finances, the chapter gains at least some coherence (153–154) before trailing off again to bring in the Duke Philippe d'Orléans and his new private secretary Choderlos de Laclos (157–158). Few readers will be surprised that a chapter like "Killing Time (1789)" (210–234), devoted to a few days immediately before the 14th of July, appears to be more coherent, to achieve a better control of events and their relevance. The symbolic value of July 14, after all, is such that the preceding days are inevitably overshadowed by this day in which the essence of the French Revolution seems to be condensed up to the present. Even so, the narrative approach is pretty abrupt and overly obvious at the same time. In a conversation with Robespierre on July 11, Desmoulins, leaning out of the window, suddenly says: "What's going to happen? [...] Revolution is inevitable". Robespierre hardly has a chance to respond with anything else than an almost tautological "Oh yes", decorated with a gratuitous higher meaning: "But God works through men" (216). Also, the evidence for an imminent revolution is squeezed from fairly well-known materials: price of bread, foreign troops, solidarity of the French Guards with the workmen (220). Desmoulins' "precipitate entry into history" (220) takes place in a fashion in which unintentional parodistic elements are hard to ignore. Someone slaps a pistol

---

111 I am quoting and following Damasio here again, for whom *The Feeling of What Happens* is the crucial criterion of a possible – and of course always problematic – sense of the real. Cf. Damasio 2000.

into his hand. When he asks whether it is loaded, somebody gives him another pistol (221). Again, private life intrudes in a decidedly less than functionally intelligible fashion (224–226). The following chapter "Virgins (1789)" (237–279) plunges, to some extent, into (anti)revolutionary activities, including those of the famous Marquis de Lafayette, but leaves them as more or less isolated events. Apparently, the narrative would need some analytical or even theoretical perspectives in order to prevent its dispersal into fragments which only historical knowledge, but not our reading experience, would certify as significant. The private point of view of Gabrielle, Danton's wife, in "Liberty, Gaiety, Royal Democracy (1790)" (280–312, especially 280–295) cannot make up for the lack of a wider range of perspective, however relative or provisional. Paul Feyerabend has insisted that such wider range can neither be supplied by trying to find out the intentions and convictions of the huge number of people involved nor by taking symbolically stylized expressions like "la prise de la Bastille" for granted.[112] It is true that the main protagonists of the revolution – Mantel has singled out Danton, Desmoulins and Robespierre – engage repeatedly in political discussions and strategy debates. But to a perhaps much larger extent, their minds and talks appear to be fueled by personal sympathies, antipathies and animosities. Thus, in a crucial phase, Danton tells Robespierre that he will not be a member of the Committee of Public Safety again. His reasons: "The business wears me down [...] I hate your bloody agenda and your minutes and your procedures." Robespierre "yell[s] at him" that he finds that attitude "extremely exasperating", but cannot oppose Danton with more than an abstract appeal to "vertu" ("Love of one's country. Self-sacrifice. Civic spirit"). Danton counters with the fairly gross sarcasm that the only "vertu" which the committee understands "is the kind I demonstrate every night to my wife" (690). And so on.

It certainly is difficult to *paint the inner turmoil* of these protagonists and to *trace its transitions into judgments* concerning the state of affairs and into *decisions for action*. Mantel, however, definitely misses a good chance to demonstrate the *elaboration of inner tensions* into a product oscillating between a *worldview* and a *theory* for which the revolution provides the *cognitive center* in the case of a second-line but not unimportant couple. We are dealing with Jeanne-Marie Roland de la Platière, mostly called Manon Roland or Mme Roland (1754–1793) and her husband Jean-Marie Roland de la Platière (1734–1793) who reached the rank of Minister of the Interior under Louis XVI and killed himself when he learned of his wife's execution. Well-educated and widely read, in-

---

112 "[...] in reality, nobody took the Bastille by storm". See Feyerabend 1999: 27, fn. 2, quoting Ilya Ehrenburg.

cluding treatises on education, ancient writers, "a great deal of Rousseau", Buffon's *Histoire Naturelle* (omitting information "she did not want", 380) and the "systems of Helvetius" [sic], 376, 379), Manon Roland's first remarkable experiences seem to consist in two sexual assaults by the apprentice of her parents, completed later by her husband for whose body "she was unprepared" (381). She falls for the Enlightenment ideas she reads about, "dreaming of Liberty", forcing "herself to dwell – on what was great in Man, on progress and nobility of spirit, on brotherhood and self-sacrifice: on all the disembodied virtues" (379 – 380). Then there happens the slightly comical and paradoxical conjunction of the American War of Independence and her marriage to M. Roland (380 – 381). In any case, however, pushed also by a social ambition fed by aristocratic insult (384 – 385), she has a mind for which the 'education' through well-articulated ideas and the interpretation of other people's thought appears like a quasi-natural need.[113] With her husband in particular, "she knew his thoughts before he knew them himself" (435). She is proud to "grasp the essentials of a complicated matter within minutes" (381), she "reasons" and has her "ideas about the state of France", starts out writing for various newspapers (382) and directs "le salon de Mme Roland" quite successfully (383). When imprisoned, she immediately starts writing again, thinking about "a justification, a credo, an autobiography" (725). The combination of psychological intensity, intellectual greed and social ambition should make for an excellent case study in the transitionalities of consciousness. Mantel mentions justification, credo, autobiography. But she does not endow them with contours.

In the Cromwell novels, Mantel has succeeded much better in relating history, biography and consciousness and thereby produced senses of the real without postulating some definable reality. Or, in other words: Northrop Frye's dictum that, whatever reality is, it's not *that*, remains valid. But, more importantly, ontological skepticism does not rule out phenomenological certainty, does not preclude the development of senses of the real. These emerge in the challenge which events pose for a biographically embedded consciousness. Both history and consciousness continue to present their provocation of incommensurability. But in the dramas of consciousness in and through which characters relate to themselves and others historical profiles emerge as transitory and provisionally structured situations of urgency.

---

113 The Rolands, especially Mme Roland, are given therefore their due in Furet and Richet 1968: 40, 176, 181–182, 217–218.

2 Biographical Patterns, Models of Consciousness and Historical Significance in Dickens

In the nineteenth century, the European novel faces a two-pronged challenge. The controlled construction, through human agency, of situations deserving the name of the real, runs into trouble by what is broadly called complexity. "When any society", A. J. Penty said in and for that period, "develops beyond a certain point, the human mind is unable to get a grip of all the details necessary to its proper ordering." More pointedly, Carlyle has pinned down the mental consequences: His nineteenth century is "destitute of faith, but terrified of skepticism".[114] This is one explanation of the need for *Weltanschauungen and* the difficulties of formulating them. On the side of individual inner worlds, not only for general psychoanalytical reasons centering in notions like repression, the self-observation of the mind has to grapple with the near-certainty that the more it intensifies the monitoring of its own activities, the more extensive the areas of inaccessibility will grow. For that situation, Matthew Arnold has reactivated the metaphor of the "buried life", the poem of that title being followed naturally, as it were, by one with the title of "self-deception".[115] Looking at George Eliot and G. H. Lewes simultaneously, we have encountered one version of the conceptual admission and the narrative absence of the unconscious already.

Dickens has probably taken the most radical steps in order to cope with the double challenge. He normally handles the complexity of the world by replacing it with modalizations of situations as comic, homey, uncanny, threatening, mysterious and the like, and, analogously, by populating the world with characters intrinsically interesting as transformations, adaptations of the older humor traditions. And he tackles the self-observation of the mind with a narrative trick: He suggests that the unconscious emerges in the intensification of stock emotions, not in the exploration of areas of the mind hitherto ignored.

Once in a while, however, Dickens takes a shot at complexity as the consequence of systemic developments and at the consequences of complexity for consciousness, thus anticipating the career of a notion characteristic especially of the twentieth century. For a discussion, I have not chosen texts which, like *David Copperfield* and *Great Expectations*, adopt the biographical form in its

---

114 Quoted by Mill 1991: 26. For the assessment of nineteenth-century *Weltanschauungen* see Mill 1991: 62–64.
115 For Penty see Williams 1963: 189; and see Arnold 1979: 286–291 and 292–293.

https://doi.org/10.1515/9783110581836-013

most explicit, but also its most improbable, that is to say fairy-tale-like form. In *Bleak House* (1853) by contrast, Gridley, a minor character, presents a succinct analysis of the basic situation: "The system, I am told, on all hands, it's the system. I mustn't look to individuals. It's the system."[116] Gridley is particularly infuriated by the solicitor Tulkinghorn ("I mustn't go to Mr Tulkinghorn") in whom, in fact, we witness the deterioration of legitimate and unavoidable *systemic self-reference* into *self-referential fanaticism*. Tulkinghorn, the family solicitor of the Dedlock family, selects even Lady Dedlock as a target of his investigations, pursuing her "doggedly and steadily" (371, cf. 530–532, 602–604), ultimately driving her to her death. One wonders how adherence to a systemic code can lead to its betrayal, to the double-crossing of a client.

For a while, this situation looks like a confirmation of twentieth-century systems theory in that individuals do not find themselves in any meaningful or substantial relation with social systems; they rather 'merely' belong to their environment. Luhmann indeed has convincingly argued that this location is advantageous: Placing people there, the theorist can do without problematic, mostly one-sided anthropological assumptions, and can liberate his attention for the manifold possible descriptions of the richness of the world.[117] The environment or periphery of systems differ, however, both psychologically and 'geographically', strongly from the spaces defined by systemic operations. Environment and periphery are not given. Nor do they regulate or determine the places where individuals might or ought to position themselves. They may stimulate curiosity about positions conducive both to professional improvement and personal development. But, depending on accessibility, on what appears as risks for or even threats to individual integrity, they may also encourage individual retreat. In Dickens, this descriptive freedom becomes ambivalent, to say the least. As the example of Tulkinghorn shows, it is doubtful whether the codes on which the self-reference of systems (here the legal system) is based and according to which they perform their operations are clearly given. The difference between self-reference and dogmatism, between necessary basic distinctions and narrow, unwarranted exclusion seems to collapse. Sticking exclusively to a systemic code and to professional habits means regressing into the old humor-type of the person seemingly consisting of one salient characteristic only: Tulkinghorn, even when sitting at a dinner-table, "never converses when not professionally consulted" (Dickens 1963: 24). Abbreviations in official letters, in this case by solicitors

---

116 Dickens 1963: 204–205. Collins 1971: 66, amongst others, finds this fanaticism of legal self-reference almost unbelievable.
117 Luhmann 1995c: 53, 55–56.

Kenge and Carboy, border on perversity (37–38). If, however, the difference between self-reference and dogmatic exclusiveness collapses, any descriptive choice hides an indefinite amount of ignorance. If threats and risks loom large, the individual may try replace curiosity by an emotional self-immunization against the possible inroads of systemic demands. In *Bleak House*, the ignorance of how the legal system 'really' operates, drives consciousness into a self-referential closure of its own: Esther Summerson, whose perspective makes up half of the novel, withdraws into a world of emotions from which the richness of the external world is excluded:

> To see everything going on so smoothly [...] to consider that, while the sickness of hope deferred was raging in so many hearts, this polite show went calmly on from day to day, and year to year, in good composure; to uphold the Lord Chancellor, and the whole array of practitioners under him, looking at one another and at the spectators as if nobody had ever heard that all over England the name in which they were assembled was a bitter jest, was held in universal horror, contempt, and indignation; was known for something so flagrant and bad, that little short of a miracle could bring any good out of it to any one; this was so curious and self-contradictory to me, who had no experience of it, that it was at first incredible, and I could not comprehend it. (Dickens 1963: 320)

This type of reaction, then, programmatically springs from a consciousness filled with emotions, capable only of the crudest distinction between something feeling good or bad. Esther knows about and acquiesces in her ignorance, thus turning it into a form of stupidity: "I know I am not clever [...] and you must be patient with me, like a dear" (27). Instead of a well-differentiated consciousness, we get a taste of a "very affectionate" disposition (29) for which "crying and sobbing" (29, cf. 30) turn into preferred activities. Such a disposition makes her "enchanted" with Harold Skimpole whose personality profile consists in a crass egoism masking itself as naiveté. Generally, the persons Esther has to deal with turn into pawns of emotionalized desire or repulsion. Allan Woodcourt, the young doctor, is introduced as being seven years older than herself, a broad hint that she sees him right away as a candidate for marriage, an implication which becomes even clearer by her pretended denial: "Not that I need mention it [Woodcourt's age], for it hardly seems to belong to anything" (225). In a similar fashion, she interprets Lady Dedlock's face as a mirror for herself. Although she has only "casually met her eyes", she is "fluttered and troubled", "thrown into this unaccountable agitation", because in the mirror face of the lady she sees "scraps of old remembrances" (235–236, cf. also 240): Esther is in fact the lady's daughter (378).

Filling a novel with modernized versions of *humor*-characters and their predetermined consciousness, mostly presented in dialogue anyway, continues into

Dickens' last completed novel, *Our Mutual Friend* (1865). Twelve years after *Bleak House*, however, the awareness that individuals are dealing with a socio-economic system inexorably following its own code and course has hardened into a certainty which precludes the emotional intensification of consciousness one still finds in the earlier text: Bella Wilfer, quite in contrast to Esther Summerson, insists repeatedly on her predominantly financial egoism as the only feature directing both her behavior and occupying her mind. To a large extent, the cash-nexus-mentality has also taken possession of the *humor*-characters. (In Dickens criticism, a lot has been made, and justifiably so, of the symbolic connection between dust, excrements, and money. In Book Three, the "Golden Dustman" Mr. Boffin figures in the titles of three chapters.). Certainly, with an inheritance one can outmaneuver the system. But in this novel it takes a repeated change of identity (John Harmon / John Rokesmith / Julius Handford) which borders on criminal behavior. Humane qualities in Harmon and Bella Wilfer are very slow to appear and must be teased out, or created, especially with Bella, in manipulative ways. She even marries Harmon under his false name of Rokesmith. The police steps in, but this new type of situation is resolved in the traditional Dickens way of combining *humor*-characters with a fairy-tale atmosphere.[118]

In spite of unpleasant characters, in spite of the cash nexus partly plaguing even these, all of this implies, even if it does not spell out, a benevolent *Weltanschauung*. In spite of failures like the Lammles, it appears possible that consciousness can embrace or, if necessary, be beaten into conformity with the capitalist way of the world; it appears plausible that the multifariousness of conscious events and the pain of maladjustment can be neglected, under such circumstances, without great psychological cost. But there is one exception which disturbs this picture profoundly. The schoolmaster Bradley Headstone represents and unfolds that disturbance in the full range of transitionality from the elementary dynamics of conscious events down to interactive situations ultimately exploding in violence. What is more: While the unconscious cannot be represented, it is fairly obvious that a consciousness running wild, and the violent behavior following from it, are the offspring of unconscious energies. From the beginning, Headstone is presented mainly in the medium of what one might call semi-consciousness to which disturbed somatization is added later on. Headstone "had acquired mechanically a great store of a teacher's knowledge", with the mechanical quality insisted upon repeatedly. The care for this "warehouse" of mechan-

---

118 Dickens 1955: 726. See 625–627 for the marriage 710–716 for police complications concerning a "matter of Identification" (715) and its resolution in the *humor*-context of the Boffins 720. One can only agree with the narrator: "All this was most extraordinary" (716).

ical knowledge "had imparted to his countenance a look of care", with the result that there was a "kind of settled trouble in the face". Filling the mind with mechanical knowledge, however, is tantamount to the "[s]uppression of so much to make room for so much" (Dickens 1955: 216). And it shows: The schoolmaster walks "with a bent head hammering at one fixed idea [...] brooding and brooding" (329). Because of the pressure of unnamed problems, he has a dry mouth and "difficulty in articulating his words" (331). Once the central problem is named, his love of Lizzie Hexxam, a love frustrated by the light-hearted Eugene Wrayburn, the somatic symptoms become glaring: "And his face turned from burning red to white, and from white back to burning red, and so for the time to lasting deadly white" (332). "The wild energy of the man, now quite let loose, was absolutely terrible". The pressure is such that Headstone himself cannot but formulate a rudimentary theory of the unconscious: "No man knows till the time comes what depths are within him". He knows because "the bottom of this raging sea" has been heaved up ever since" (379). Goaded on by Wrayburn, his "state" becomes "murderous" (515). Somatic symptoms (sudden nose-bleeding, giddiness, 601, 702) deteriorate. He attacks Wrayburn and injures him terribly, but the competitor for Lizzie survives (655–656). Once violence has been triggered, it can easily be released again. It is not quite clear whether Headstone fears betrayal or blackmail by Riderhood (738, 745). In any case, the two come to blows and die in the dirty water of a lock (748). The unconscious is not accessible. In its place, violence and fixed ideas have entered the historical scene.

3 Diagnostic Power and Practical Relevance: Some Further Steps

What, if any, consequences can be drawn from Dickens' novels? The form of Esther's consciousness in *Bleak House* does of course not follow inevitably from the ignorance of central social processes. But it is *one* plausible form provoked by an increased lack of coordination between consciousness and environment. And it is a plausible form starting from which one can construct other plausible variants characterizing roughly the period normally identified with the nineteenth century. For that purpose, the pattern of *Our Mutual Friend* might fit even better. Clearly, the unconscious comes into play. But it cannot be represented or sufficiently structured. Therefore, the impact which it exercises on consciousness and the ways in which the latter engages with situations out there cannot be reliably predicted. The ultimate shape of the triangle they form in any concrete situation remains open. This picture differs from later official psychoanalysis. In Dickens, the emphasis is less upon civilization and its discontents, but rather on the explosive potential which the lack of definiteness of the unconscious, the contrasting rigidity of fixed ideas and the frustrations felt in social situations entail. Dickens does not elaborate on this – Headstone remains the isolated freak. The *Weltanschauung* remains basically benevolent. But it is disturbed in principle by the cash nexus and liable to violent situational disturbances. More importantly, it is no longer possible to spell out its elements because it is mainly embodied in character types of the past. Consequently, it would take quite an effort to describe and represent it explicitly. The characteristic feature of the ninetenth-century situation seems to be that the transitionality of consciousness tends to end up in *Weltanschauungen* which, especially if formulated explicitly, betray the effort and strain it takes to construe them. On the side of art, this should also explain why, in spite of the many programs of realism and naturalism, ninetenth-century aesthetic appearances were so often driven into "phantasmagorias".[119]

With such generalizations I am exposing myself to heavy speculative risks. But the effort to distinguish Dickens and others from eighteenth-, twentieth- and twenty-first-century characteristic forms should yield very practical insights into the (literally) burning problem of relations between conscious orientations and history. And, for a beginning, there can be little doubt that, while Kant seems to have coined the term *Weltanschauung*, its problematic epistemic career

---

119 An important and I think correct thesis in Adorno's aesthetic theory. See Adorno 1970: 156.

https://doi.org/10.1515/9783110581836-014

takes mainly place in the ninetenth century when the systems philosophy especially of German idealism, while remaining fascinating, yet gradually has to loosen its grip on the dynamics of history. The same happens to the concept of ideology. Stemming from the eighteenth-century context of Condillac, developed by Destutt de Tracy (*Eléments d'idéologie*, 1801–1815) in the very early nineteenth century as a 'neutral' and 'objective' analytical tool, it acquires a negative tinge as false consciousness especially with Marx and Engels. Later, as I said before, it is almost invariably on its way to a polemical combat term: Ideology rests always with the other. Insofar as the twentieth century may have been stumbling, in spite of its catastrophic totalitarian tendencies, into attitudes of "anything goes", it primarily witnesses the declining importance of both *Weltanschauung* and ideology, simply also because they can be diagnosed at will and almost everywhere. The absence of convincing forms for both leaves cognitive gaps refilled by all kinds of more or less arbitrary constructions. That is why, from a present-day vantage-point, it would appear that the twenty-first century is going through a well-nigh perverse and mad renaissance of both *Weltanschauungen* and ideologies.[120] The Western world in particular is paying heavily for having been beaten, and indeed having beaten itself, into accepting almost any version of transitionality, of the chaotic basic dynamics of consciousness into the products of a rage for order. This phrase occurred first, it seems, in the last stanza of Wallace Stevens' "The Idea of Order at Key West" where it is still granted the distinction of being "blessed" (1934). This possibility, for the time being, has completely vanished. In the domain of consciousness, the "death of outrage" has certainly taken place. The hysterical mind, occupying a kind of central evolutionary place in Edgar Morin's anthropology, presents itself, in situations made up of elements of economic globalization and stubborn mental provinciality, in a naked historical form. "Anything goes" has asserted itself with a vengeance. The topic will be taken up in chapter 4.

In *Bleak House* and *Our Mutual Friend* we witness the genesis of this situation. The latter novel especially draws attention to the latency of an explosive potential in the relations between unconscious energies transformed into fixed ideas and the 'ideological' images of dominant realities out there. This is a situation completely unknown in the eighteenth century where a socially oriented and relevant structuring of consciousness does not of course eliminate frictions between the individual and its environment, but creates the impression of their overall social intelligibility. The eighteenth century certainly knows (what we

---

120 See Pfeiffer 2015: 168–169 in the chapter on dramatised theories of significance. For what follows I have borrowed the expression "death of outrage" from Bennett 1998.

have come to call) ideologies and dogmas. But we would not normally call them *Weltanschauungen*. Renaissance artists in their turn, Wolfgang Hildesheimer has said, operating on the basis of more or less self-evident total conceptions, were less explorers in the abstract than finders in the concrete. The inventors of that time were less guided by intellectual speculation than by the urge to get information.[121] Shakespeare, in his turn, handles the notorious Elizabethan worldpicture, which he often is supposed to have illustrated (not to say taught) in and by his plays, with remarkable carelessness, using it in whichever direction dramatic interest dictates. It is a total conception loosely, not assertively believed in. Nineteenth-century *Weltanschauungen*, by contrast, rather betray a highly suspicious, strained effort at unification.

In a more general historical way, I follow Jacques LeGoff who has maintained that European thought is "eternally" characterized by one feature: its "scholasticism". He does not of course target the dogmas of this medieval movement but rather its legacy as a style of thought relying on a thorough and strict categorization of what may count as reality.[122] That categorization may take many historical forms and intellectual directions. It can figure as theories, ideologies, dogmas and the like. For the nineteenth century, *Weltanschauung* seems to be the best term. In this respect, even a comparison between Dickens and Hegel, preposterous as it may sound, makes good sense. Certainly, in Jaspers' psychological scheme, *Weltanschauungen* are brought forth in any period. And yet, the tensions in which consciousness (the spirit, *Geist*) finds itself between chaos and form seem to take their most telling form in Hegel (or for that matter in Kierkegaard). Jaspers draws attention to Hegel's ambiguous and wavering attitude towards 'reality'. Its neglect is engineered by a highly sophisticated conceptual machinery. Even so, it belongs typologically to the simplistic emotional version of Esther Summerson. For her, the status of reality depends on its emotional acceptability with rare, but built-in social extensions (the medical profession of her husband Allan Woodcourt is socially important). For Hegel, reasonableness inhabits a totality for which all kinds of "trivial" defects do not matter. In both and many other cases, the reality which really matters is reasonable. In both and similar cases, the reasonableness is bought at a high price. The passage in Jaspers concerning Hegel deserves a longer quote:

> By distinguishing being, existence, reality as different concepts and by accepting the philosophical worldpicture as a successive, step-like order of realities, the word reality may signify a common sense, down to earth concrete reality, or some philosophical essence, that is

---

121 Hildesheimer 1980: 42–43.
122 See LeGoff 1986: 100.

to say the only "true" reality within concrete reality. On the other hand, we observe a deep immersion into what appears as concretely and perceptibly real in Hegel, but then also, and this is crucial for us, a curious lack of sensitivity for empirical factuality, indeed an indifference and contempt for it. Instead of mastering the givenness of the real (something he does, but not in principle), instead of experiencing and studying the real problems, he is satisfied with the mere dialectical relationship of the concepts used for grasping them. Thus, anything may be interpreted as being reasonable. In reality, whatever may happen, this philosophy is capable of justifying it as the only reasonable reality.[123]

Obviously, it takes a considerable effort to wipe out all the factors which might disturb the reasonableness of what Hegel posits as relevant and real totality. In many of Hegel's writings, even in the *Aesthetics*, one has only to think of the world-representational status of the Protestant Prussian state which, Hegel claims, prevents us from becoming 'Catholic' again, a state of mind which for Hegel apparently belongs to the past only. Dickens' Esther Summerson and many other of his characters have to make a similar effort to shut unsuitable elements of all kinds, including other people, out of their desired world picture.

In any case, the "revolutionary break" within nineteenth-century thought does not happen as a break in types of thought. It rather consists in drastic conceptual shifts within the same type, namely *Weltanschauungen*. Karl Löwith, among many others, has described the replacement of Hegel's active (for Jaspers: hyperactive) spirit by varying totalizing views of the (Christian) individual and its 'existence' in Kierkegaard or of social practice in Marx. Hegel's spirit as the subject and substance of history does no longer count as a foundation but at best as a problem in the face of both social (the French) and technological revolutions. Renan's question: "De quoi vivra-t-on après nous?" has not been answered but

---

123 Jaspers 1960: 370. Incidentally, Jaspers characterizes Hegel's notion of thinking very much along the lines of consciousness ("Denken") and its transitionality ("Nachdenken" and "nachfolgendes", "reflektierendes" and "vernünftiges" Denken) adopted here (Jaspers 1960: 365 – 366). The tension between concrete, perceptible and experienced reality and a reasonable reality (appearing arbitrary to many readers and critics) has haunted Hegel criticism. Two (perhaps somewhat unusual) witnesses would be Arnold Gehlen's *Wirklicher und unwirklicher Geist* (originally 1931): "That the absolute was spirit was for Hegel as evident as for any mystic: who dares to say today to have understood that?" (Gehlen 1978: 134). And there is, very importantly I think, T. M. Knox in the introduction to his translation of Hegel's *Aesthetics*: The "great strength and interest" of the lectures "lies not in their main philosophical and historical thesis, but in what constitutes the bulk of these two volumes, namely the examples and illustrations drawn from India, Persia, Egypt, Greece, and the modern world, and in Hegel's comments on this detail. These comments on art, perhaps especially on painting and literature, must be fascinating to a student of art, however much he may wish to dissent from them" (Knox 1975: vol. 1, v. See also Knox' comments on terminology viii-xiv.

rather buried under a plethora of theories and models of thought.[124] Given their lack of orientation, the twenty-first century, for the time being, has replaced those by naked and violent fanaticism.

Jaspers, too, has adopted a critical position with respect to Hegel's conceptualization of reality. It is unclear whether he does the same in his presentation of Kierkegaard's conceptualization of the self. There would have been enough reasons for doing so. Like Hegel's oscillation of reality, Kierkegaard's spelling out the possible ingredients and dynamic forces of the self has remained fascinating as a (subject-based) version of a *Weltanschauung* (Jaspers 1960: 419–432). He himself, like Hegel, is fascinated by the dynamic movements in which both the self and its relation to itself develops. But there is also a tendency, again as in Hegel, to proclaim some of these movements and forces as *essential* ingredients of the self. The self, in order to be itself, needs something with respect to which it can position itself as self. For the child, there are the parents, for the man, there is the state; with God in the position of an infinite vis-à-vis, the self itself becomes much more of itself (420). On the one hand, the consciousness the self develops of itself is so concrete that no writer has succeeded in describing it. The self is immersed in the fullness of empirical life. On the other hand, it is also supposed to become, in its very complexity, transparent to itself. If it does not succeed in that, melancholy as a profound ('existential') condition sets in (422–423). And yet, thirdly, self-transparency can never be complete. Consequently, there will always be a remnant of melancholy (423). Mental shapes are infinite in their variety, "more numerous than flowers" (quoted 423). But this variety is also transformed into relatively stable and permanent forms. Kierkegaard seems to be particularly gripped by what he calls the demonic, an orientation of the self, fluctuating in itself, but also defined as the defiant determination to be and to stick to an accidental self, to a provisional version or stage of the self to be left behind (429). As such, it is an effort to escape despair. Despair springs from the desperate, tormenting wrestling with accidental qualities trying to take over the self (426–428).

As this summary probably indicates, even Jaspers has a hard time making sense of the back and forth in Kierkegaard's strained efforts to do justice both to an endless variety and to a need for essential forms which, it would appear, are ultimately conquerable only with and in faith (424, 426). In faith, the believer enters into an absolute relation with God, in the demonic domain human beings

---

124 Löwith 1964: 7–9. See also first part, chapter III on the dissolution of Hegel's mediations by Marx and Kierkegaard, 158–191, and the affinities between the two: "Remote as they are from each other, they are also close to each other in using and departing from Hegel in their attack on the powers that be" (179).

only reach an absolute relation with an accidental stage of the self (429). The chances, in Kierkegaard, for the transitionality of consciousness to attain to one or the other absolute relation seem to be unevenly distributed. Kierkegaard's list of possible transformations, as he calls them, reads like an enumeration of human psychosomatic pathology or, as one could also say, of variations of Morin's hysterical consciousness: overexcited sensitivity, irritability, neurasthenia, hysteria, hypochondria (423). Conversely, the effort to achieve faith must take an unlikely amount of energy. Its psychological basis is seriousness – Macbeth is a prime example for all seriousness having gone (432), his criminal career providing proof *ex negativo* for its desperate need. Generally, however, one would assume that in the development of literature towards modernity, "the importance of being earnest" has dwindled away. Kierkegaard, by contrast, tends to overestimate the persistence of seriousness in the cultural products called art. The assertion that Mozart's Don Giovanni is transformed by the music from a single individual into the voice of the spirit, that through music he acquires "aesthetic seriousness" (whereas Molière's Dom Juan comes along with an almost ridiculous ethical gravity or in downright comic ways), that he represents and lives an "ideality", namely the "spiritualization of the flesh out of the spirit of the flesh itself", or, in still another version, that he is the demonic in the shape of the sensual – this assertion is certainly tempting. But it presupposes a metaphysical function of music. It also implies, more particularly, a very exalted and representationalist notion of the media qualities of opera. This notion, to say the least, would have great difficulties to compete with a more detailed comparative history of media effects than the one which Kierkegaard offers with respect to the Don Juan figures in Molière, Mozart and, in passing, Byron. In such a history it would turn out, I think, that music, even with the support of language in opera, does not represent emotions, but that it presents and enacts emotional intensity which the listener may, but need not associate or identify with specific emotions.[125]

---

125 See Kierkegaard 1975: 107, 109, 129, 132, 135, 136, 139. Insofar as I am downplaying "the importance of being earnest" with respect to consciousness and conceptions of the self (including, as much as possible, elements of a deeper self and even the unconscious as far as they can become part of the conscious self) I am not following Böhme's notion, derived from Kierkegaard, of being and existing seriously (Böhme 2017: 202–203). Furthermore, with respect to Kierkegaard, a representationalist notion of opera will normally assume that opera represents emotions and even ideas or, as in Kierkegaard's interpretation of *Don Giovanni*, the essence of some (here erotic) desire. I do not go along with that. See Pfeiffer 2002: 182–222. See also Löwith 1964: 179, 207. In the spring of 1939, when he finished the first edition of the book, Löwith could still reasonably believe that we "are indeed still living off this [nineteenth] century" (9). In various ways, this is true. But it also appears clear that Nietzsche's diagnosis of gen-

On the whole, for the English nineteenth century, Darwin appears to have been one of the few thinkers who tried to resist the temptation of transforming his theory and his empirical findings into a wholesale *Weltanschauung*, much as others took care of precisely that and offered Darwinisms, Social Darwinisms and counter-Darwinisms of all kinds. There can be hardly any doubt, for instance, that the mixture of scientific-empirical stance and unbounded speculation in, say, the works of Herbert Spencer or in the equally monumental *Philosophy of the Unconscious* (1869, extended 1876, 1889) of Eduard von Hartmann has produced *Weltanschauungen* bought at the cost of obvious biases sometimes bordering on obscurantism. Hartmann recognized that he had basically written a "metaphysical novel". He clearly saw that the *Philosophy of the Unconscious*, his most successful work, which its subtitle in fact defined as an "effort towards a *Weltanschauung*", was certainly not his best.[126]

The effort it takes to preserve relics of seriousness of a nontrivial kind in conscious processes and at the same time block its march towards dubious forms of ill-founded *Weltanschauungen* shows with symptomatic force in a writer whom I have already twice taken to task for his presentation of forms of consciousness mainly concerned with a stylistic ordering of existence, a writer who, however, was not able to banish the inroad of seriousness in dysfunctional or perhaps even remotely demonic forms. I do not know why Colm Tóibín has written a 'novel' exploring the mind of Henry James. But he certainly has produced a text in which the *cost structure* of the mind's basic *processual complexity* is laid out with exemplary precision and tact: We watch complexity in action, here in one of its most attractive forms as literary creativity, and we follow a transitionality moving, at great effort, towards safeguarding some seriousness and, at greater effort, towards hiding an even more important demonic relation to the self.

The twilight of the nineteenth-century triangle, based on some laborious and vague *Weltanschauung*, of an implicit unconscious, looming large but not thematized, of consciousness and of social situations out there has been sketched in Tóibín's intriguing text on Henry James *The Master* (2004). Incidentally, *Bleak House* plays a minor role there in that it turns – one would suspect provocatively

---

eral permissiveness ("nothing is true, everything permitted", quoted by Löwith 1964: 207) fits much better into the latter twentieth and early twenty-first centuries and is related to the relativistic implications of theories, to say nothing of models of thought.

126 Quoted in the article on the work in *Kindlers Literatur Lexikon*, 12 vols., Darmstadt: Wissenschaftliche Buchgesellschaft 1970, vol. VIII, 7478–7479.

for James – into the preferred reading matter of two minor characters.[127] More importantly, becoming acquainted with Paul Bourget (credited after all with the development of the so-called psychological novel), James thinks that Bourget notices nothing really crucial about him (James): "His list of Henry's attributes, were he to make one, would be simple and clear and inaccurate. He did not observe the concealed self, nor, Henry imagined, did the idea interest him". James is pleased with that because it allows him to remain "invisible" (Tóibín 2005: 226). This motif turns into a *leitmotif.* In his long conversations with another 'fellow'-novelist, Constance Fenimore Woolson (1840–1894), who committed suicide by jumping or died by falling out of a window in Venice, neither "spoke about their private lives, their hidden selves" (230). The self, hidden or not, is also shut out from the talks between the brothers Henry and William, although the problem plays a huge role in both their works and although age and illness might argue for a certain urgency of the topic (William has a heart disease and wants to go on a cure in Bad Nauheim, 323). Henry opts for silence and hushing things up when his sister-in-law wants to reopen talks about Henry's relations with his sister Alice or tries to make him interested, like William, in the hype of spiritualist séances (319). Matters are made even worse by William's criticism of Henry's 'English' fiction. William asserts that the English have no "spiritual life, only a material one. The only subject here is class and it is a subject of which you know nothing [...] your style has suffered from the strain of constantly dramatizing social insipidity" etc (335).

Tóibín does not hesitate to add further suspicious touches to this picture. Clearly, a certain miserliness or at least meagerness is built into Henry's regard and attention for other people. This is almost embarrassingly clear in the way in which he reacts to Constance's death and the light her death throws on their relations while she was alive (251–255, 262, cf. 119–122 concerning Minnie). The reasons why Henry (and in this case William, too) did not volunteer in the American Civil War like their brothers might have been equally embarrassing. Although Tóibín does not say so clearly, the complex of the hidden self and the reluctant or merely superficial, emotionally distant sociability of Henry point to a probable core: his homosexuality which is neither totally unconscious nor allowed a role on the stage of consciousness. There are some broad hints: Oscar Wilde's trial looms large, and, after some very tentative perceptions of Hammond, the servant he has while staying at Lord Wolseley's (39, 44), the fairly long description of the relationship with the sculptor Hendrik An-

---

127 See Tóibín 2005: 333, 350. I am grateful to Michael Lackey for drawing my attention to this important text.

dersen reads occasionally almost like a direct statement (278–312, see for instance 286, 310–311). A statement, to be sure, from the narrator's side. James does not allow himself a clear perspective, instead, like Dickens' Bradley Headstone, he somaticizes sometimes ("with no idea why his eyes had filled with tears", 310). Only in the solitary confinement of his bed does he indulge in mental images of his friend undressing and standing "naked studying himself in the mirror" (311). An earlier scene where he has to sleep in the same bed with the well-built friend of his cousin and sister is granted equal mental freedom: "He wondered if he would ever again be so intensely alive" (98).

The impossibility, both personal and historical, of building homosexuality as a conscious element into his conscious and his social life brings James closer to Dickens, that is to say the historical position of a somewhat special individual, the writer. Phenomenologically, one would probably describe the raw quality of James' mind as the creative version of elementary, amorphous consciousness. Tóibín insists repeatedly on the "randomness of the mind's workings", on the almost daily involvement in a "new set of musings and imaginings", making James wonder "how an idea could so easily change shape and appear fresh in a new guise" (49, 67, 125). At the same time, on a first and for James most important level of transitionality, consciousness adopts a both well-ordered and still productive movement once James starts to think about a publishable story (67, 125, 147, but see also 235–236). In any case, contradicting to some extent his brother's criticisms, Henry can write complex *and* saleable stories. As I tried to show in the discussion of *The Portrait of a Lady* and *The Golden Bowl*, however, these texts thrive upon a promising sort of vagueness especially in the representation of consciousness. If we combine this analysis with the present one, we seem to be driven to the assumption that his *homosexual orientation hedges in the formulation and even the mere implication of a worldview with unsurmountable difficulties*. The "thing that he most needed to write would never be seen or published, would never be known or understood by anyone" (9). That is why James, in literary respects, develops a style of vagueness which can pose as higher, if remote wisdom (that is the picture of Irving Howe, see above 47 but also Tóibín 2005: 147, last paragraph) or as sophisticated and irrefutable complexity. But that is also why he must keep his private life at a minimum of sociability because otherwise his enforced liking for secrets (Tóibín 2005: 5) would be threatened. That means that whatever James' *Weltanschauung* might have consisted in: Building it into texts and life did not only require energy, but a lot of effort and strain. This is still nineteenth century, but it is that century coming to a close.

4 The Pseudo-Freedom of Consciousness and its Cost-Benefit Analysis in the Twentieth Century

This chapter is supposed to bring the *conceptual backdrop and tensions* of the preceding one into sharper focus by setting up a *symptomatology of representative nineteenth- and twentieth-century intellectual work* (mainly J. S. Mill, Feyerabend, Valéry). In the twentieth century, the strained character of *Weltanschauungen* has become hard to ignore. That century might be called an age of *theory*. Theories do not normally aspire to the universalism inherent in the older form. Where this still happens, as in Heisenberg's world formula, a feeling of futility is apt to develop rather quickly. It is certainly more common to look upon theories as "intellectual tools". They must be set up in greater number and used in any field in order to cope with the "multifariousness" of objects. This has destroyed the "ontological monolith" which these objects seemed to constitute in former times.[128] Theories may occasionally still resemble and embody those "key attitudes" by which the making or unmaking and the status of a scientific-philosophic person is determined. Normally, key attitudes, linked explicitly with *Weltanschauungen* by Arnold Gehlen, live on as empty models only, because the state and status of the sciences do not allow an extension of their insights into a full worldview or ethical system any more. There may be compromises: It is possible that the functionality of guiding ideas, so-called *idées directrices* ("Leitideen"), is still oscillating between key attitudes and 'mere' ideas.[129]

In a slightly strained pun, one could say that, for twentieth-century thought, a multiplicity of theories is needed in order to handle the multifariousness of multifaceted objects. In order to reintroduce uniformity and avoid chaos metatheoretical movements like the philosophy of science were set up. But even these were and are restricted to the formulation and enforcement of methodological rules. They are not authorized to define the nature or essence of things. Moreover: It was precisely this methodological universalism which drew fire from critics like Paul Feyerabend. The latter, to be sure, often criticized for preaching an unqualified "anything goes", claimed irony for this phrase, asserting that "anything goes" must be the impression gained by a terrified rationalist from Feyerabend's arguments. In his self-interpretation, Feyerabend has, however, continuously elaborated upon his basic maxim that principles of research

---

128 See Iser 2006: 3, 5.
129 Gehlen 1971: 286–287.

https://doi.org/10.1515/9783110581836-015

cannot be formulated independently of concrete research problems. This looks like a somewhat euphemistic veiling of the hard claim that for any methodological rule, however basic, there are circumstances which tell us not only to disregard the rule but to actively follow its opposite.[130] Feyerabend recommends the use of several theories, even allegedly dated and scrapped ones, for the analysis of one problem, in order to squeeze out as many aspects as possible. He argues convincingly that no theory can be in full control of all the facts belonging to its range of validity, because some of these facts are invariably shaped or deformed by older theories more or less forgotten (Feyerabend 1999: 34, 67, 71).

By and large, I think that Feyerabend is very persuasive as a theoretician and historian of science. But that is not important here. He has explicitly transferred his somewhat (in his own words) anarchistic theoretical pluralism, which I have reduced here to a few bare essentials, into the socio-political domain. It might come as a surprise, then, that *Science in a Free Society*, against Feyerabend's intention and apart from its variation of persuasiveness, rather opens up views on the risks of pluralism. In his last published book, *Zeitverschwendung* (*Killing Time*), he describes his terrified awakening from the dogmatic turn which the pluralistic intention may take. One the one hand, his picture of consciousness is close to what I have tried to outline in the first chapters as "dramatic narratives". In writing, the point is that the plethora of ideas and impressions should be ordered like colors and forms so that they do not lose their "dramatic potential". On the other hand, he refrains from ascribing 'hysterical' qualities or a hypertrophic elaboration to that drama in the way of Morin or E. O. Wilson or also in the way of Jaynes' modern vestiges of the bicameral mind whom I am following here to some extent. Instead, he prefers an ordering of dramatic conscious events through the transformation of this potential into socio–political energies. This is precisely what gets him into trouble. His last, unfinished and unpublished book, probably to be called *Conquest of Abundance*, was supposed to show how lay people and experts go about reducing the mass of impressions their minds and perception are continuously exposed to. Feyerabend wanted to expose the genesis of abstractions, the ways in which they are supported by general ways of talking and by forms of life and in which they change under the pressure of arguments or practical compulsions. He wanted to demonstrate the ambiguity of all concepts, images, and ideas. It dawned upon him, however, that his own concepts like democracy, tradition, relative truth were marred by the same rigidity he had criticized in so many others.[131]

---

130 Feyerabend 1999: 11, 21–22.
131 Feyerabend 1995: 144, 245–246.

This, however, was the trap he had already fallen into in *Science in a Free Society*. More explicitly and at greater length this book insists on the role and the intelligent use of *traditions* in thought and behavior. Any society should have as many traditions as possible, because plurality eases the task of assessing their relative value.[132] Reason and practice are not essentially different, they are two types of traditions, theories being meaningful only in the framework of a tradition (Feyerabend 1982: 148). Traditions are neither good nor bad, they simply exist (68). Feyerabend assumes that most countries have developed fairly reliable mechanisms to protect their traditions. In order to make them creative, they rather need techniques to loosen their rigidity (22). On the basis of equal rights of access to the centers of education and power, a free (not planned, directed) exchange of ideas is best (71–73). Problems can then be solved by the decisions of the people who experience them, not by preconceived theories which, of course, may influence the decisions (77).

This is, as usual, a bare outline of Feyerabend's very detailed arguments. Heated debates broke out around them in the eighties and nineties of the last century. For their time, the partly ferocious character of debates was understandable. Today, I find it difficult to see more than an effort, on the part of the critics, to preserve the universalism of *Weltanschauungen* in the shape of scientific methodology. By and large, there is more to say for than against Feyerabend's argumentative drift. In the context of my concerns with consciousness, questions pop up in a different quarter. I approach them with limited praise for the way in which Feyerabend has handled astrology in the book (chapter 6, 181–189). He points to the evidence which justifies the belief that the positions of planets, of the moon and the sun influence human lives. He is probably also right in emphasizing the "delicacy" of that influence (183–184). The problem with astrology, however, does not lie in this evidence, but rather in the detailed net of assertions, that is to say the highly elaborate character typologies, to say nothing of forecasts, derived from the basic assumptions. It is very difficult to say how far one can go from basic assumptions to detailed descriptions of, for instance, behavioral regularities.[133]

---

132 Feyerabend 1980: 19. See the parallel plea for a plurality of theories in Feyerabend 1999: chapter 3.
133 One of the most interesting tests in that respect was performed by Gunter Sachs (famous and notorious for many things, in the mind of the mass public probably and unfortunately above all for his marriage to Brigitte Bardot 1966–1969) with the help of the Institute of Statistics of the university of München and others and the data collected above all in Swiss archives. See Sachs 1997.

It is, in other words, not the fact, but the *concept* and the *degrees* of influence which are at stake. This applies also to the concept of tradition. In a *general* way, we can assert that we are embroiled in all kinds of traditions. But their *individual* efficiency, their presence, shape and strength in the mind, depending also on the sphere of life in which they are supposed to be active – these are entirely different matters. Moreover, Feyerabend has not sufficiently distinguished tradition from custom. This might appear as a minor point, but it is an important one in Feyerabend's own traditions and orientations. Both in *Against Method* and in *Science in a Free Society* John Stuart Mill's *On Liberty* (1859) plays a decisive, but again conceptually vague role. (In the German version of *Against Method*, he calls that text "superb" [großartig], 167, in the German version of *Science in a Free Society* even "immortal" [unsterblich], 69.) Mill in fact engages in a searing criticism of custom. Some "rules of conduct" must be "imposed", because otherwise "restraints upon the actions of other people" could not be enforced. "What these rules should be, is the principal question in human affairs." It is at the same time one of those questions "which least progress has been made in resolving."[134] "People are accustomed to believe, and have been encouraged in the belief by some who aspire to the character of philosophers, that their feelings, on subjects of that nature, are better than reasons, and render reasons unnecessary" (Mill 1991: 10). Such is the "despotism", the "sway of Custom" that the "contest" between the progressive principle, either as the love of liberty or of improvement, and "the despotism of Custom" "constitutes the chief interest in the history of mankind" (78). In his analysis of habit formation, Mill takes individual consciousness, then, into consideration. He foregoes, however, any closer examination of its role. That is why his own ideal, that of an individuality resembling very much Wilhelm von Humboldt's notion of an all-round development of a personality and his or her abilities (cf. 64), comes dangerously close to just another example of habit formation. I leave aside the much-debated questions to what extent Mill has defined his own central terms (self-protection, harm to others, utility, social tyranny or tyranny of the majority, the permanent interests of man as a progressive being and so forth) and to what extent the situations targeted by crucial expressions can be clearly imagined: How do we know that we are only "pursuing our own good in our own way, so long as we do not attempt to deprive others of theirs, or impede their efforts to obtain it" (17)? When and in which situations can we be sure that the assertion of our individuality does not "primarily concern others" (63)? Why should we agree to Mill's assertion that "society has now got fairly the better of individuality", that "the

---

134 Mill 1991: 9.

danger which threatens human nature is not the excess, but the deficiency of personal impulses and preferences" (68)? Some people would think that it is just the opposite which is the case. Mill sketches a history of individuality which one can call adventurous at best (68–74). It culminates in the thesis that "Eccentricity has always abounded when and where strength of character has abounded; and the amount of eccentricity in a society has always been proportionate to the amount of genius, mental vigour and moral courage which it contained" (74–75). One would have liked Mill to provide at least a rough idea about where the evidence for such a thesis might come from.

Even if true, that thesis carries consequences which probably Mill himself would have been appalled at. Robert Paul Wolff has very critically attached the label of "the sanctity of idiosyncrasy" to them, a criticism which, in its turn, has provoked some severe countercriticism. I do not see, however, what could prevent me from aggravating that phrase and say "sanctity of idiocy" instead.[135] This is because we have to reckon with an unintended, (in the sense of my title) potentially catastrophic consequence of both Mill's touting of eccentricity and Feyerabend's 'creative' use of traditions: With both binding methodologies and, in Georges Devereux' sense (see the next paragraph), generally accepted life forms having disappeared, *any* idea concerning these, including ideas one would have considered idiotic, 'chaotic', or outrageous at other times, can claim attention, justification, legitimacy and implementation.

This appears to be the situation we have fallen into in the early twenty-first century. Or at least: This is a simplified version. It can be refined; in particular, it can be reinforced from an angle perhaps least expected. First, the motivation for having chosen Feyerabend must be made more transparent. Feyerabend represents the twentieth-century predicament in a very clear way. In terms of larger configurations of thought, he illustrates the transition from the precarious totalizing claims of *Weltanschauungen* to the selective power of multiple theories and "traditions" and their objective correlative in a pluralistic ('democratic') sociopolitical context. In this transition, the universalism of worldviews cannot be replaced by a universalism of (scientific) method. In terms of the mechanisms of consciousness, Feyerabend embodies a twentieth-century tendency to interpret the multifarious dynamics of the mind as a potential of creativity ultimately transformed into the productive competition of theories and traditions. While this is not impossible, it is difficult *not* to see creativity also as a euphemism.

---

135 Wolff 1969: 19. I am concerned only with this thesis in Wolff. For the assertion, contradicting Mill, of a trivializing mass production of individuality in modern times see for instance Gehlen 1957: 114 (and other essays by this author).

An optimistic fallacy looms large: neither scientists nor the supposedly free society can control an anarchic *and* stultifying turn in what is all too easily seen as creativity. Nor can they really protect against the returns of dogmatisms which contemporary societies need in order to make up for the lack of real orientating power of the creative ways.

Feyerabend, then, is also representative of the twentieth-century situation in the sense in which Georges Devereux has put it in painful, not to say brutal clarity. In what one could call a cultural psychoanalysis of the West he diagnoses an incoherence and lack of form in the "Western ideology" (including the sciences in a broad sense). Religion has become the only strict and coherent ideology (we can note here that this certainly applies more to 'Eastern' religions like Islam than to Western Christianity, but at this point this is not very important). The prestige of religion does not reside in any substantial contribution to Western life forms. Rather, it is the only systematic ideology still commanded by Westerners who only seem to know what they do *not* want. Consequently, they lack what Feyerabend amongst others had hoped for but, as he came to see, could formulate only in dogmatic terms: a creative ideology of freedom and a strong commitment to their own life forms. In spite of his brutal diagnosis, Devereux assumes that only the West will be able to formulate an ideology corresponding to a rational ego-ideal and not to an irrational superego.[136] Clearly, this has not happened so far; given what keeps happening in the (Western) world, it is receding into an indefinite distance all the time. It would be too easy to push Devereux into the role of the entertaining outsider; writers like Houellebecq (and a series of others on which he draws), have described the suicide of European culture, the sale of values without substitute, in equally clear words.[137]

The probability of such a figurative 'suicide' has been enhanced by a discourse type, since the eighteenth century, which was meant to prevent it. I am talking about the development of legal discourses, including a multitude of prison reform projects, all of them intended to replace the chaotic ways of punishing wrongdoers by penalties (mostly capital punishment) doled out without any sense of proportion, or adequacy, between the seriousness of crime and the severity of punishment. The old practice was totally arbitrary and, one could say, monotonous, because, as I said already, the death penalty was imposed most frequently in order to punish crimes of totally different calibers. Even the movement called, somewhat misleadingly, legal humanism from roughly the Renais-

---

136 Devereux 1998: 163.
137 Some years ago I added my own version of (part of) the self-destruction of Old Europe to this picture in terms of the intellectual migration. See Pfeiffer 1988.

sance onwards, had excelled by demanding punishments conspicuous mainly by their barbarous cruelty. The Scottish legal historian Douglas J. Osler has done extensive work on that.

One would normally assume that efforts towards a relative sense of proportion between crime and punishment would produce standards of judgment far superior to the indiscriminate, but basically totally arbitrary lack of an adequate relation between the two dimensions. In the eighteenth century, indeed, an immense amount of work was devoted to the noble purpose of adequacy and proportion. Moreover, we would normally praise the further effort to induce, by a just verdict and forms of imprisonment adjusted to them, something like an inner reform of the culprits.

The essential feature of especially the British paradigm change of law in the eighteenth century, however, consists, to take up formulations of John Bender, in *imagining* the new sense of proportion between crime and punishment and, especially in Jeremy Bentham, in the phantasm of the *geometrification* of penitentiary architecture supposedly creating the possibility to supervise and control the inmates by one guard only. I am more interested in the first aspect. As Bender shows, we have to see the imagining as a kind of cooperative work of many discourses involved "in the ongoing process of cultural construction." Novels especially, from Defoe to Fielding, are "the vehicles, not the reflections, of social change" and of "institutional formation".[138] Since Bender is primarily interested in the imagining of the new prison, he does not talk about the strange case of Dr. Johnson and Mr. Chambers, that is to say Dr. Samuel Johnson, the great literary practitioner and emblem of mid-century literature, and Sir Robert Chambers, the second Vinerian Professor of English Law in the University of Oxford. To all intents and purposes, Johnson appears to have helped his friend Chambers to write up "A Course of Lectures on the English Law", Chambers' main duty to be performed on and for his chair. In spite of substantial (also editorial) work especially by Thomas H. Curley we do not know much about why and how this collaboration came about, who precisely took care of which task. Chambers may have been overawed by his great predecessor on the Vinerian chair, Sir William Blackstone. If he was, it did not prevent him from becoming a 'creative' legal scholar in his own right, doing important work for the 'juridification" of the empire, especially India. On the other side, we must assume that Johnson was in no way inhibited to let his legal 'opinions' run freely into and through the text. This was a course on English, that is to say mainly Common Law.

---

138 See Bender 1987: xv, 1–3. Bender's first chapter describes prison conditions in the old institutions in great detail.

One the one hand, Common Law demands great intellectual skills in order to set up, in the absence of huge masses of written and interpreted laws, meaningful, plausible, better still provable relations between a crime situation and a criminal. That is why at the basis it is still surprisingly close to legal humanism, especially with a somewhat indiscriminate advocacy of the use of capital punishment. Moreover, there are ample ambiguities concerning the question whether and to what extent Norman law conformed to or violated the older Saxon common law. There are tensions sapping the very basis of law and justice: Are they to be sought in an ultimately religiously grounded very conservative view of social institutions culminating in the absolute power of the king or in an elastic and pragmatic adjustment to historical forces? With Bengal and the American colonies, Chambers and Johnson seem to opt for the elastic solution; with events on the home front, they tend to judge much more harshly. There are interpretational difficulties galore: What kind of document do we face with famous or rather notorious *Magna Carta?* Has it really anything to do with justice, as the magnates claimed, or does it document a ferocious power struggle which ultimately deprived King John (John Lackland) of his kingdom?[139]

The preceding remarks are not of course intended as a criticism of this work which, in quite a few cases, surpasses its predecessor, Blackstone's *Commentaries*, both in subtlety and intellectual cogency. But it is equally clear that modern legal argument is on its way to interpretation-based *opinions*, thereby unintentionally pushing ahead with the split, barely visible in the eighteenth century, more distinctly recognizable in the nineteenth, and finally helping to produce the opposition between theory without action and action justified by arbitrary opinion.

In a situation arrived at in a historical logic of that kind, Feyerabend's creative ideology of freedom does not stand much of a chance. The most detailed and comprehensive analysis of implications, costs and benefits of this Western logic from great conceptions including or at least implying action-directing power to worldviews detached from action and at best abetted by petty opinions had indeed already been performed before Devereux and Feyerabend. Experts and amateurs of intellectual history agree that it was Paul Valéry (1871–1945) who deserves the title and honor of having been *the* representative figure of European intellectuals of the first half of the twentieth century. An intellectual here would probably mean a person able to practice both the close-distance observation of one's own processes of thought, including creative-artistic ones, an absorbing interest for philosophical, scientific etc theories of all kinds and an

---

139 See Curley 1998: 84–107.

awareness of their larger cultural and political implications. In the intellectual field there is nothing which would equal or even come close to the 29 volumes, each about 1000 hand-written pages amassed over more than 50 years, producing a phenomenology of conscious processes and products from the smallest units of thought to the elaboration of far-ranging poetry (Valéry was one of the last poets able to make a living in this field) and combining this with the practice of analysis, criticism and theory in an amazing number of areas. For some of his efforts in the latter respect, Valéry has been criticized by the specialists. François Lhermitte took Valéry to task for his "strange abstraction" of a pure ego within or at the basis of all the transformations of consciousness; René Thom warned against withdrawing behind mathematical formulas which one does not really understand; philosophers grumbled about what they saw as Valéry's disparagement of their discipline. The general and damaging question "Valéry, what for?" ("Valéry, pour quoi?") can be and has been asked.[140]

My own view, while granting the legitimacy of such criticisms, deviates from that direction. I take Valéry to have performed a series of crucial experiments: Is it still possible to observe the working of consciousness *and* to think through human concerns without falling prey to either the universalist assumptions of worldviews or the self-referential closure in which most modern realities ('systems') and the theories about them find themselves? Is it possible that theory can learn from its objects even if it has to constitute them in the first place? Here, right at the beginning, a distinction between theory and theorizing comes in. Since, as Gehlen has said, it is the process of discovering and not the result of possessing knowledge which is exciting, stimulating and invigorating, Valéry replaces theory with a mixture of experience and theorizing. Theories, if they were possible, would have to do with "l'usage du possible", because the given, especially in living 'systems' and their environments, is only a transitory slowdown within a range of possibilities. For Valéry, the question of a modern German sociologist about the degrees of the reality of systems ("how real?"), would have been meaningful indeed.[141]

This is no idle speculation; it rather follows fairly inexorably from a very detailed theory and phenomenology of consciousness which Valéry has tackled and developed over many years and for which his occasional ideas about a pure ego or consciousness are not essential. He has in fact described this effort in a

---

140 For Lhermitte and Thom see Robinson-Valéry 1993: 146–147, 208, for the what for-question the volume without editor.
141 Valéry 1957: 1026 ("La politique de l'esprit"); Gehlen 1975: 30. See also Valéry 1957: 986 for the demand for a "theory of theory" ("la théorie de la théorie") and, for the 'reality' of systems, Nassehi 1992.

letter as his only constant and his only permanent instinct (Valéry 1960: 1504). From the outset, the enterprise proceeds on the horns of a dilemma: The analysis of the mental functioning needs language and writing to acquire some intelligible and more than just momentary form. But it also has to protect itself against the "parasites" of language which tend to impose their readymade "illusions", in particular illusions of stability and permanence (1960: 1504). These appear impossible because the basic and incontestable fact about the mind consists in the activity of billions of cells (1969: 1478, 1481, 8/271).[142] It is true that internal and external pressures, starting with the one for survival, have contributed and continue to contribute to a certain ordering, to classification and regularity (3/80, 5/576, 6/318). Valéry imagines – and there is indeed, as his critics have said, not that much evidence for this – that the "moi pure", "l'absolu de la conscience", "la pure et simple conscience" (1957: 1227, 1960: 1504–1505) can be taken as a structural potential which controls and directs, to some extent, the multiple variations in the specific content of thought processes. But he is much more interested in that variation of content in which even the purported absolute consciousness is hardly more than a "relais" dealing with the power of transformations in consciousness as a theater of transformations (1957: 920–921, 1021, 11/71, 20/105). *Association*, that is to say the habitual connection between various images and ideas, has come to channel the variation of content into intelligible forms: "Une chose fait *penser* à une autre. C'est là le mécanisme de l'esprit" (10/212). But that does not produce fixed values for the transparency of the real or the success of communication. It is only in the relatively rare cases where strong practical needs have asserted themselves that we can count on a kind of 'intersubjective' stability of consciousness (3/2, 9/628, 21/916). Even so, "toutes les liaisons psychologiques" depend on time (6/848, cf. 6/882, 908, 7/55). Any state of consciousness, however transformed into linguistic, pictorial or musical form, is just "le sommet d'une pyramide de conditions" (10/297). In anticipation of the situation in the twenty-first century, one would have to add that the acknowledgment of practical needs, the respect for what we are supposed to call necessities (cf. Shakespeare, *2Henry IV*, 3.1.92–93: "Are these things then necessities?/ Then let us meet them like necessities") has in many cases itself turned into a matter of endless interpretation and therefore into a source of serious stress. That stress is already clearly visible in Henry IV but does not yet really form part of the historical *episteme*. Later, however, stressful tensions can always flare up: Consciousness needs language to become meaningfully aware

---

142 References with year and page are to *Œuvres*, references in two Arabic numbers are to volume and page of the *Cahiers*.

of itself, but consciousness and language are also always non-congruent, if not incongruous: "Il faut choisir entre l'inexact de l'expression et l'incommunicable de la pensée" (20/373, cf. 1/142–144, 150, 698). Language – a point indefatigably repeated – presents a collection of speech habits which hide the underlying discrepancies produced by consciousness (cf. 1/291–293, 309, 439–441). Words like *dieu, vie, réalité, univers, beauté, raison, pensée, esprit, être, infini, cause, hasard*, should be always put in inverted commas (19/53, cf. 13/593). In short: Language allows us to talk about things which we are somehow acquainted with but know little or nothing about (29/84).

We know when we are able to do ("Je sais ce que je sais faire", 27/750). In the background of 'abstract' terms like those above, in the background of twentieth-century pluralistic theorizing, there lurks therefore an unknown amount of ignorance. In the background of terms for sociopolitical affairs where practice makes for some knowledge and competence at least, there looms impotence because we do not know enough and, instead, are guided by fairly crude interests ("nous sommes aveugles, impuissants, [...] dans un monde que nous avons équipé et dont nous redoutons à présent la complexité inextricable", 1957: 1016). For all we can tell, quite in contrast to what systems theory admits, complexity is inextricable because both sides, complex 'realities' and the complexity of conscious as well as unconscious processes, have turned into a knot which we cannot disentangle. But the starting point lies in consciousness. Valéry tries to locate it in pictures of the mind resembling Morin's hysterical mind quite considerably: "Et ce sont là les produits connus de l'anxiété, les entreprises désordonnées du cerveau qui court du réel au cauchemar et du cauchemar au réel, affolé comme le rat tombé dans la trappe..." (1957: 990, cf. 1001: "L'homme est cet animal [...] qui s'élève sur tous les autres par ses ... *songes*, – par l'intensité, l'enchaînement, la diversité de ses *songes!*"). Theories like conflicts multiply and explode (cf. 1957: 989–990 for uncountable dogmas, ideals, dogmatic variants). In living systems ("le système vivant"), there is always "un élément d'imminence, d'instabilité toujours prochaine" (1957:1027). In the essay "La crise de l'esprit", the European Hamlet goes on a sightseeing tour of the Calvary, the Golgata of European and, by extension, American thought (1957: 993–994). This is the point of departure in which a twentieth-century "politique de l'esprit" finds itself.

For such a policy, the distinction between theories forming part of the gallery of ghosts and theorizing as an effort towards the controlled openness of thought participating in the vital concerns of its objects is essential. Valéry thinks that the ancient Greeks and their 'science' have come closest to a method for that. I take it that this is also the cardinal point in the great effort to regain Greek rationality which was recently undertaken by Arbogast Schmitt. In his picture, Plato and Aristotle advocated a "philosophy of discrimination" in which perceptual and conceptual work are in constant interplay. What matters is the concrete, but also conceptually consensual act of knowledge (Schmitt 2012: 78, 136). So far, so good. In comparison, however, Valéry appears to insist more on the different domains of reality in which the Platonic-Aristotelian method does or does not work so well. If we follow Schmitt in the assertion that the final criterion of all rational argument does not consist in Descartes' clarity of evidence for our mental representations, but rather in the concrete, definite and conceptually consensual content of any act of knowledge (Schmitt 2012: 236), do we also have to buy his assertion that, as long as we concentrate on something as something definite, it does not matter whether that something is "a human being, an animal, a point or a line" (234)?

It does matter. It does not seem so difficult to reach conceptual agreement about what is perceived as point, line and circle. But it *is* difficult to agree – and by agreeing escape the danger of falling into a sea of fictions (as I might rephrase Hamlet) –, for instance on what constitutes individual happiness within the complexities and conflicts of a state (Schmitt 2012: 421–423, 442–443), on the relations between economy and ethics (433–434), on "rational self-realization as a condition for the merging of personal advantage and the social whole" (506–508), to say nothing of "a culture of emotions and its aesthetic, ethical and political meaning" (341–380). Likewise, many people would agree to the assertion that there is an "inner rationality and intelligence of emotions" (342). But that does not at all mean that we can fix the conditions which enable us to judge "a situation, another human being, a social group etc in all the aspects relating to practical action in the community in their specific character and value" (379).

For Valéry, it is Europe which has pushed farthest efforts toward the control of what counts as evidence for consciousness and the forms it takes in systematic thought and theory. We do not have to accept his thesis that Asia can boast of a "connaissance substantielle de la vie" much more than Europe or America (1960: 1553). Indirectly, Valéry moves away from the Greek model. While the Greek model of scientific thought was and continues to be important, it tends to neglect what I called the distinction between theory and theorizing. The latter term is meant to catch the quality of an *event* (1960: 920), hopefully an exciting one, in which thought does not destroy, but participates in the vital significance which the object of knowledge embodies. Event is of course a common, but also a treacherous term in historiography. Its psychological-epistemological dimension is all too often lost sight of. Valéry uses Leonardo da Vinci as a crucial example in order to illustrate the virulence of this dimension. Leonardo practiced a lot of formal and neutral, for example mathematical-geometrical argument. But he was also keenly interested in the relationships of living forces which cannot be grasped by formal language nor by general language altogether. He tried to visualize, to construct, to decorate, to develop a sensibility for the balance between arbitrariness and necessity, thus turning into a cutting-edge model for what the sciences should and could be today (1957: 1250–1253).

In Leonardo, such combinations are clearly visible. Valéry tries to discover analogies in thinkers one would not readily associate with that dramatic event quality of theorizing. Case studies of theoretical events include Newton and especially Descartes. With the latter, Valéry is not so much interested in the story of his stay in Neuburg on the Danube where the illumination for the central tenet of the *Discours de la Méthode* is often said to have dramatically taken hold of him.[143] Valéry denies that the notorious "Cogito ergo sum" is the result of a valid logical argument and conclusion: "Il n'y a pas de syllogisme dans le *Cogito*, il n'y a même point de signification littérale. Il y a un coup de force" (1957: 806–807). The egotistical-oracular formula derives its power from Descartes' talents in *geometry* which, plunging into an intoxication with his own superiority, he transferred into *philosophy* (1957: 843). We are dealing – and this is the event quality in Descartes – with the experience of a gestural-discursive transfer of mental power and fascination. Or take Bergson. We might admire the acumen of his theory of laughter. But we feel at the same time that this theory cannot be *true*. It dodges "le problème réel" which consists in the dynamic, 'event-like' interpenetration of diaphragm, nerves and thought. At best, Bergson's theory can be seen as a preparation for an attack on the real problem (1957: 884–885).

But is this saving, projection and transformation of the dramas of consciousness into the theorizing about objects and problems enough for a "politique de l'esprit"? Where does this leave us then with regard to the intricacies and entanglements between the workings of consciousness and, apart from but also partly within science, with the *mondes mythiques* of *le monde social, le monde juridique, le monde politique* (1957: 1033)? These worlds are certainly not purely imaginary. But in their encounter with consciousness, in its turn energized by a sensibility which supplies consciousness with its strength of transformation ("puissance de transformation", 1957: 1028), we must continuously handle, as I said above, two types of complexity which threaten to flow together. The essay "La politique de l'esprit" in any case ends on a note of resignation, not of resilience: We must preserve at least "la volonté de lucidité, la netteté de l'intellect, le sentiment de la grandeur et du risque" (1957: 1040).

---

143 See Dieter Henrich's contextualization of this and other stories in an effort to find more than just arbitrary motivations in the genesis of the crucial ideas of philosophers in Henrich 2011: 34–35, 84–86, especially 84 for the role of Euclid. See also the older work by Weischedel 1966: 108, supporting Valéry's thesis.

This is a far cry from the optimism of free speech which Timothy Garton Ash has displayed in his recent book which came out while I was writing these lines. Garton Ash has a lot of practical communicative experience (for instance in and with China); he is fully aware of the many obstacles which very often thwart the theoretically obvious communicative potential of the digital age. Still, he is convinced that we can find, across cultural trenches, a normative consensus of how dialogue and debates can be conducted without violence. It is not necessary to agree. But it is necessary to agree on how we disagree. That these are demands with a long history does not invalidate them. But they are hollowed out by the changing internal logic of products of thought, especially the drying out of built-in dimensions of action which accompanies the transition from *Weltanschauungen* to theories and later to models of thought (see next chapter). Once the connection between significance and action is endangered or cut, almost any commitment, majority or minority agenda can claim a legitimacy which, in its turn, can be exploited, in a feedback loop as it were, as a justification for new action. Thus, a vicious circle gets going compared to which rules on how to agree to disagree look fairly pale.[144]

---

144 See Ash 2016.

5 The RAF, a Twentieth-Century Reality Shift, and a Contemporary German 'Novel'

Valéry, then, is pleading for a dramatization of consciousness and knowledge, but he does not, or only skimpily, depict those dramas. Insofar, he presents a rather distanced, 'intellectualized" version of processes and products. More importantly, however, he *embodies* the crucial connections between the objects of investigation in this book, especially those still ahead, objects which at first sight might look very different indeed. He represents the later stages of what is commonly called *liberalism* which, very broadly speaking, makes itself felt for the first time in the movement ordinarily described as the *Enlightenment*. In any case, we are now in a position to turn around the perspective again and to compare these conceptual configurations and drifts with the implications chaos and catastrophe tend to assume in advanced contemporary literature. After that, taking its inspiration from Valéry's cutting-edge but solitary embodiment of processes and products, the discussion will move on to public extensions, in the shape of selected Enlightenment configurations, exemplary situations of liberalism and, for diagnostic refinement, renewed comparative confrontations with literary and other texts.

Recently a giant book by Frank Witzel (*1955) came out in Germany, winning the German Book Award for 2015. It can be seen as a novel-like drama assessing the dramas of the twentieth century, especially those of consciousness, and sketching contours of what might be ahead in the twenty-first. Witzel starts out with an analogous framework in what could be called a dramatic encyclopedia of both experience and knowledge, using quotations from texts by Adorno, Camus, Bourdieu, Rorty, Bloch and William James, to point out both the indispensability and the unavailability of holistic, unified or merely coherent notions of history and (auto)biography. This is particularly striking, because the main 'historical' development and event, the rise of a terrorist group like the RAF (Rote Armee Fraktion) in the Germany of the late sixties and early seventies must indeed be seen as a paradigmatic and dramatic break and shift in the organization of modern realities. The break is not restricted to West Germany; in various forms, its impact and repercussions still determine to a large extent crucial dimensions of what counts as real in the contemporary world. (In a superficial sense of event, 9/11 is certainly a much bigger event than phenomena like RAF; in terms of shifts in mental maps, however, all the necessary ingredients are there, especially the absence of stopping rules for the claims to legitimacy, importance or merely attention. More on that later.) At the same time, Witzel's book is unique in that this event of capital historical importance is seen mainly

https://doi.org/10.1515/9783110581836-016

as the drama of consciousness in a teenager, a drama couched frequently in religious or psychiatric discourse. On the one hand, this entails a derealization of layers of history, like politics, normally thought important. On the other hand, the powerful immediacy of almost anything in the adolescent and also juvenile mind, in which the distinction between the literal and the metaphorical has not yet fully taken place, cannot be dismissed, in an adult perspective, as mere illusion or fantasy. Rather, it feeds into and intensifies the reality effect of other layers. Music, especially Anglo-American rock music, assumes prime importance here. Like terrorism, it exudes and attracts by a power which none of the usual societal control mechanisms can contain. The book amasses a huge amount of parallels. They do not add up to any coherent view of history and biography, sometimes they can hardly be taken seriously at all, like the parallels between the (lyrics of the) Beatles' *Rubber Soul* and religious matters, especially those of thaumaturgy (Witzel 2015: 400–425). But they collect patterns of possible evidence. Some of these, after all, demonstrate greater persistence. As a consequence, images of history and biography both monstrous and realistic are assembled. It is plausible, for instance, that the teenager, mired in a disorientation which his environment does not reduce but rather increases, sees a parallel between his situation and the emergence of the RAF. The teenager's only knowledge and source of security consists in the conviction that there are no sufficient grounds for whatever happens. This conviction is tiring. The appearance of the RAF, by contrast, turns into the concrete image of people being in *and* overcoming the same situation. The teenager could not have conceived the group, and yet, with his own experience of insecurity increasing, "he invented it" (360). But again, this is no mere invention. It rather can claim to be a representative pattern of the times. Witzel's book is located precisely at the explosive intersection of the history of consciousness (its typical form or product of transitionality being theories weak in orienting action, to say nothing of their lack of ethical guidance), of historical trends (the ageing of traditions, whether in schools, universities or social institutions at large), and the enhanced susceptibility of the teenager's mind, its increased readiness to mix possible layers of reality (from the most trivial daily chores to emotions sublime and ridiculous at the same time) and blow them up into forms of radical social energy. Consequently, chances for an "official historiography" have become slim or nil. It is only possible to use one's own history as a shape for the past (761). But the personal history is of course not personal only. It is soaked in the imaginary *and* real terrors somehow happening out there. And, somehow, the "suspension of chronology" (526) has to be handled in some way. Witzel has interspersed this side of his book with chapters and scenes of later interrogation and questioning, in which the former teenager is pushed by the examiner (some unidentified police or similar official) to explain his past behavior and motivation. The effort remains of course largely futile.

Likewise, the images of evolution, ego-consciousness and a history of emotions in chapter 54 (extracts from the "small dictionary of metaphysics", 362–389) are highly heterogeneous, embedded as they are in speculations from the inflammation and bacteria of the body, to an intriguing philosophy of things and (earlier, 351–352) of the Other according for instance to Martin Buber and Emmanuel Levinas. Even so, some of them add up to diagnostic evidence not to be dismissed as arbitrary speculation. There are somewhat weird ideas, for instance, on the functions of hats (387). There is the striking, if still somewhat weird image of evolution in a four-verses wordplay from "singes entre singes", "signe entre singes", to "singes entre signes" and "signe entre signes" (365). There is the equally striking analysis of individuality and its lack of cultural relevance. Individuality is still cherished, and yet, "waiting for our next application, "we creep through cities looking more like perfectly administrated rehabilitations centers" (382). Emotions have been deprived – Dickens' *Bleak House* betrays a clear early awareness of the situation which Esther Summerson still cultivates as an ideal – of their "objective correlatives" into which they can be invested. T. S. Eliot's Hamlet-criticism has been generalized into a hallmark of culture. We would need therefore "purgatives, laxatives, and emetics" for our accumulated and luxuriating emotional repertoire (381), in order to try once more to determine their motivation, justification, time and cultural locus. In a very important book, Peter Sloterdijk has tried to figure that out for wrath, the most uncanny of human emotions.[145] In the process, the specificity of emotions has been eroding too. Witzel's vague image, namely that something will out but cannot (so we take tranquillizers instead) is therefore quite appropriate. The mind needs to be soothed because it finds out that neither thoughts nor emotions are present in an intelligible form. In their absence, the mind develops what I would call secondary symbol languages and associations (Witzel 2015: 384).

It is important to keep in mind that I am not trying to tie Witzel down to such or other theses. Their enumeration may look arbitrary. But in the long run, they appear to be used in order to encircle more durable perspectives. The organization of the text and its network-like density does turn them into the kind of resting-places for the reader's consciousness in William James' sense from which it is hard to escape. Much in the way which I have sketched the historical status of theories, Witzel devotes a later, highly parodistic chapter, headed by an allusion to Marx and his theses on Feuerbach, to the "theorists who have only interpreted

---

145 Sloterdijk 2006.

the world differently" (608–614). Theorists know that names are not identical with concepts. Real history thus disappears behind historicity (608–609). This failure occurs in particularly damaging form with respect to the significance of death, where theorists have not only not been able to provide real "advice", but did not even produce a fascinating, spiritualized transcendence or metaphysics. For death, people had to stick to religion, for the rest theorists went for an unending rehash of the old Greeks, mixed with a few ideas of the Enlightenment (611). At some point, however, they came to see that the subject, imagining and conceptualizing its objects of knowledge, had to be replaced by intersubjective forms of coming to terms with others. This led to a fatal last step: Truth turned out to be a linguistic construct. Its acceptance hinged on social agreement (613–614). Taking up Witzel's idea of a fascinating theory: It would indeed be fascinating to confront that rudimentary sketch not with the rehash, but the rehabilitation of Platonic-Aristotelian thought in Arbogast Schmitt's *magnum opus* on modernity and Plato as two paradigms of rationality. For Schmitt, it is absolutely clear which type should be preferred.[146] Witzel, in his turn, appears to endorse the view on the historical functionality of 'theory' adumbrated in the preceding chapter.

The essential point in the almost endless accumulation of theories and ideas, however, would seem to be its provocation to reorient thought and accordingly consist in the development of *models of thought* ("Denkmodelle", see 717). These are not be confused with ancient to roughly eighteenth century total images of world and humankind (like the great chain of being), nor with the totalizing *Weltanschauungen* of the nineteenth century, nor with the plurality of theories in the twentieth. They must remain free from "big words" like (fall in) love, alcoholism, depression, cancer, terrorism (755), freedom, truth, redemption, ecstasy (766). But it is possible to hold that, while Freud was certainly not right with some of his doctrines, psychoanalysis still provides us with a useful model of thought. It is equally plausible to maintain that Marx was quite right in fundamental respects, but still is not useful as model of thought (or "ideology"). We do not have a "system" of thought on which we can rely (717).

Rather, we should inquire into what, in neurobiological talk, is called binding power – this time not the binding power *of* consciousness, but the binding power (the fascination) of phenomena *for* consciousness. The central binding power in the book is certainly music, vaguely prefiguring but not determining the shape of problems and experience. Musical practice forms indeed an integral part of Witzel's artistic education and competence. The binding power of music –

---

146 Schmitt 2012, *passim*.

prefiguring but not determining, inviting but not enforcing imaginations and identifications of all kinds – can be misleading. I take it that the example of *Rubber Soul* by the Beatles is meant to suggest the theological abuse of the identification potential (see above). But the efforts to come to terms with that potential, to gauge its relative strength in different rock bands occur with conspicuous frequency: The consciousness of the teenager simply cannot abandon the effort to squeeze something meaningful into or out of the songs, texts, and their interaction of a long array of groups. The Beatles, the Rolling Stones and the Kinks appear to play leading roles in that respect. But if one cannot get rid of music, it is also well-nigh impossible to use it in the construction of models of thought – unless it is used as a necessary element of indeterminacy in such models and as an equally necessary form of commitment without definition. With Witzel, the twenty-first century has become aware of one of its central dilemmas: We are pulled hither and thither by phenomena, like music, with high binding power but low enunciation and orientation, and by phenomena, like models of thought with a high degree of intellectual elaboration and low binding power.

The category of binding power must be used not only because its relevance for the attraction of phenomena like music is fairly obvious. Its importance follows also from a phenomenology of consciousness in which transitionality plays a specific role. Witzel exploits the metaphorical potential of doors in order to indicate its peculiarity. Playfully and undogmatically he suggests that one might change Lacan's famous phrase and say that the unconscious is structured like a door. Doors seem to be related to the innermost being of the human psyche to such an extent that the mentally ill often see their personality core endangered by openings like doors (holes, passages, membranes). Doors are necessary for rooms and no mere addition or weakening of structure (634). Their various forms like Asian sliding and Western leaved ("French") doors are culturally and psychologically significant. Sliding doors seem to deny themselves the status of a door, refusing to evaluate space, treating both sides as equivalent. Oriental curtain doors block the gaze, but not the crossing. Western leaved doors tend to encourage thinking in dichotomies ultimately turning into heaven and hell (the access to heaven is visualized as a door), good and bad, matter and spirit, body and soul, inside and outside; 636). In the event of a catastrophe like an earthquake, the doorframe is often the only and therefore protective element which remains more or less intact. Small wonder that, starting with the Bible, an extensive symbolism has developed around doors (634–635).

These may be idle speculations, coming, as they do, from a grown-up teenager in the special department for personality disorders of the university hospital Hamburg-Eppendorf and delivered in a speech on the lack of chronology in life (chapter 85, 621). But they are taken up in various forms and on varying occasions. In the musical context, but also in some forms of prose (like the fascinating and incomprehensible sentences of Peter Handke), the transitions, in both directions, between the unconscious and consciousness are taken up again near the very end (792). Much earlier, we get quotations from a "Small Dictionary of Metaphysics". One is concerned with the smooth and the confused or blocked transitions of thought after wake-up. In a block, the speaker/writer is tempted to give up the effort to think altogether, but then feels the temptation to profit from the peculiar productivity of dim thought (368, cf. 756). Then, again, the father of the teenager (probably) describes how, after "an hour of relative unconsciousness", he will start thinking wildly and in fragments, in a kind of looking around or browsing, like browsing in the central register of a country (582–583).

Which, if any, consequences could we draw from Witzel's pictures of consciousness and its products? If consciousness works in these ways, then products of thought should reflect at least to some extent its multifariousness. This diversity cannot be rechanneled into a unified conception of the world and of human beings. That means that the time of total conceptions and *Weltanschauungen* is definitely over. Not only that: Terrorism, which may *mean* many things in terms of causes and conditions, *implies* that the definitional power of what is supposed to or should be called realities (especially social and political ones) can now be arrogated by any group or individual feeling like it. Total conceptions of the world and human beings were normally buttressed by religious and ethical demands; *Weltanschauungen* could at least claim that patterns of legitimate action could be deduced from them; theories lost that strength but replaced it, successfully for a while and perhaps to some extent even today, by methodological rigor and predictive potential. The product logically resulting from the phenomenology of consciousness in Witzel's book would be, as suggested before, variable models of thought, that is to say an elastic and possibly multiple ordering of diversity, but not its erasure.

What does that imply? Certainly, the "nihilistic acceptance of everything" denounced by Gehlen rears its head.[147] But Witzel also presents so many confrontational debates that simple acceptance cannot be the last word. I would like to illustrate Witzel's implications with three examples. First example: Remembering Feyerabend it would appear that his reasons for always working with more than one theory (or now model of thought) have become even stronger. One of Feyerabend's arguments, in chapter 3 of *Wider den Methodenzwang* (*Against Method*), concentrates in a criticism of the practice that normally one theory only is compared to facts or rather observational statements (Feyerabend

---

147 Gehlen 1973: 40.

1999: 43). But facts and theories are much more closely connected than this practice would lead us to assume. In particular, any description of fact is saturated with theories which may differ radically from the theory to be tested. Moreover, there are facts which can be stated only with the help of other theories, facts which therefore would not be at the researcher's disposal if other theories were not brought in (Feyerabend 1999: 43–44).

Feyerabend illustrates his position with respect to the Brownian movement in physics. I am of course not competent to judge that in any way. But I am sure that the saturation of so-called facts in the humanities and social sciences with previous theories or other theoretically relevant assumptions is much more conspicuous, comprehensive and convoluted than in physics. Let me briefly provide some examples. (Before I do that, it is useful to remind ourselves that the logical consistency of the conclusions Feyerabend draws from this situation leaves quite a bit to be desired.) I think it is true to say, for instance, that the judgments of scientists and doctors, of experts in general should not (with Feyerabend 1980) simply be accepted. It does not follow, I think, that the public or smaller non-expert groups like publicly elected committees have to examine those judgments as closely as possible. In fact, I think that such procedures would be quite dangerous.)

Second example: A few years after World War II, the famous German sociologist Helmut Schelsky published a collection of essays called *Looking for Reality*. The subtitle seemingly made it clear that essays and title were meant to refer to the West Germany of the time (*Collected Essays on the Sociology of the Federal Republic of Germany*). The Preface stated explicitly that Schelsky considered the essays to be "documents of the time" (mainly from the end of the war to about 1955). Each generation can handle only its own experienced past. The Introduction insisted even more emphatically on the narrow timeframe for which the analyses could claim relevance. Schelsky had been struck by the speed "with which entire sociological libraries had been turned into rubbish and wastepaper by the war and its consequences".[148] Yet, inevitably (I would say), the reach of theories and analyses was widening – it was widening in an altogether indefinite way. The essay which provided the title for the volume ("The Loss of Reality in Modern Society", 394–409, from 1954) in particular reads mostly like an analysis of global developments, even if the empirical research for it was conducted in German (possibly remote) provinces. On the other side, taken globally, one has the strongest feeling that crucial theses of the essays were patently wrong. One might have the further feeling that they are not

---

148 Schelsky 1979: 9, 12.

even true for all of West Germany. Schelsky's central assertion holds that the structural tensions between basic analytical categories like family, workplace, forms of community, city and country, young and old, men and women, entrepreneurs and workers "have lost a large part of their accuracy, their power of distinction, and simply reality" (Schelsky 1979: 397). They have all been swept away and replaced by huge and anonymous superstructures (a term imported from US-American sociology, 398). Schelsky has increased the difficulties to find out about the precise reference of these terms by propagating, in the end, a return to old structures and values like primary and intimate groups, personal relations between an authentic I and a genuine you, a return to friendship, marriage, collegiality, and professional communities (408 – 409).

Apart from the vague utopianism creeping in towards the end, all of these categories are fed by different sources. Schelsky certainly has caught an important trend in most Western societies of that time. But he remains sorely deficient in comparative power and precision. Without denying the general relevance of his judgment for West Germany and in varying extents for most of the Western world and probably an indefinite part of the rest of the world as well, one just has to take a look, with respect to country and city, for instance at Raymond Williams' *The Country and the City* (1973) in order to get a partially overlapping, partially contradictory set of implications. This is my third example. Williams holds that "the English experience is especially significant in that one of the decisive transformations, in the relations between country and city, occurred there very early and with a thoroughness which is still in some ways unapproached".[149] In Britain, the traditional peasantry for instance disappeared already with the Industrial Revolution. During the imperialist phase, the country changed again drastically in that dependence on a domestic agriculture dwindled rapidly (Williams 1973: 2). One can extend such arguments into a culture game by collecting the stereotypical complaints, throughout the centuries, that the good old country life has disappeared; the literary historian will remember that Oliver Goldsmith saw, in *The Deserted Village* of 1769, "the rural virtues leave the land" (Williams 1973: 10, 9 – 12). By the eighteenth century, nearly a quarter of cultivated land was owned by four hundred families, about half by five thousand (60). The large landowners constitute the top echelon of the rural social structure, but their income, especially with the advent of the nineteenth century, is also involved in government and bank stocks, in canal and railway shares, in the profit from harbor facilities and mines and so on (186). As such, this group as well as others seem to demand a more distinctive and detailed sociological approach than

---

149 Williams 1973: 2.

the one presented by Schelsky for West Germany. Apparently, "pride, greed and calculation are active among landowners as well as among city merchants and courtiers" (28). Classical pastoral and rural literature in general, down to Thomas Hardy, seems to have been busy excising tensions "until there is nothing countervailing", and let selected, purified images as it were stand by themselves (18, cf. 22, 35–36).

The quotes from Williams are not intended, of course, to refute Schelsky. But they should demonstrate the need to work with more theories than only one for one phenomenon. Basically, they argue for a preference for models of thought. To rest satisfied with an exchange of products of thought, however, would get us mired even deeper in the arbitrariness of the *practice* of both theories and models of thought, an arbitrariness which we saw emerging as the price to be paid for "science in a free society". If we are thrown back on models of thought, the question of the authority, of the *enforceability* of rules and practice comes to the forefront and tends to become more important than efforts at ethical norms mostly suspended in thin air. This is where Witzel's combination of models of thought and confrontational debate takes on its central importance. Chapter 8, with the example of Hume and others, will have to say more on this.

Witzel's combination, in any case, implies and demands an effort towards the reevaluation of *liberalism*. As a product of thought changing with the times in which it is produced, liberalism oscillates uneasily between a *Weltanschauung*, a series of theories and varying models of thought. The following chapter will briefly sketch intrinsic weaknesses which haunted liberalism from the beginning. The backfiring of liberalism in the conception and practice of theory and models of thought emerges in Williams' picture of rural life (and investigations like Karl Polanyi's *Great Transformation*) insofar as any decision taken tended to produce more or less the opposite results from those intended. This holds, with a vengeance, in particular for the poor laws which, instead of improving the lot of the poor, made their situation even worse. Increasing poverty, as Williams put it, "became a system of pauperism" (Williams 1973: 103). For literary people, this may be less obvious, because there is hardly anything in literature for instance to record the passing and death, by expropriation and a kind of legalized seizure, of villages (Williams 1973: 98, 102).

6 The Drama of 'Liberalism'

Witzel's great book can also be read as the (much more than) biographical delineation of West German history, with the teenager as almost a victim, from the authoritarian situation after the war to tentative forms of liberalization in the later 60s and early 70s. Obviously, this book could and should also be viewed as another biographically shaped chapter in the history of liberalism. Turning this argument around, we could also argue that, by and large, novel-writing presupposes some form of liberalism. We hardly find it in absolutistic or similar regimes. Some of its varieties must therefore be tested for their mode of existence and historical power.

The death of liberalism has often been announced. Like the news about Mark Twain's death in 1897, it is vastly exaggerated. Its mode of existence and orientating efficiency, however, are entirely different matters. The term is far too important to be dismissed from our conceptual repertoire. On the level of conscious processes, it can be used to designate our phenomenological self-awareness suggesting their relative freedom. This translates fairly easily, on a first product level, into the feeling of personal freedom as opposed to the often traumatic experience or imagination of enslavement. The complex of images and sensations associated with human bondage feeds the 'hysterical' drive of the mind for freedom. At the same time, liberalism tries to mute the aggressive sting which the hysterical drive normally displays. In that respect, Gehlen's characterization of liberalism as an optimistic and harmless way of uniting all kinds of individualisms into collective happiness and, as such, as a prepolitical good spirit and nature, seems to be correct.[150] Even so, parallel to the basic 'mood' of the mind, liberal thought runs through many political orientations. Discontent with its elements of *laisser faire* and its practical deficits have certainly contributed to the backlash of radicalisms terrorizing our time. As a *style* of thought, liberalism runs within and parallel to most modern forms of literature. These could not thrive without at least some loosening of despotic governmental regimes. (In the next chapter, I will treat the Enlightenment as a historical exemplification of liberalism insofar as the effort towards the building of a variegated, but also coherent body of thought is concerned.)

Its wide and flexible usefulness as a product of thought has made the term indispensable and suspect at the same time. As a *basso continuo* in the mind, it provides a direction for the self-interpretation of conscious processes; as a mode of thought, it appears as a functionally most suitable term for the institutions of

---

150 Gehlen 1972: 63.

https://doi.org/10.1515/9783110581836-017

modernity. At the same time and on all counts, liberalism could be denounced as a prime agent of self-deception. I want to take a closer look, therefore, at the historical beginnings of liberalism in which such tensions came to the forefront. In what follows I want to show that the relations of this *Weltanschauung* with the socio-political situations out there which it was meant to structure, to plausibilize, to promote, to criticize or to harmonize did not advance to a level of productive mutuality. Connections between the three domains were and continue to be tenuous and unstable. They lead up to the conceptual and logical dead end which marred J. S. Mill's classic analysis *On Liberty* discussed before.

As a *Weltanschauung* committed to the improvement of individual lives and human rights as well as to socio-political, 'democratic' betterment, liberalism emerges mainly as a late eighteenth-century development. Some see, as far as England is concerned, democratic stirrings already in the Magna C(h)arta Libertatum of 1215 – a preposterous misjudgment if there ever was one. Others include movements like the seventeenth-century Levellers whose radicalism, however, appears hard to reconcile with what we have come to demand as liberal tolerance. The picture is, to say the least, complicated and blurred. It seems reasonable, by contrast, to consider for instance the Habeas Corpus Act of 1685 as a predecessor of liberalism. T. B. Macaulay, in his *History of England from the Accession of James the Second*, has noted that this law, "though passed during the ascendency of the Whigs, was not more dear to the Whigs than to the Tories. It is indeed not wonderful [sic] that this great law should be highly prized by all Englishmen without distinction of party: for it is a law which, not by circuitous, but by direct operation, adds to the security and happiness of every inhabitant of the realm."[151]

---

151 Macaulay 1849: vol. 2, 238. I should mention here that Judith Shklar, in her famous essay "The Liberalism of Fear", does not think that liberalism qualifies as a *Weltanschauung* (she uses the German term which she reserves for a whole "philosophy of life"). Liberalism for her is 'only' a political doctrine trying to secure political and economic conditions which make the exercise of concrete personal freedom possible. But she also recognizes the existence of a liberalism of natural rights targeting the fulfilment of an ideal normative order, of perfect societies of citizens pursuing their own lawful aims in harmony with a higher law. And she sees that there are a few more varieties like the liberalism of personal development which Mill took over from Humboldt. Cf. Shklar 1989: 21–38. There is a translation of that essay in a very good collection in German edited by Hannes Bajohr with essays by Michael Walzer, Seyla Benhabib and Bernard Williams. Thanks again to Jo Ludwig for drawing my attention to that book.

Criticism of the varieties of (humanitarian, political, economic) liberalism set in around 1900 at the latest. In 1909 J. A. Hobson for instance published *The Crisis of Liberalism*; for Germany see e. g. Hermand 1989. During the summer term of 2017 the Mosse Lectures at Humboldt University Berlin were devoted to evaluations and criticisms of liberalism.

Macaulay normally enjoys the dubious reputation of being the main representative of the Whig interpretation of history. That interpretational mode, seeing
past events and trends from its own vantage point fulfilling the desires of the
present, assumes a direct line between these events and its own aspirations.
Macaulay's introduction presents the classical formulations:

> I shall relate how the new settlement was, during many troubled years, successfully defend-
> ed against foreign and domestic enemies; how, under that settlement, the authority of law
> and the security of property were found to be compatible with a liberty of discussion and of
> individual action never before known; how, from the auspicious union of order and free-
> dom, sprang a prosperity of which the annals of human history had furnished no example;
> how our country, from a state of ignominious vassalage, rapidly rose to the place of umpire
> among European powers; how her opulence and martial power grew together; how, by wise
> and resolute good faith, was gradually established a public credit fruitful of marvels which
> to the statesmen of any former age would have seemed incredible. (vol. 1, 1)

Here, we have the liberal *Weltanschauung*, clad in English clothes, on the brink
of ideology. But again, this is not now important. What counts is the oscillation
of the "liberties of England" (Macaulay 1849: vol. 1, 126), indeed their being
picked to pieces and crushed in the 'chaotic' wear and tear to which the imagined liberties are exposed. If, at some point, Habeas Corpus was highly prized
by all Englishmen, the later liberties were used and misused for any purpose
ready at hand. Looking into a few histories of England, we do get a dramatic picture of how a body of ideas which might have ascended to a liberal *Weltanschauung* is distorted until it is hard to identify intelligible elements. With Macaulay, that process is already in full swing. In terms of contemporary reactions, it
is especially the closeness, future or past, of the French Revolution which provokes contradictory attitudes even in one and the same person (e.g. Edmund
Burke). While remaining a burning ('hysterical') issue for individual minds and
their interests, liberalism is thus prevented from acquiring at least a minimal
consistency as a socio-politically accentuated *Weltanschauung*. Later historians
certainly try to instill some order, to smooth out discrepancies between individual interests and images and to salvage the awareness that there is something
like English liberties with more or less success. But the discrepancies persist.
G. M. Trevelyan, to name a famous example, takes what he calls the beginnings
of democracy as a unifying perspective. That perspective, however, is undermined right from the beginning by the stark contrast between an unusual degree
of individual freedom and strong oligarchic power structures represented mainly
by the landowners. To some extent one gathers the impression that English liberties can be talked about primarily in the sense that King George I had been so
indifferent to things English that he left interior policies entirely to his ministers.

The British state of the middle-eighteenth century could be described, Trevelyan thinks, as the rule of aristocracy interspersed with minor forms of social unrest.

The oligarchy of the Whigs, in due course and with its spirit exhausted, came to an end, the old Tories were dead, a new party was not born yet. For a while, as Trevelyan puts it in a nice image, the English were sheep without a shepherd, or rather: Their shepherds were playing cards while the wolves were already at the gates. William Pitt, Trevelyan thinks, said the simple truth when he asserted that he knew he was the only one who could save the country.[152] Pitt could be seen as the embodiment of liberalism ("the great Commoner" as he was called), acceptable to all and desired by many. But even Pitt – apart from the conceptual problem that one representative, splendid as he may have been, is not enough to justify the use of a term designating a movement – was not able to reconcile the diverging interests. George III, after ascending the throne, took government into his own hands, forcing his ministers into their old role as servants to the King. Pitt, according to Trevelyan who is normally see as the last representative of Whig, 'liberal' historiography, made matters worse because of his "more than aristocratic personal pride" (Trevelyan 1947: vol. 2, 620). Instead of acting as an umpire, he increased confusion (620). His second term (1766–1769) with a cabinet supposedly above parties, grew into an all-round disaster (621).

Meanwhile, the war of independence started in America. Democratic programs began to appear (Trevelyan 1947: vol. 2, 633). Together with the French Revolution, however, the war brought all political changes in England to a standstill (632). George lost his power in the wake of an illness which was honored with a film (*The Madness of King George*, 1994), an oligarchy, this time the Tories, took over. This change hardly mattered, since power remained in the hands of the landowners anyway (634). But liberalism in the sense that liberties were there which could be claimed had reared its head and continued to do so. It seems symptomatic that during this time the Catholics of England and Ireland demanded back the full civil rights which they had lost. In this case, King, Tories and the majority of the population were united in their resistance against the Catholics, a resistance blown out of all proportion because it was mixed up with the large-scale hatred of Tom Paine's 'democratic' preaching and the hodgepodge of political and religious fervor against the 'Papists' in Ireland. The second wave of efforts toward democratic reform (Price, Priestley, cf. Trevelyan 1947: vol. 2, 637) remained largely "academic" or restricted to a small minority. The upshot: "Exploitation, hatred and mutual suspicion broke apart a beautiful life of

---

152 Trevelyan 1947: vol. 2, 603, 613.

togetherness which until that time had been the hallmark of English life in the eighteenth century" (638).

To repeat and to sum up: In Trevelyan, who counts as the last great Whig, i. e. liberal historian in England, we get a picture of liberalism as, first, the potential for a historically plausible and indeed urgent *Weltanschauung* which could be easily presented in a more comprehensive way by looking into the great economic thinkers of the century. This framework, however, is picked to pieces by the hysterical and antagonistic violence with which it is burning in individual minds. In the process, the difficulty of finding arguments for causes however justified in some way or other becomes glaring. Trevelyan, or so it seems to me, writes out of the mood of the disappointed liberal, with most hopeful steps in the right direction leading nowhere. It is instructive to compare his version of that period with another one offered by the German historian Kurt Kluxen which looks as if inspired by the Habermasian theory about the changes of the public sphere in processes of European modernization. Kluxen thus pays stronger attention to political movements, their institutions and their media. Even so, one 'anarchic' individual turns into the centerpiece of his narrative. For Kluxen, the period of the candidacy and arrest of John Wilkes led to the massacre at St. George's Field where, out of about 20 000, eleven people were killed. Ultimately, Wilkes was successful with another candidacy in spite of parliamentary manipulation against him. With Wilkes becoming a celebrity, his most active adherents founded a "Society of the Supporters of the Bill of Rights" (Kluxen 1976: 469) and another one for "Mr. Wilkes and his Cause". The latter collected about £ 20 000 to pay his debts (469). In 1774, Wilkes became Lord Mayor of London. Conflicts persisted. The crucial question concerned the specific rights of the electorate. This included questions of the freedom of opinion and of the press (470). Around 1776, these internal conflicts were exacerbated by those with the North American colonies. A number of pamphlets was thrown into the fray. The Whig gentry, basically open for reforms, was suspicious of London radicalism. The range of reform ambitions shrank, especially when the Catholic problem became mixed up with the Gordon riots in June 1780 (a Protestant rebellion against an emancipation law for Catholics) and partly, for instance with an attack on the Bank of England, got out of control (474). Radicalism, not so terribly radical anyway, aiming at most at a constitutional reform, hardly had any effect. "Its importance emerged in retrospective view only" (474). Kluxen consequently detects plebiscitarian elements and new forms of political fight. But they function more as an announcement of things to come in the nineteenth century than as realities of the eighteenth (476).

In the nineteenth century, indeed, this dead end between the hysterical agitation of consciousness in its aggressive form and the depressing development of the world out there became visible to such a degree that something had to be and was done. With the eighteenth century drawing to an end, the signs became very ominous even then. There was a dramatic increase in population especially around 1780 (Hill 1977: 65, 68); there was a steep increase in prices not at all matched by increases in wages. The notorious Speenhamland System, originally intended as a local measure of relief mainly for agricultural laborers in Berkshire, spread rapidly across the country, confusing the problem of wages with parish relief or the Poor Law. The results were disastrous: "Speenhamland demoralised the countryman" (Hill 1977: 65). He might work as much as possible; he would not get more than a fixed wage. The outlook was bleak: After the Great French War (1793 – 1815), the country entered "one of the grimmest periods in modern British history, years of distress and class hatred, darkened by sullen discontent and periodic riots in the industrial areas" (Hill 1977: 68). One important countermovement consisted in the intensification of the hysterical consciousness adopting a religious form. Or, as Asa Briggs put it in a more neutral form: "Against this background of rural poverty, it is not surprising that a religious leader with a spiritual mission to the poor emerged [...]" (Briggs 1985: 176). Against this background, it is also not surprising that the nineteenth century was almost compelled, or condemned to formulate and articulate an antidote, that is to say liberalism as a full-blown *Weltanschauung*. John Stuart Mill's *On Liberty* (1859), mentioned before, provides the classic example. Although, as Raymond Williams insisted upon, eighteenth-century literature might well have paid attention to forms for instance of rural misery and did not, literature does pay attention to the misery of work and public institutions a century later. But this does not, of course, rehabilitate liberalism as normally conceived and practiced. One reason for that was stated back in 1873 by Sir William Harcourt. Liberty, he told a gathering at Oxford, does not consist in making others do what you think is right. "The difference between a free Government and a Government which is not free is principally this – that a Government which is not free interferes with everything it can, and a free Government interferes with nothing except what it must." As far as the safety of society will permit (a central argument also in Mill), a liberal government will try to allow everybody to do as they wish.[153] The moot point here is of course that safety is not enough and that other criteria – like equal access to opportunities of various kinds – are difficult to define and, above all, to operationalize.

The systematic problem then with *Weltanschauungen* lies in the unresolved tension between the view of the world and the program of action. Normally,

---

153 Quoted in Tyrrell, Jr., 2012: xii.

a *Weltanschauung*, openly or indirectly, will contain such a program. Normally also, this does not pose much of an urgent problem, because the program need not spell out all of its (organizational) hazards. It will normally be tested and tried at some later point. Then, additional assumptions can be adduced in order to hide weaknesses in the transition from view to action. Theories and models of thought, in comparison, do not usually talk about programmatic aspects at all. This does not mean that these have been sufficiently dealt with. It rather means that the effort has been tacitly given up: Anything goes, yes, but not anywhere.

7 What Does Enlightenment Enlighten Us About?

There are probably neither periods nor movements which demonstrated the same intense interest in both processes and products of thought and their inter-relations like the so-called Enlightenment especially in eighteenth-century France. This comes hardly as a surprise. What with the self-observation and the self-reference of the mind having become steadily more important and impossible to get rid of any more, the question of its relation to products of thought and what they represented socially, politically and otherwise could hardly be ignored, especially when the represented institutions betrayed weaknesses and instabilities. Hilary Mantel's picture of the French Revolution mainly in the form of portraits of the revolutionaries should have provided ample evidence for that.

In the interest of getting close to the thought of those involved with English eighteenth-century liberalism (which one could call with Shklar a political liberalism) I have been presenting a very 'concretistic' picture so far. The title question of this chapter now alludes to John Bender who asked a similar, but more abstract question with the formula "Ends of Enlightenment". He argued correctly, I think, that we live "with residual versions of these ideas, actors, and institutions in today's world", perhaps even "in the modes of cultural unconsciousness and fragmentary recollection".[154] In terms of content, "these ideas" consist in the necessity, formulated amongst others by Kant, of universal criticism especially of what seemed to show up as superstitions, in projects like a new ideal citizen on both sides of the Atlantic, in the definition of moral sentiments and the new media suitable to express and circulate them, in new, mostly 'empirical' criteria with which to test the credibility of important narratives. I will move freely between these two levels. They are also represented (as types of thought products) by Judith N. Shklar's "liberalism of fear" with its highest aim as the avoidance of cruelty on a livable basis of political and economic security, and Hannah Arendt's "liberal republicanism" with its public political and communicative practice protected by the law and ultimately based on a philosophy of history.[155] I want to move freely between the levels since the very range of aspects brought to bear on liberalism by Arendt and Shklar alone is an index of not just a historical, but an almost logical wear and tear of such a type of thought. This wear and tear may or may not depend on the causalities or contingencies of the origins of the various liberalisms.

---

154 Bender 2012: 1.
155 The comparison has been made with exemplary clarity by Axel Honneth in his preface ("Vorwort") to Bajohr (ed.) 2013: 7–25.

https://doi.org/10.1515/9783110581836-018

In any case I feel entitled to regard the Enlightenment as an important part of liberalism. Shklar is right to insist upon the fact that, in terms of political *world* history, liberalism in any sense is a fairly rare phenomenon. But since it is important (as I think), it is also important to track it down wherever we can reasonably detect it and to see how far it will work. As I hinted at, discrepancies between different versions of liberalism and their origin (e. g. assumed to have happened after the European religious wars) are historical matters of often but not always great importance. Conceptual or definitional problems, however, *are* worrisome, because they spring from the very effort of defining something moving from concrete to abstract levels so quickly and unavoidably[156] that one aspect seems to get not honored but destroyed by the next. This is due to the complexity of almost any issue we face in liberalisms. As I tried to suggest repeatedly before, Arbogast Schmitt's version of Plato and Aristotle propounded an unsurpassed model of rationality as a philosophy of discrimination, as the 'art' of identifying both things, objects and more 'abstract' matters *adequately through continuous and comparative conceptual work*, culminating in the concrete, definite and conceptually consensual content of any act of knowledge. But the more the sciences extended their domain, the more curiosity brought about an expansiveness of the real at the same time enjoyable and frightening, the more a certain relativity of truth claims asserted itself as well. Both science and the Platonic-Aristotelian model then had to defend themselves against the suspicion of not embodying only rationality, but also adopting variable strategies of rationalization. Moreover, rationality and rationalization also appeared to depend on the domain of reality to which they were applied. It did and does not seem so difficult to reach conceptual agreement about what is perceived as a point, line and circle. But it *is* difficult to agree, for instance, on what constitutes individual happiness within the complexities and conflicts of a state, on the relations between economy and ethics, on rational self-realization as a condition for the merging of personal advantage and the social whole, to say nothing of a culture of emotions and its aesthetic, ethical and political meaning. And it is not easy find out which implications and risks one is bargaining for in adopting any specific version of liberalism. Take Shklar's cardinal criterion of finding guarantees for the exclusion of cruelty. One might agree about physical cruelty, although even that is to a considerable extent disputable, given at least some historical and cultural relativity of how pain is felt. The question of emotional cruelty is, I think, much more difficult to ascertain, since, apart from the

---

156 This might have been one of Shklar's reasons to mention and concede a place to liberalisms of natural rights or laws or of personal development and more at all.

even greater differences in history and cultures, the grasp of its complexity and variability has been practically destroyed in divorce cases in courts of law. Or, if we can still grasp it, we can certainly not handle it in ways acceptable to all parties concerned. There is, finally, ample evidence that the main commitment of Shklar was not directed at a waterproof liberalism both theoretically discriminating and practically feasible, at a liberalism which, by taking into account political and social conditions and thus fend off cruelty and injustice as much as possible, would realistically increase chances of a truly liberal state. Both Seyla Benhabib and Hannes Bajohr, in the German volume dealing with Shklar's liberalism of fear, argue very strongly and convincingly that Shklar was much more interested in a kind of moral psychology which might be far more capable of dealing with the ambivalences, the opaqueness and stubbornness of the human psyche and its emotions. She tried to get at a non-trivial experience of life the elements of which – in a parallel with Jaspers' phenomenology of the mind (see first part, chapter 2 above) – she would rather find in the great works of literature. Bajohr quotes from Shklar's book on *Ordinary Vices* that whoever really wants to find out about the bourgeoisie should ask Molière and Balzac.[157] In such works, however, we would look in vain for concrete programs of action or explicit standards of morality.

The Enlightenment, in particular its French version, in its turn is instructive, because we obtain a complementary picture of that situation. Its themes, as outlined above with John Bender, appear plausible (as any prolonged look in any comprehensive survey will tell us too). But the ways in which they appear in the explosively increased textual and performative possibilities of the eighteenth century makes them enormously difficult to handle consistently. The risks of heterogeneity in any term important for the self-interpretation of humans, especially the terms for morality, are sometimes embodied in one person. I am thinking especially of the enormous and cognitively dissonant potential of contrasts, not to say conflicts of implications in Diderot. On the one hand, Diderot is interested more than anybody else in connections between processes and products of thought. He wants to know which worldpictures would be developed by people without eyesight or hearing ("Lettre sur les aveugles à l'usage de ceux qui voient", "Lettre sur les sourds et les muets"). Texts like "Le rêve d'Alembert" sketch dimensions of (the relatively new word) "sensibilité" from materialistic and physiological levels up to mental and emotional potentials. A dialogue like "Paradoxe sur le Comédien" asserts propositions about emotional control or the absence of emotion which would look inhuman not only in most of Dider-

---

157 Bajohr 2013: 164; Benhabib 2013: 71–73.

ot's plays, but also and even in other essays like the texts on natural human goodness ("bonté"). In most of these cases, Diderot does not seem to care very much about full consistency or solutions purged of all impurities. Diderot offers a *Weltanschauung* (probably more than one), but he also foreshadows the poly-perspectivism of models of thought.

For a reading of for instance *Le Neveu de Rameau* the difficulties begin right away with deciding who might be meant by "lui" (probably the nephew) and (more difficult) "moi". In most of Diderot's texts, there is no dearth but rather a superabundance of competing starting points, aspects of an argument and possible conclusions. Barbara Stafford for instance thinks that Diderot unfortunately did not succeed in bringing sensual and intellectual forms of cognition into productive and dialogic communication with each other. For her, the nature of the visual is trivialized. In their book on the culture of diagram (2010) John Bender and Michael Marrian do *not* see, however, the enterprise of the *Encyclopédie* blocked by an opposition of word and image. Their long chapter on visualization does not opt for harmony nor for non-communication but rather for the heterogeneity of those perceptions with which intellectual interpretation must work. Diderot was convinced, they say, that each organ possesses specific nerves for special functions ultimately to be brought to coherence by the brain. This is the basis for his special hopes in the efficacy of the theater, because there, within the realm of art, perceptual diversity or rather perhaps heterogeneity is offered to the highest degree. The combinatorial power of the brain is challenged to the utmost.[158]

In what one calls, I take it, great moments of the theater, this may indeed happen. Even so, Diderot's ambition for the *Encyclopédie* to produce not only a survey of the sciences in their interrelations, but also a well-ordered catalogue of the confusing variety of the world and the even more confusing varieties of its perception appears preposterous. What we really get enlightened about is Diderot's virtuosity in changing the basis of changing worldviews. He may start out as a materialist, for instance in the trilogy of 1769, but also as an idealist, as in the essays on human goodness or also, in tendency, in his "drames bourgeois". Paul Vernière, in characterizing Diderot's philosophical works, makes do with the suspicion that there might have been, in Diderot, "un goût pour la mystification [...] quelque soupçon enfin des contradictions intérieures", but dismisses these suspicions himself. Diderot can talk leisurely about how to imagine God in *Pensées*

---

158 Stafford 1994: 220; Bender and Marriner 2014: 12, 23 and especially 118–129 on pantomime, theater and theatrical *tableaux* in Diderot. For what follows see also Diderot 1964: xix, 13 and Diderot 1968: 306–312, concering the "singerie sublime" of the actor or actress.

philosophiques, turn pantheist in the same work, finally adopting the atheist's role in *Lettre sur les aveugles à l'usage de ceux qui voient*. In a short text like "Eloge de Richardson" Diderot may present himself as more of a sentimentalist than Richardson himself. His most widely read text "Paradoxe sur le comédien" drives both the potentiality of human coldness and the agonies of human emotions emerging from the intestines into extremes.

Diderot's indifference with respect to inconsistencies in and between his positions is no mere intellectual relativism. It is also, though certainly not exclusively, an offshoot of what one would call a liberal life style later. Once in full swing, this connection can be exploited for the justification of ideas in terms of their value and service for life. In one of the dubious periods of German history the well-known philosopher Erich Rothacker for instance saw all of the humanities as agents and instruments of "life fights" ("Lebenskämpfe").[159] The personal infighting of Enlightenment personnel, with Rousseau involved almost everywhere, is of course also intertwined with the question of who is "dans le vrai" in terms of central propositions, in the free debate about problems, issues and whatever important matters. But behind these (on the origin of inequality, the specific beneficial or detrimental cultural function of art forms etc) there loom the spectres of how one would like to and how one could or should live.

That Rousseau, for instance, plays still such a prominent role in European intellectual history has to do not only with the content of his thought, but also with the unusual relationship between his thought, character and behavior, or rather with his ability to stage himself as his doctrines and his doctrines as himself, and with the inability of most of his contemporaries to see through this amalgamation. This assumption makes it easier to understand how and why such an entirely different kind of thinker and man like David Hume stumbled into a relationship with Rousseau. After Rousseau had been expelled from his Swiss exile, Hume was asked whether he could help to find another exile in England. Hume complied, his main reason being his respect for what appeared and appealed to him as Rousseau's higher mentality. This mentality Hume did not define in terms of Rousseau's ideas, but rather his character "which makes him shun obligations and dependencies", an attitude which Hume said he had always striven after himself. In terms of philosophical interests, the two had little in common. It is striking how skillfully they avoid any dis-

---

159 Rothacker 1965: 107–113. It is clear that for Rothacker, whose book was first published in 1927, the term *Weltanschauung* is generally valid, since it exists only in this aggressive and forced way. But Rothacker does score valid points too: How is it that even a good thinker can never convince his adversary (111)?

cussion of their ideas. In Hume's first letter to Rousseau (July 2, 1762) he stresses his own "love for philosophical retreat", his "neglect of vulgar prejudices" and "disdain of all dependence" as the bonds presumably uniting them. He assumes that "my conduct and character entitles me to a sympathy with yours".[160] Hume certainly also praises Rousseau's talent, the eloquence and power of his ideas and especially of his language. Clearly, however, something like extravagance, wildness and exaltation (Schulz 2012: 36) prevents him from a full appreciation. A more serious, but not at all detailed criticism of Rousseau's ideas sets in soon (36: "mistakes"). But it is definitely Rousseau's personality and way of life which strike Hume as well as others most strongly (eccentricity, love of solitude, nature, character, appearance of misanthropy and so forth). Rousseau, in his turn, is not interested in the ideas and controversies negotiated on British soil. He talks about the concrete conditions for his life in England very quickly and almost exclusively: He needs country life, with blossoming trees, he cannot stand the black fumes of cities. Problems like an income for Rousseau from the sale of his books by London booksellers quickly take over (30, 35, 45). Once he actually arrives in England on January 11, 1766, worries not only about a general orientation of life, about a life form, but about any detail concerning concrete living conditions come to the forefront (beginning January 18, 1766, 70–71). The most frustrating problem is represented by Rousseau's 'housekeeper' (Thérèse Le Vasseur) who, as Rousseau insists upon, must also sit at table, although, as he admits, she is quarrelsome, malign and too stupid to know which year, day, or month they are living in (72–73). The second strongest influence on Rousseau seems to be his dog Sultan (87). Within days, Rousseau is transformed, for Hume, into the probably "strangest contemporary on earth" (81, letter to his brother February 2, 1766). Rousseau seems determined to live on a remote farm in Wales. Even so, an English royal pension seems still possible (82–83). In spite of devastating character judgments by Baron d'Holbach and others, Hume keeps thinking or pretending, declaring his stubbornness to be a proof of sincerity (89), that he can manage the relationship with Rousseau. That one however switches, starting with matters of health extended into the writing of books, more or less into the mode of constant complaint (96, 104–106). Soon, Rousseau suspects Hume of opening his letters (112–113) and of trying to dishonor him (125). In any case: There is, as Sabine Schulz notes in her edition of the letters written for this affair, "no trace of any concrete philosophical debates". Rousseau especially seems to have been exclusively interested in pushing his

---

160 Schulz 2012: 13, 17. Hume's first letter to Rousseau is quoted (I hope correctly) from the facsimile (19–21).

conduct of life, his break with all the rules of society, his refusal of a conformism practiced by quite a few of his Enlightenment adversaries.[161]

Whatever may have triggered the rapid alienation between Hume (as well as many others) and Rousseau: Their lack of interest, in the midst of what one would imagine to have been an intense debate of Enlightenment ideas, of philosophical exchange and communication, in the ideas of the other, remains striking. I would like to propound the thesis that, while the case may be peculiar, that peculiarity is just a special form of a wider and significant development which has come to hit the later twentieth and the early twenty-first centuries with a vengeance. I would define it as the cognitive depletion of ideas, as their loss of binding power for consciousness and as a shift of interest to life forms conducive to individual interest and well-being, but not really amenable to general justification. In our time, fundamentalist movements and dogmatisms of all kinds can exploit this situation by pretending that their ideas and life forms are still capable of full justification. Movements and attitudes which feel compelled to argue against that and the actions which seem to follow automatically from such premises, cultures which, like most Western cultures today, are hampered and handicapped for instance by an imperialist past, are not able to oppose this strategy with a cultural self-confidence of their own, inevitably find themselves in the disadvantageous situation described by Georges Devereux (cf. above 142– 143) of not knowing what they want, of not only being attacked from the outside but being put in question from within by many of their own members for whom an assumed consistency between conscience, conviction and action as the hallmark of culture has gone to pieces.[162]

This line of argument needs of course some more preparation. Western cultures – unless they are really committed to the Adorno and Horkheimer "dialectic" of the Enlightenment beset with ambivalences reaching back to the *Odyssey* and the destruction of authentic human relations – do not normally admit that this consistency, that is to say some convincing connection between thought and action, began to go to pieces already within the Enlightenment movement. This is precisely what the Hume–Rousseau case but also the example of Diderot are supposed to urge very strongly. The Enlightenment fell prey to the self-deception that the 'encyclopedic' collection and arrangement of knowledge, that a meth-

---

161 Cf. Schulz 2012, Nachwort, 509, 512. Schulz is very much committed to a balanced picture, takes however Rousseau's "paranoia" for granted (513).
162 That self-criticism of the West, weakening its position perhaps more than attacks from the outside, can be found in the most unlikely places. See for instance the Secret-Service/Soviet double agent Bill Faydon in Le Carré 2009: 407, who does not speak of the decline of the West but its death by greed and constipation and calls that a partly aesthetic, partly moral judgment.

odological universalism could be installed as the legitimate successor of the conceptual universalism of total conceptions of the world and the place of human beings in it like the great chain of being. However: A systemic form of that communication like the *Encyclopédie* enterprise, with its numerous writers as observers and self-observers, subjected ideas to a permanent wear and tear from which they could not recover and be recycled back into something like the great whole of yore.

Once such a development has started it gathers a momentum and a speed which can propel it ahead of its own time. I guess that Voltaire was still untouched by that development. In spite of a sufficient number of conflicts with authorities, he was able to offer bits and pieces of wisdom which seemed to be broken out of an older and greater whole somewhat changed in its leading tenets (for instance deism instead of monotheism) and in the emphasis on details (tolerance, caution, restraint and the like). Taking them together, his ideas may look confused and yet suggest that they form part of a meaningful ensemble. In particular, he appeals to the nineteenth century because he can be seen as an early hero in the public space which this century had to structure in its own way, a task to which for instance government propaganda made large contributions. The nineteenth century, bringing the climax of Voltaire's reputation, could reasonably see the apparent ensemble, squeezed into neat little communicative packages ("Il faut cultiver notre jardin"), as a *Weltanschauung*, its own preferred product of thought.

Rousseau, by contrast, started out on his writing career from a position of a far more acute cultural maladjustment. He tries to counter stigmatization by pushing an obsession with equality. In order to impose his doctrines, a drastically increased effort of argument had to be invested. That is why, for the twentieth century, his doctrines came to resemble theories. With his reputation therefore coming to a climax, that period indulged in orgies of Rousseau exegesis. In contrast to the status of theory in the twentieth century, Rousseau did not yet sever theory and action completely. What the last century did not and probably could not appreciate sufficiently, was the amalgamation of polemic and aggression with theoretical claims. The aggressive stance diverts attention away from and hides the weakness of theory. It betrayed a latent separation of the two domains which in the Hume affair came almost out into the open.

Diderot's style of thinking, as described above in its rapid production and dropping of ideas, anticipates and produces features of models of thought. In comparison with Voltaire and Rousseau, Diderot comes closest to the situation our thought is hedged in by.[163] The main difference seems to be perhaps the pleasure which Diderot apparently still was able to experience in writing as an exploration in all directions, as a yoking together of heterogeneity. For us, doubts concerning the relevance of an all-round inflation of models of thought, may, as often as not, interfere more easily with the pleasure of production. The melancholy of writing, latently present at most times, becomes endemic once its self-thematization sharpens the suspicion that the risky boldness of exploration is hard to distinguish from arbitrariness.

But Diderot has gone in fact even farther in providing us with concrete images of how models of thought occupy consciousness and communication. The characters in his longer prose texts for instance appear to be committed to a thorough, indeed almost unending discussion of ideas. Sometimes these ideas look important, sometimes they do not. In reality, in doing that, the characters are pleading for the acceptance of their life forms. Hegel apparently detected this exploitation of a literary-philosophical form in *Jacques le fataliste et son maître* and *Le Neveu de Rameau* and portrayed it accordingly, whether directly or indirectly inspired by the two tales, in his *Phenomenology of Spirit*. Jacques the servant and his master do not figure, for Hegel, as characters interesting in themselves or because of their opinions and their adventures, but rather because they represent forms of consciousness, namely the conscious experience of what servitude and rule have come to mean as existential categories. In the midst of talk and events mostly absurd and not to be taken seriously as a narrative anyway, there emerge the real agencies of life forms. The master, having gained reputation and power for instance in battle, can demand the recognition of his superiority for a while. Gradually, however, the distribution of power is turned around: The master comes to depend on the servant in order to satisfy his need for luxury. That might amount to the latter's conquest of independence. But it does not really liberate the servant because without a master with needs to be satisfied his own existence, power and person would shrink into insignificance. The ambivalent life form with partial dependence and independence serves both better.

Hegel has placed Diderot's *Le Neveu de Rameau* into differentiations of life forms even more squarely. Moreover, the ordinary interpretation of the nephew as a parasite would already allow me to tie him up with this topic. In Hegel, he figures prominently in the second main chapter on spirit ("Geist"), for non-Hegelians certainly a misleading classification. Hegel, however, corrects any misunderstanding quickly. The spirit is very concretely defined: As a "real sub-

---

163 I owe the splendid idea about the significance of Enlightenment reputations (Voltaire, Rousseaau, Diderot) to Hans Ulrich Gumbrecht and our talk in the Mainz Hilton Hotel.

stance", it is the "people", as a "real consciousness" it consists in the "citizens of the people". It is a spirit which "exists and is in force". In its general form as a "reality conscious of itself" it may be called the "law", which the citizens know, and the "customary morality" ("Sitte") which they follow. It is impossible to follow Hegel's construction in detail. Be it said that there is a place for the divine law, the power of the state and the family. The family in particular, as the real spirit reflected in itself, represents the simple identity of the moral substance, especially in the relation between brother and sister – both being of the same blood but not desiring each other. The feminine in the form of the sister comes closest to an idea of the moral substance.[164] Consequently, Antigone, although consciously violating state law with the burial of her brother, remains within the true morality because morality has split into two laws, while consciousness can only identify with one of them. Antigone chooses the family's, especially the brother's part. Taking action involves the "true self", at the same time, with respect to the other part of the law (state law), such an action leads her into guilt. Indeed, the moral consciousness is more complete, its guilt purer to the extent that it knows it is confronting the power state and state law (Hegel 1970: 251–252, 263, 265).

Rameau's nephew finds himself in an entirely different situation. In what one must call Hegel's historical dialectics, the nephew lives in and is shaped by the age of *Bildung*. In the context of German intellectual ambitions, this is a highly tricky term. Very briefly: In the first main propagator of the term, Wilhelm von Humboldt, it indicates the need and the possibilities of the full development of the individual person. The term carries a connotation of autonomy which, in its turn, implies a certain distance to utilitarian or conformist attitudes. That is why it can be used later on, when socio-economic and political pressures tended to produce discomfiture and more in the progressing nineteenth century, as the hallmark for culturally well-educated and knowledgeable persons whose expertise with respect to an autonomous realm of culture lifts them out of the dreariness of material life. Using a term I promised not to use: *Bildung* can easily turn into an ideology.

For Hegel, it does not represent the "true spirit" ("wahre Geist") anymore. Rather, it belongs to the alienated spirit. This is, in principle, not a bad thing, since the spirit has to exteriorize itself into the "real world" before it can come back into its own (Hegel 1970: 275). Exteriorization, however, is not just an external process, it transforms the subject. Ideally, in the process of *Bildung*, individuality forms itself into what it is as such. Exteriorization is the means or

---

164 Hegel 1970: 251–252, 255, 257.

transition into what the individual really is (277). The reality of the individual, whether in work or enjoyment, is general (280). On the other hand, Hegel recognizes that there is (under capitalist conditions?) something like "pure *Bildung*" ("reine Bildung", 290), in which reality and thought are not transformed back and forth. They become indistinguishable, because they can turn into their own contraries. "In this world", we experience neither the real essence of power and riches, nor their well-defined concepts. Nor do we get an adequate awareness of good and bad, of noble and base (293). General talk amounts to judgments tearing things apart ("zerreißende[s] Urteilen", 294). The torn consciousness is the consciousness of absolute falsification: It brings together thoughts which, for an honest consciousness, are far apart. Its language therefore is the language of (arbitrary) wit ("geistreich", 294).[165]

This is the talk of (let us assume) Rameau's nephew. The shamelessness of admitting that much is its main title to truth. For the rest, Hegel quotes the passage about the musician who sings thirty arias, Italian, French, tragic, comic, of all kinds of character, sometimes as bass, sometimes as falsetto, furious, mild, commanding, mocking (294). For the calm, honest consciousness, this talk offers a weird mixture of wisdom and baseness, of true as well as wrong ideas, of a total perversity of feeling, of perfect turpitude as well as total openness (294, a second quote). The consciousness of disunity, aware of itself, laughs mockingly at existence and the confusion of the whole and about itself. The simple consciousness, however, cannot simply demand the dissolution of this false world. It must ask the spirit of *Bildung* to abandon its own confusion and to win a higher level of awareness. This looks like a difficult task indeed and, to my knowledge, has not yet been achieved.

Rather, the Enlightenment experienced the transformation of wit from a substantial faculty of cognition into a converting machine for anything into anything else, including its opposite. (In poetry, this had happened even earlier, in England for instance with the 'metaphysical' poets of the seventeenth century.) In such a situation, the drive to change life forms will be reduced, because no cogent reason for one or the other alternative will emerge. The nephew, while turning around any proposition, stays put in what Hegel would have called his false world.

As I have suggested, it is hard to imagine two thinkers more different from each other in any respect than Rousseau and Hume. Yet essentially Hume's phi-

---

165 The interpretation in terms of capitalism and its reality was put forward for instance by Georg Lukács in Lukács 1967: 552–693. Lukács speaks of a "perpetuum mobile" of opposites being transformed into each other (507). For the original quotes from *Le Neveu de Rameau* see Diderot 1962: 413, 468.

losophy moves into the same direction as Rousseau's mixture of doctrine and self-staging in the *propagation* of his conduct of life. Hume does not push a specific life form, but his analysis of consciousness leads, in a fairly inexorable logic, to a *recommendation* for a mentally and physically salutary way of life. Hume's analysis of consciousness can sustain comparisons with our modern ones: In the incessant dynamics of the mind, no conscious element (normally called an idea) can assert and maintain itself for long. The first sentences in the *Treatise of Human Nature* state quite clearly that impressions and ideas, imagination and memory do not differ very much as categories or concepts. They differ with respect to their intensity of presence ("force") and "liveliness". Occasionally it seems that the imagination is only a synonym for memory, senses and understanding, that is to say "the vivacity of our ideas". Since, moreover, there are affective layers in any thought or movement of reason, Hume is less interested in the distinction between reason and passion, between experience and observation, but rather in styles of handling whatever comes up as an impulse, more or less strong, of action or thought.[166]

The conclusion of the first book in particular intensifies the energetic aspect of conscious processes and thereby increases the difficulties of their control. "Nothing is more dangerous to reason than the flights of the imagination, and nothing has been the occasion of more mistakes among philosophers" (Hume 1978: 267). But a converse strategy would be equally dangerous: To "reject all the trivial suggestions of the fancy, and adhere to the understanding, that is, to the general and more establish'd properties of the imagination" would entail "the most fatal consequences" (267). This is because the understanding, "when it acts alone and according to its most general principles, entirely subverts itself and leaves not the lowest degree of evidence in any proposition, either in philosophy or common life" (267–268). The understanding is a purely critical, strictly speaking destructive faculty because it can call into question anything. The understanding, founded on imagination, never observes "any real connexion between objects" (260). In appealing to the understanding, we end up in "total scepticism" (268). We could try and save ourselves "by means of that singular and seemingly trivial property of the fancy, by which we enter with difficulty into remote views of things" (268). The fancy, lively as it may be, does not grant us "so sensible an impression" as those things which we find "more easy and natural". From such a view it would follow, however, that "no refin'd or elaborate reasoning is ever to be receiv'd". We would "cut off all science and philosophy" and would moreover contradict ourselves: If we proceed on

---

166 Hume 1978: 1, 265.

one singular quality of the imagination, namely the fancy, and eliminate all the others, we must base this procedure on a preceding complex reasoning which must have been "sufficiently refin'd and metaphysical". If we now condemn refined reasoning "we run into the most manifest absurdities". If we admit it, "we subvert entirely the human understanding". Hume's train of thought here may not be entirely cogent in this last conclusion, but the overall dilemma seems inescapable: "We have, therefore, no choice left but betwixt a false reason and none at all. For my part, I know not what ought to be done in the present case" (268).

The confusion of consciousness may turn into torment because, in spite of a certain readiness to "reject all belief and reasoning", of looking "upon no opinion even as more probable and likely than another", basic questions keep haunting the mind: "Where am I, or what? From what causes do I derive my existence, and to what condition shall I return?" (268–269) Such questions cannot be stopped, but they can be interrupted. This is where the form of life comes in. Since reason cannot cure the ills it produces, "nature" (or rather culture) must step in. Hume does not advocate a specific life form. Within a loose ('liberal') framework, preferences for various leisurely activities can and ought to be enjoyed as an antidote to the dead ends of consciousness. Hume cures himself of his "philosophical melancholy and delirium, either by relaxing this bent of mind, or by some avocation, and lively impression of my senses, which obliterate all these chimeras" (269).

This may sound overly trivial. But Hume is trying to organize a complex interaction between the seeming stability, but also the pressures of everyday life, the necessary but unreliable syntheses of the imagination and the flight of ideas indulged in by the fancy. It would be easy or at least easier if one could break the relentlessness of performance demanded by these activities from time to time by a relaxing "carelessness" and "in-attention" (218). But these become effective only if they are tied up with another type of activity: "I dine, I play a game of back-gammon, I converse, and am merry with my friends" (269). Once they get on his nerves, a reverie in his room or a "solitary walk by the river-side" (270) will be beneficent.

Yet the "former disposition" of questions and argument cannot be eradicated so easily. The mind cannot rest for long: "I cannot forbear having a curiosity to be acquainted with the principles of moral good and evil", as well as for lots of other things including "the condition of the learned world" (270–271). In such a situation, philosophy must have its comeback, albeit in a different function. We must decide about a guide teaching us *how* to ask the questions which will not go away. "And in this respect I make bold to recommend philosophy" (271). Philosophy does not give us true answers to these questions, but "presents them only with mild and moderate sentiments" (272). Philosophy deals with tough questions, but it is not, for all its debates, vitally important, "its opinions are merely the objects of a cold and general speculation [...] Generally speaking, the errors in religion are dangerous; those in philosophy only ridiculous" (272). Philosophy, whatever its epistemological achievements or failures, both activates and defuses the emotions. Hume interpretation has been concerned for a while now with the role of what Hume also calls "calm" or "cool passions" within a "politics of culture". Writing texts in which the emotions or passions are both socially and psychologically crucial thus creates a manageable space between the delirium of ideas and the threat of melancholy looming large once the agitation of consciousness has exhausted itself. Writing takes care of the need for a cultivated presentation and negotiation of emotions.

8 The Paradox of Liberty and Authority

So far, Hume's picture of human existence appears to be a fairly liberal one. The interplay of thought, passions and physical or socially relaxed activities seems to allow for that reduction of affective charges in consciousness which make social life possible and even agreeable. There is, however, a presupposition which, while clearly delineated in Hobbes, came to be neglected or even forgotten from the Enlightenment via John Stuart Mill down to present-day societies. J. G. A. Pocock (and similarly for instance Quentin Skinner) has characterized that presupposition as "the paradox of liberty and authority."[167] The point is that in order for the individual to cultivate his or her *passions* in socially compatible ways, the state has to make sure that its jurisdiction concerning individual *action* is, like a seat-belt, securely fastened. In Hobbes, this led to the separation of persons into a private and public half, into a domain of private secrets and strictly regulated public behavior. The state is a space of moral neutrality; as far as private secrets are concerned, the individual is a free human being. As citizens, however, people are subjects.

Clearly, that zone of inner freedom remains a space of variously structured or unstructured unrest. It is only one step from Hobbes to the Enlightenment where the separation of human being and subject is no longer understood and where the private domain of thought switches to the idea that the human being must develop its full potential within and through the state.[168] It certainly formed part of Hilary Mantel's novel on the French Revolution to give glimpses as intense and variegated as possible of the energies and tensions from individual consciousness via programs to action. Hume's position in the history of this 'misunderstanding' is ambiguous. One the one hand, the person must go through a process of cultivation and/or self-education in order to bring the passions into a socially compatible shape. But the passions are extremely volatile and dynamic; they run into each other in such ways that it is often impossible to tell where one ends and the other begins (Hume 1987: 366, 529). Therefore, society must support the self-regulation of the passions. The task is anything but easy: Society finds itself also in a ceaseless process of differentiation and transformation which function as shaping influences on the malleable passions. This double movement appears to have been responsible for a double way of argument. In the *Enquiries*, Hume tries to ward off the suspicion of "sceptics, both

---

167 Pocock 1985: 60. See also the subtle analyses of Glaubitz 2003: 57–60.
168 This is a capital point in the "pathogenesis of civil and bourgeois society" analysed by Reinhart Koselleck 1973: 29–311.

https://doi.org/10.1515/9783110581836-019

ancient and modern", that all moral distinctions arise from education and were later invented and encouraged by "politicians, in order to render men tractable and subdue their natural ferocity and selfishness, which incapacitated them for society". He maintains that "nature" must already have made distinctions, "founded on the original constitution of the mind", that otherwise words like "honourable" and "shameful", "lovely" and "odious" etc would not have made their way into human vocabulary. From that (slightly dubious) claim he deduces that the "social virtues must, therefore, be allowed to have a natural beauty and amiableness, which, at first, antecedent to all precept or education, recommends them to the esteem of uneducated mankind, and engages their affection." We can therefore see the "public utility" of these virtues and, since we have a "strong connexion with society" and perceive the impossibility of "solitary subsistence", we become favorable not only to our own happiness and welfare, but also to "the practice of justice and humanity by which alone the social confederacy can be maintained." A few pages before, however, Hume had placed the emphasis rather on the "necessity of rules, wherever men have intercourse with each other", since they find it impossible "so much as to murder each other without statutes".[169]

Yes, indeed, but which kind of statutes? A few pages before again, Hume asserts, more realistically I think, that whenever "a number of political societies are erected, and maintain a great intercourse together, a *new* set of rules are discovered" and are called the Law of Nations. Amongst these rules, however, we may find fairly *immoral* ones like "reasons of state" which may, in particular emergencies (only?), dispense with the rules of justice (Hume 1975: 205–206, my emphasis). Apparently, the fairly monolithic power and jurisdiction of the state with respect to actions of its subjects in Hobbes is imperceptibly dissolving in Hume. From now on, it is the *authority of rules* primarily in the form of laws which is and will remain at stake. G. Böhme has made the telling comment that even the transcendentalist Kant takes concepts to be rules according to which our imagination shapes the objects the concept seems to designate. And he has added: "You follow rules – or you don't." Depending on what one wants to achieve, it is better to respect or to ignore them. There is, of course (or so one would think), the resistance of society to tolerate a simple living out of the impulses in the mind. What we say will normally have to fit some context. Persons have to wear a mask, a *persona*, which covers up the chaos of their minds and what is merely private about them. [170] The problem just is that

---

169 Hume 1975: 210, 214–215.
170 Böhme 2017: 115 (with quote), 126, 129.

fewer and fewer people, even from within, say, Western societies, are willing to respect what others call the rules. More precisely: In an age like ours which has replaced reference to the richness of the world with the self-reference of systems, it has become rather difficult in many areas characterized by *referential opacity*[171] to know what the rules 'really', that is reliably consist in. Nowadays even soccer players complain about the 'unruly' behavior of their fans. In the case of laws, it is both their interpretation and their *enforceability* which keep creating unending difficulties. At the same time, the Christian and philosophical imperative to explore interiority and thereby to find perhaps at true or better self, confronts the person with a chaotic diversity, vague tendencies, contradictory impulses and paradoxical situations. In varying forms, the clash between these dimensions will be the problem at the center of the following third part.

The Enlightenment authority, whether we choose reason or something else, did not, in any case, prove sufficiently strong. The crisis, undermining already the Enlightenment itself, has been described very often and at great length (as a general crisis of the European spirit: Paul Hazard, as a rather diabolical dialectic of the Enlightenment, that is to say a kind of in- or even perversion of its original goals: Adorno/Horkheimer) without, in most cases, sufficient attention to the internal structural weakening of crucial orienting concepts in products of thought. Since the Enlightenment, these products have been floating helplessly between *Weltanschauungen* (with their heyday in the nineteenth century), theories (prevalent in the twentieth), and models of thought (produced *en masse* in what we broadly call the present). All of them stand in dire need of an overarching supplementary guide to action. To assume that a discourse like ethics can take over this function is a mistake. The energy landscapes of consciousness (here characterized mainly with the analogy of hysteria) cannot be controlled by products of thought, including ethics, undermined as they are by their own pluralistic drive and their internal gaps. Western societies are paradigmatically (certainly not exclusively) hit by the conjunction of the paradox of liberty and authority and the diminishing orienting power in action in the transition from total conceptions to models of thought. They have to come to terms with a situation which runs counter to one of their basic principles of rationality and legitimacy, namely that there must be sufficient of reasons for any action to be called legitimate.

---

171 The term is Quine's and defined by him in a strictly logical way. However, Quine himself has prepared the way for cultural and very generally ontological relativity. See Quine 1962: 158 (on a "nonessentialist view of the universe" and "an ontological crisis" always looming large). See further Quine 1960: 144–151, and very pointedly concerning the "inscrutability", indeed the "nonsense" of reference in the absence of clearly defined "coordinate systems" the title essay of Quine 1971: 26–68, especially 48–50.

Part III **A Case Study: Chaotic Consciousness and Catastrophic History, Discordant Evolution and Political Overreaction: Oswald and Nicholas Mosley**

1 Catastrophe Practice: Frameworks and Presuppositions – From Individuality to Scripts

The British novelist and writer Nicholas Mosley (*1923) is important because both his life and his work offer a most elaborate and detailed model of the processes/products configurations presented so far. In him, the eldest son of a father, Sir Oswald Mosley (1896–1980), mostly known as the leader of the British Union of Fascists in the thirties of the last century, the Hume situation delineated above produced a feeling of an unbridgeable distance between human beings and whatever they might claim as their own. Nicholas Mosley (= NM), in his writings, starts out with the distance which consciousness must necessarily adopt with respect to itself, whether in observing itself or in trying to tap its own resources. He ends (for instance) with an absolute and unmanageable contrast between political propaganda and criteria for action, ultimately between war and peace. In fact, the absolute contrast between war and peace not just on the obvious or trivial levels, but in relation to a human psychology based also on the workings of consciousness, is something like a leitmotif in most of Mosley's works.

In its most impressive forms, NM has sketched the trajectory from consciousness to larger and larger behavioral patterns in a series of five texts normally named *Catastrophe Practice* after the first volume of that title and characterized, misleadingly as their author well knew, as novels. The first volume of this series, *Catastrophe Practice* (first published 1979), has indeed provided me both with an idea and the title for my own enterprise. The last one of these five texts, *Hopeful Monsters* (first published 1990) can be read as an almost systematic exploration of the ways of transitionality, sometimes condensed in a single sentence: "Is it that there are wars and so we have these images, or that our minds have these images and so there are wars" (Mosley 2000: 210)? To opt for the second possibility would make it easier to understand the transition from hysterically charged conscious processes to social and larger forms of aggression. NM has prepared for that transition also by suggesting a certain closeness and affinity of psychoanalytical content (early childhood frightening experiences) pushed into the unconscious, but having a strong impact on conscious processes (Mosley 2000: 54). Furthermore, it would appear that the transitional charge of consciousness is underpinned and set in motion by bodily sensations: "I had an almost physical sensation of being pulled in different directions at once: an arm here, a leg there: perhaps I would disintegrate: perhaps there would be a mad confident voice repeating my cries as questions as I fell through the universe" (212).

https://doi.org/10.1515/9783110581836-020

To appreciate this achievement more fully, let us first take a step back. As a person, Hume was probably able to handle the occasional delirium of thought and the shakiness of thought products including social statutes, rules and institutions. There is for instance the famous report of Boswell about his last visit to Hume. Boswell was aghast at Hume's composed and indeed serene talk about both books and his own (relatively imminent) death: He was reckoning upon his "speedy dissolution". That this was probably an exceptional attitude may be gauged from the agitated and 'hysterical' response of Samuel Johnson when Boswell broached that topic to him and tried to set up Hume as a model of a personally and socially exemplary way of dying.[172] We may assume that in the nineteenth century, what with hysteria and neurasthenia identified now as specific illnesses, the turbulences of mind had become more difficult to manage – not because of stubborn and obvious symptoms, but because of their combination of persistence and elusiveness. However that may have been: On the surface, the nineteenth-century nation state was capable, often with the help of the newly established government propaganda, to create the impression of stable institutions cushioning and absorbing individual turbulence. All too often stability, however, was a risky combination of bureaucratic rigidity and ignorance. We are experiencing the consequences today with renewed intensity.

British upper-class society from at least the eighteenth to the early twentieth centuries was conspicuous by assuming that instabilities of the mind as well as of action and institutions could be controlled by sticking to what they called the rules of the game. Significantly, this is the title of the first volume of the biography which NM wrote about his father Oswald (= OM). The assumption was that both for private life and its public dimensions action, however painful for the parties involved, was acceptable as long as it proceeded along the lines of the rules. OM was not convinced about the 'fitness' of institutions but thought he himself could mend that.

There can be little doubt that such rules exist(ed); there can be little doubt either, however, that the rules, whatever their individual use in problematic situations, were far from ordering life either aesthetically, morally or politically in any reliable way. The 'catastrophes' resulting from minor or major failures of the rules (not only, but with OM predominantly in the political domain), cannot always be avoided. Therefore, catastrophe practice or training seems to take on a primary 'educational' importance. The original catastrophe (or, given NM's Christian leanings, the original sin in human life) occurs in the split which separates, in and with consciousness, human beings from their own thoughts. These are

---

172 See Hume 1963: v–xvi, xv, and Boswell 1999: 304.

normally emerging and disappearing too fast for any authentic intimacy to arise between the thinker and the thoughts. NM does not speculate about, for instance, an evil spirit or, more neutrally, the use of public languages to account for that split. The first text in the series, *Catastrophe Practice,* rather suggests that, given the lack of order and the speed of conscious processes, an element of anonymity will normally creep into them. The main marker for this is the expression "as if", later supplemented by "to mime". Both might be the most frequently used terms in the whole book. In the "Plays for Not Acting" we are watching a small group of people whose thoughts and actions are continuously undercut by "as if" and later variations of "to mime". These and a few other expressions indicate that persons are never sure to what extent they can ascribe their thoughts and actions to 'themselves' and call them their own. The distance of persons towards themselves increases in so far as they appear in several plays, but each time in another of a set of limited roles. Characters speak as if they were quoting somebody or something (Mosley 2001: 113), "as if [they] were trying to get back to a script" (22) – a script which never precisely formulates what they want (or rather: might want) to say. In contrast to the claims of the upper class characters often act and speak "as if they are uncertain of the nature of the game" (95) and "as if a cue has been missed" (102). The themes (if the term is still appropriate) of the dialogue tend to become trivial or weird: two men climbing the north face of the Eiger without safety net (120), a man on his honeymoon finding that he wants his wife to die, with the two still conceiving a child (121). It is also possible that there is a military framework surrounding the talks in a hotel-like atmosphere (e. g. 121). Manipulating the brassiere of a woman called Sophie turns into an isolated ritual (137, 143).

The problem starts in the brain: "The brain is in two halves, so the left doesn't do what the right is knowing" (48). NM apparently thought that this 'alienation effect' might pose serious problems for an audience. So he surrounded the plays by explanatory essays (using indeed the Brechtian version of the alienation effect, 8 – 9) in which he insists on the adaptability of his plays for his purposes. In tragedy, the person felt him- or herself to be a both free and responsible agent; melodrama flourished because it presented the helplessness of humans to an audience which, however, could continue to watch the plot as something that could not happen to themselves (7). Comedy presents "anxiety allayed by laughter", "ambiguities were lulled, but remained unassuaged" (8). The theater, the introductory essay concludes, has always been accustomed to observe how people behave; "what might now be observed, is people's observing" (12).

But what people observe are the pervasive as if-structures already mentioned. Moreover, meanwhile they have come to know about it. (Extending Damasio's notion of extended consciousness a bit further so as to include reflective qualities and powers, one could probably claim that we can see a reflective consciousness aware of the oscillation between the truly personal and script-like as-if action emerge first and forcefully in Shakespeare.) That is why lulling ambiguities and allaying anxiety do not work so well anymore. Quoting Sartre extensively, NM raises the question whether being-at-one was a "characteristic of the unconsciousness of a thing"; having human consciousness might mean, by contrast, to "have a division between a self that was conscious and the self it was conscious of: consciousness consisted as it were of this gap: it was a lack, an anxiety" (77). NM tries to refute Sartre, but the refutation is directed mainly at Sartre's idea of individual nothingness (no-thing-ness) and despair which is not the primary problem here (77–79). In a leap to the question of Western culture NM quotes Jacques Monod as saying, rather in the way of Devereux quoted before, that Western societies still "present as basis for a morality a disgusting farrago of Judaeo-Christian religiosity, scientific progressism, belief in the 'natural' rights of man and utilitarian pragmatism" (quoted 79). These societies do not see, as I argued before, that, with the domination of theories as products of thought at the latest, a thorough revision of ethical premises – or rather: a rethinking of the place and occasion of ethical argument – is called for. NM, going beyond that, asks the question which has been in the center of the epoch of theory: Just what might the new covenant Monod speaks of between theory, scientific method and daily life consist in (80)? It is possible that art can really do something about this situation in that the image of feeling created by art seems capable of encompassing the whole mind of man (a hope expressed in Susanne K. Langer's theory of the mind in the form of an essay on human feeling, Mosley 2001: 86, 89) with art presenting the world in a heightened perception and knowledge of the world as rational experience. Langer's thesis certainly corresponds to parts of our experience of art. But whether it applies to all of it, whether art has not also partly become one of those "deafening" means of communication appears to be left undecided (87).

In an essay following the play *Landfall* in the middle section of the book, NM appears again haunted by what he calls a taboo now: the problem that there is no language, no style in order to talk about the taboos (life evolving only at an enormous cost of waste, the small fruitful part in what is generated) in a way in which individuals "might feel at home" (155). This is very much bound up with the other central topic that people meanwhile know they are playing parts, but that they do not have control over those parts (155). The result is that dreams rush in to fill the vacuum (156). Again, NM tries to bring in "poetry" as a language dealing both with facts, patterns of facts and the minds observing such patterns, a language that must be "elusive, allusive; not didactic" (156). Hegel's effort to make philosophical language perform in that way ended up in the petrified constructions of Marxism (156–157). Nietzsche saw the chance to split human beings up and to make one part of them "step out of the continuing trapped and trapping process altogether" (159). But he made most people anxious about an elite taking over, an elite with connotations of all the taboo words of the twentieth century: "some inborn superiority of class, of race, of intelligence, of aesthetic sensibility: a conjunction between those who have these qualities and those who have power" (160). NM withholds his opinion about that: We may assume he is very reticent not only because of the ambiguous attraction of Nietzsche, but above all because that program, as we will see, went definitely wrong with his father OM.

In the play *Cell* following this essay dramatic action is conceived as virtual action in the absence of a compelling or intrinsically interesting plot and therefore mainly presented as if it were a mere stopgap. Dramatic action, or rather its paltry residues, is more or less submerged by stage directions which elaborate on the as-if-quality of what is, against all probability, still put forward (see especially 174–180). It comes as no surprise, then, that even minor actions and gestures are inevitably perceived as ambiguous ("Hortense climbs on to the bed and sits straddling Anderson; as if to steady him – or to make love"; "Hortense, on top of him, throws her head back as if in pain – or having an orgasm", 185). The short essay following the play cannot but state the obvious: "It would be unusual for these plays to be performed" (227).

Without falling into gross narcissism it is legitimate to assert that the real topic of plays, essays and a final novel *Cypher* (which occupies about 90 pages out of the book's 330) emerges in the transitionality of consciousness. If we are lucky, the movement and selection in conscious processes seem to consist of "the creating of conjunctions that can, like any other form of procreation, give not only energy but pleasure" (228). The problem lies in the forms which such transitions ("conjunctions") can or should assume. One plausible product would be acting because it combines role play with an awareness that it is both role play and more. NM calls that "knowingness" (228). However: "What is missing at the moment in even the most brilliant films and plays is any sense of what all the brilliance is about" (228). In the attempt to move between what acting is and what it is not, there would have to be the knowingness of the Brechtian Chinese actor who expresses his awareness of being observed, observes himself and sometimes looks at the audience saying "Isn't it just like that?" (229). On the other hand, there may be only "randomness of selection" in this coming to terms of consciousness with itself (231).

Given this dilemma, *Cypher* concentrates on two opposed and extreme forms of transitionality. One might consist in the mind working at and hopefully improving itself, that is to say genetic engineering (240–241), the other in social engineering. The first is quickly abandoned in the lecture of a Professor as being not yet feasible and hopeless in principle without the "qualities of imagination and intelligence" which (this is a point strongly emphasized by Leroi-Gourhan also) are necessary for the survival of a society (242). The second shows up in what is not really a narrated story but rather looks like a negative and somewhat abstract or arbitrary exploratory and experimental projection of imagined situations characterized, it would seem, with bombs going off repeatedly, by various stages of social disintegration and anomie.

2 Catastrophe Practice: Routines – Individuality Manufactured and Medialized

The idea of social engineering springs from an assumption based on an unclear amount of experience-based evidence. In terms of the transitionality of mind, it is a very large step which tends to skip the small-scale, more or less everyday routines of mind and behavior in which Murphy's Law ("Anything that can go wrong will go wrong") looms large. NM's novels following *Catastrophe Practice*, especially *Imago Bird* (first published 1980), *Serpent* (first published 1981), and *Judith* (first published 1986) make up for that and focus on the personal and social contexts in which, prepared for by the mind's lack of control, smaller and bigger catastrophes are actually manufactured. One could also describe the range of so-called catastrophes as the transition from the technical sense to the everyday sense of the term. We do have relatively straightforward narratives, with the main characters largely overlapping, in these texts. But the impression that, whatever people think and do, they are not performing that thinking and doing as something really and intrinsically their own, has become a basic and pervasive ingredient of the narratives. *Imago Bird* (with "imago" hinting both at the final and perfect stage of an insect after have undergone several metamorphoses as well as the idealized mental picture of oneself or another person, especially parent) for instance moves between the worlds of psychotherapy, personal relations, media and politics. The 18 year old main character, undergoing psychotherapy because of his stammer, is also the nephew of the Prime Minister. His perceptions chime in with the perspectives of the preceding text. Quarrels between his aunt and uncle sound as if the two had "forgotten their lines and were ad-libbing; or were waiting for the prompter to say something off-stage" (Mosley 1989: 5, cf. 9, 70 – 71). Actions, even those commonly believed to represent the strongest desires, like sexual drives, look more like accepted habits than authentic needs (cf. 17: "It was accepted that Sheila and I made love in the afternoons") and can lose their motivation accordingly. One can lose the ability "to turn into reality what my mind told me I so much desired" (18). Interaction comes to resemble "an experiment about what is acting and what is not" (89). In most cases the experiment fails because people cannot harmonize its various levels unfolded in the complex back and forth between action and observation. The "real thing" can hardly be obtained by a woman putting her tongue in Bert's ear (79). There is even more symptomatic significance in the way NM opens up a line of transitionality from consciousness to situated action. If there is no intrinsic motivation for the goal of action or the substance of desire, it is the affective charge of desire which tricks us to believe in authenticity: The elements of con-

https://doi.org/10.1515/9783110581836-021

sciousness, like thoughts, may be vague, but, given the uncertainties of the situation which they are supposed to handle, they are charged, in Morin's picture, with hysterical intensity. That is why the psychotherapist Dr Anders can ask Bert whether he really believes that people want to get out of the hell into which they often maneuver themselves in and through interaction (11). In an analogous fashion, Bert's mind is flooded with turbulence after the therapeutic sessions. Bert fantasizes himself into being Icarus or, on a more practical level, into being a fighter-pilot in the Battle of Britain (39).

The irony is that it seems only politicians feel "absolutely at home there [in Parliament and other professional contexts]; as if they had found their ecological niche and would not change for millions of years" (119 – 120). Obviously, this is deceptive; clever politicians just have perfected the corresponding forms of self-presentation. The paradox is that in reality [!], one would need at least film as a medium for the construction of the contours of self both in its conventional 'alienations' and in scenes of otherness. It would have to be a special technique of film using at least two screens in which the simultaneity of contrasts could be suggested (144 – 145).

I take this to be the reason why in the following novel, *Serpent*, films and airplanes are used as the main self-constructive media of modern times. This is especially the case if the film takes up an old story in which the construction of a self which consists of a series of obligations to otherness (mostly ideals like country, faith) is more clearly foregrounded than it could normally be done with contemporary stories. Also and quite trivially, the airplane, being removed from ordinary reality, promotes an increased readiness to let the unusual happen. Many years ago, in 1998, the German chansonnier Reinhard Mey in one of his songs ("Über den Wolken") brought home the message that, "above the clouds, freedom must be unlimited." And indeed, it may be literally and symbolically trivial to privilege the airplane as a place for special forms of communication. NM, in any case, seems to be in a hurry to establish an airplane, more specifically still its first class seats, as a place for special communicative possibilities. Thus, there is the strange mixture of medical-sexual events in the tourist-class compartment occurring between Lilia, wife of the scriptwriter Jason (who flies first-class) and an unknown "dark-skinned" man (who might be a terrorist for all we know) in chapters IV and VI. The object of the film is the Jewish mountain fortification of Masada which the fight against the threatening rule of the Romans in A. D. 72 to 74 turns both into a monument of Jewish identity, and also, owing to the mass suicide of the defenders, into a symbol of an unlimited will to freedom. The scriptwriter Jason, who has written a screenplay extensively quoted in the text, doubts that such a screenplay about the old Masada heroics can or should really be written, that a film should be made at all. The film producer Epstien, while not accepting these doubts at once, soon chimes more or less in and enlarges the list of failed films or perspectives on life as a somehow going concern. Both more or less agree that tragedy or farce, cynical or sentimental stories will no longer do as the organizing principles of films and stories (Mosley 1990: 6; cf. also 3 on the cost of treating life as going concern). That the film, should it be made, would be morally and politically objectionable, is just a conventional paraphrase for the difficulty of finding a more adequate basis and focus (89). Even so, from the talks of the film people in the first-class compartment one could after all conclude that the medium of film has more chances to deploy complex otherness. On the other hand, the tourist-class events on the plane, opening up into especially Lilia's memories, are hardly less extraordinary. The extracts from the script, in particular the debates between Josephus and the Jewish Elders in the context of the Masada events and the Roman capture of the town of Jotapata sharpen the contrast between moral values and what appears as an increasing autonomy of events or personalities. Flavius Josephus was the Jewish historian and general who took part in the Masada events. After the Jewish defeat, he is said to have escaped with 40 soldiers, practicing with them the Roman group suicide method of "decimatio", arranging this in such a way that he and a friend were the last survivors. (This became the mathematical "Josephus problem".) After his surrender, he gained the favor of Vespasian and settled in Italy. Looked upon by many Jews as a traitor, he has become a focus of fascinated interest even in modern Israel.

In the text, two movements seem to be going on. One is fed by the intensity of conflicts normally to be called psychological, sometimes perhaps, as in the reference to *King Lear* and a contemporary play, metaphysical (Mosley 1990: 116). Often, they consist of conflicting emotions in personal relations, as they do in the early, certainly sometimes also later relations between Lilia and Jason (139–142). This is a fairly straight transition from hysterically charged conscious processes to hysterically marred communication. The other movement progresses from the same starting point (hysterically charged consciousness). But it produces an awareness of the performative quality this consciousness assumes in communication and interaction. Once the knowledge about performance has become habitual, the sting of hysteria is taken out of communication (118–119): "To worry about them is cancer: to see the shape in them is life" (142). The film people find themselves in an often uncomfortable position in between. Since they normally assume they have to understand the character they are representing and playing as fully as possible, they tend to get mired, to that extent, in the psychological mess. But since performance, for them, is almost anywhere and always in front of their eyes, it is at least easier for them to reach or to come closer to that level of playful cold-bloodedness Diderot was so much concerned about in his "Paradoxe sur le comédien". In Jason's script, this situation is rehearsed on Masada when Philomela talks about former performances of *Medea* and the pathos of killing one's own children, but destroys that pathos repeatedly with 'coldblooded' comments ("in her ordinary voice" or acting "in a comic voice", 156) and a specifically biting irony concerning the "suspension of disbelief". People, she says, always believe in pathos, "If you do it well enough. It's called suspension of disbelief" (155) – a devastating comment on large parts of 'romantic', but certainly not all of literature She declares that to be a matter of language: "Language finds it easy to say what things are not: Not to say what things are" (160).

At the airport, a final twist of transitionality occurs with a particularly and indeed 'really' dangerous intricate interplay between charged consciousness and real effects. The security officer Deborah Kahn, a trained physicist, has come to suspect particularly those people as security risks whose style, pattern or type of answering appeared as if they were trying to act as though they were not acting (163). There were people who appeared "such rounded, purposive characters that they had seemed to her like puppets". Those looking completely sincere and all-of-a-piece "just because of this, might be slightly mad and therefore dangerous."

In one case, a person had appeared "so essentially and dramatically a woman that this had not seemed true". 'She' was in fact a man. Deborah's husband, a military officer and psychologist by training, puts that into the formula that "if someone seems to believe in himself too simply, he is not quite human" (164).

NM's narrative direction does not of course make nonsense of common human problems. But since they are products of a basically hysterical consciousness and therefore liable to overdo both the relevance and the topicality and to underestimate, by contrast, the degrees of obsolescence in such problems, an awareness and knowledge of their hysterical performative theatricality belongs to the picture of a larger and more desirable humanity. At the same time, in *Judith*, questions of how to distinguish between that kind of theatricality and a higher-level productive interplay of creative acting and playful behavior, of controlling hysterical conscious processes and yet not losing conscious energy and pleasure, of how, in other words, to explore an open, yet not completely arbitrary scope of human possibilities *and* substance, of how to recognize obsolescence in parts of that scope have become more pressing. It looks as if *Judith* came up against limiting factors in all these respects. NM is fully aware of the catastrophes in human life (Mosley 1991: 116–117). But the limited repertoire of alternative options depicted in three letters by the title character, each about 100 pages long, is indirectly suggested by a slightly repetitive nature (apparently ignored by

NM) of the climax which, unfortunately, comes right at the beginning and therefore tends to downgrade the remaining range of experience. The historical model here is Jean-Paul Sartre's 1953 play *Kean*, adapted from Alexandre Dumas' *Kean, ou Désordre et Génie* (1836). Sartre's play delivered a sharp analysis of the interpenetrations of theater, acting and life. The external framework of these relations is marked by the contrast between Kean sought after as a lover because of his acting abilities, but socially despised as an actor. The play is especially famous for a scene in the fourth act: Kean, playing Othello and about to murder Desdemona, suddenly stops himself in the middle of his recitation and shouts at the wife of the Danish ambassador in the audience, whom he would like to make his mistress, telling her to take the place of Desdemona and let herself be killed tenderly. The offstage conflict widens, including finally all of the audience. The conflict is clearly delineated, the boundaries, however, in Kean's case, between acting, playful and aggressive behavior are fluid. NM basically presents that fluidity in a staging of *Judith and Holofernes* with a stronger emphasis on creative acting and ease of transitions (7–11). To a considerable extent, the productive undecidability of acting and non-acting is also prefigured in Ariane Mnouchkine's film *Molière* in a scene in which Molière teaches his future wife 'how to do' a love scene. In *Judith*, the transition gets under way with the actor conveying the impression at some point as if he was wondering about the lines he had to say, "as if he might at any moment break off and exclaim – Listen to this! Or even – what frightful rubbish" (7–8). Judith, who is an understudy for the star actress and a handmaiden in this production, describes the powerful impact of "this acting or non-acting" (8, cf. 10). Her service in the removal of Holofernes' codpiece triggers the main transition: After playing their love scene both seriously and as a joke, Judith and Holofernes – or should one say: the actors supposedly having taken these roles – barricade themselves in the dressing room. The way in which NM subtly describes the undecidability of acting and non-acting transforms the worn clichés of life (whether in so-called real life or literature) into what suddenly appears as the powerful sublimity of rubbish (10).

Such sophistication is much harder to achieve if so-called real life must be approached in dead seriousness because the creative ambivalence of acting is either absent or unevenly distributed. This applies to the rest of the main narrative elements in Part I (relations with two men called Desmond and Oliver), but also, if perhaps to a lesser extent, to Part II, when Judith goes to an *ashram* in India. The guru, also sometimes called God, practices a kind of acting and non-acting; manipulative techniques and dubious messages ("Truth is that of which the opposite is also true", 130, cf. 159 and 164: the story of an allegedly dead woman brought back to life by 'God', 178–180: the "bizarre way of his discourses", 184–186: the special blessing ritual), however, would appear to diminish its value. Judith answers the question of how she finds the *ashram* with a highly non-committal "all right" (156). An element of the habitual, mechanical and casual creeps into the narrative elements. That includes the casual indifference of thinking about "making love" with men Judith hardly knows, a habit conspicuous in Part I, but returning several times in Parts II and III (147, 177, 216, 272, 274). It includes the illogical conclusion that something like the *ashram* Garden cannot be a fraud simply because it says "Of course, if you like, this is a fraud" (204). Apart from the initial acting/non-acting oscillations, NM's explicit glance at transitionality is fairly commonplace too: "Humans have this drive to commit themselves, to give themselves over, to a cause, a god, a fatherland, a lover. They join groups, parties, armies, treadmills; their aim is to become identified, loyal, fixed, all-of-a-piece" (61). Part III offers a lot more of this non-committal philosophizing which, towards the end, leads into a kind of medieval allegory. Close to an US-American airbase beleaguered by anti-nuclear demonstrations, Judith runs into a "toy village" where only a church "seemed to be a real church" (286). In one of the (formerly perhaps real) buildings, Judith comes across a sheep, alive and with two heads. A child is climbing down from above, describing himself as one of the "hopeful monsters", something "born which things outside are not quite ready for" (291). One is grateful for the irony in which the assumption that it might have come down from the "Tree of Life" which seems to grow all around is couched (290, 297).

I am not objecting of course to the lack of explanation in these narrative meanderings. But while some statements are clear and unequivocal, demanding and guiding further interpretation ("You once said, did you not – Ecstasy and despair are the only two emotions worth having", 284), others are apt to provoke the emphatic feeling that more explication might be a consummation devoutly to be wished (for example concerning "Bert's machine for demonstrating Catastrophe Theory", 275), but that no suggestion whatsoever is forthcoming.

3 Hopeful Monsters: Discordant Evolution and Steps towards Mutation

The fifth and last text of the series is of an entirely different caliber. It is not explicitly called a novel, although, in terms of narrative coherence, it would qualify more than any of the other four for the status of at least a novel of letters – the novel comes in the form of very long letters which the two main characters write to each other. The very last chapter, however, introduces a "correlator (as it were)" who later supposedly turns out to be Jason, one of the main characters in *Serpent* (Mosley 2000: 528, 546–547). This construction is highly improbable. Although the text, with respect to the main (invented) characters, completes the other four by providing us with the history of Max Ackerman and Eleanor Anders in the form of a kind of prehistory of the (invented) characters in the preceding novels, this final narrative arrangement creates havoc with the distinction between fictional and non-fictional narrative. The arrangement asks, but does not answer the question concerning the relation – as editor, inventor or something else – of Jason to the letters. Put more modestly: For the purposes of this text, the distinction is tacitly declared to be more or less irrelevant.

What are these purposes? *Hopeful Monsters*, again in contrast to the others, is soaked in and saturated with 'history'. Set mainly in the period and locations of the German Weimar Republic, the Spanish Civil War, World War II and the England of these times (including scientific work in Subsahara Africa and a Sahara crossing), it exudes a sense of historical reality not by saying what historical events are supposed to be precisely made of or mean, but simply by presenting the events, quite independent of any meaning, in the form of intimate and more or less inescapable personal experience. Thus, right in the beginning, the Kapp Putsch and the murder of Rosa Luxemburg (18–19) come menacingly close to Eleanor: Her mother is a "disciple or devotee" (5) of Luxemburg who in fact shows up in the Anders apartment in the Cranachstraße in Berlin, the street where Luxemburg also lived from 1902–1911 (6). The protagonists thus are part of an indefinite historical density and intensity. Eleanor and Max, after years of separation and on opposed sides in the Spanish Civil War, in fact meet and marry in Spain. They repeatedly hope for some meaningful pattern to emerge either through their personal self-creation or through coincidental and also converging events; they are occasionally confident that there is a way out of the "maze" (366). But history seems to be the wrong candidate. Immediately following the expression of hope we find the lines:

https://doi.org/10.1515/9783110581836-022

> History is put together from what people want to say or to remember: but how little of what
> is written seems to do with what an individual on the spot has experienced! History for the
> most part is made up from the public professions of politicians, but politicians are not pri-
> marily concerned with truth, so history becomes *a statistical amalgam of special pleadings*
> (367, my italics).

Even so, some historical events remain one of the main sources offering senses,
however problematic, of the real, provided they are able to transform the elementary transition of consciousness from hysteria into adventure, terror or fascination (mainly in the form of reading adventures) into some more public communicative shape. With this novel we have reached a vantage-point from
which the desirable form of transitionality appears as the replacement of excitement on the hysterical level with the excitement in the adventure of ideas. One
could also speak of a transformation of *uncertainty:* Uncertainty changes from a
stressful into a fascinating problem.

I am alluding above all to Heisenberg's uncertainty principle. With Eleanor
and Max, this connectivity, or elective affinity between hysterical consciousness
and communicative forms both fascinating and public is in fact also the hallmark of the second source of reality effects: science.[173]

For Eleanor and Max, the exciting connectivity is indeed hard to avoid. Eleanor's father is a philosopher (of science) in Berlin who exposes her, for example, to Einstein's General Theory of Relativity when she is about nine years
old. Max' father is a neo-Darwinian Professor of biology at Cambridge; his mother belongs to a group of London intellectuals who are among the first people in
England to deal with Freud's psychoanalysis. Darwinism is challenged by the
neo-Lamarckian Austrian biologist Paul Kammerer who shakes the scientific
world with the inheritance thesis of acquired characteristics. The book does
not take a definite position on whether Kammerer was really refuted. Nor is
there any indication that Max did *not* repeat Kammerer's crucial experiment successfully (79–80). In any case, the 'scandal' ended with Kammerer's suicide. For
Max, Kammerer is also highly interesting because of his 'affair' with his mother
with whom Max, on his side, had a brief incestuous relationship (78, 190, 330).
For Eleanor, relativity theory becomes provisionally intelligible as an extension
of selected conscious images (for instance a small group of people on a vast and
lonely plain who can never see anything outside the curve of their universe, 13).
Max, in his turn, is 'prepared' for the fascination of science by fairy stories, fan-

---

173 I am grateful to Mr Dietrich Menn for allowing me to make use here of the paper on the
topic of science in *Hopeful Monsters* which he wrote for a seminar of mine on Contemporary British Literature.

tasies and myths which his mother reads to him as a child (41). She is also connected to the Bloomsbury group and its interest in psychoanalysis. Max is understandably gripped by this doctrine because it stresses the role of frightening childhood experiences. He does not remember them, but feels, however vaguely, their strong after-effects. At the same time, he is looking for connections between psychoanalysis and biology (53–55) or, later on, for relations between history, psychoanalysis and evolutionary biology. In my framework, the ambition of Eleanor and Max would be called universalist. Their hopes, however, do not materialize. First, it dawns upon them that consciousness creates everything: "but for us to become used to this, we have to become used to some breaking up, reforming, breaking up, of ourselves" (473). In physics, we can accomplish this reform of consciousness to some extent, because physics involves mathematics to which, with more or less training, consciousness can become attuned. This is why in such cases we seem to be able to relate the structures of the mind, the Platonic mathematical world and the physical world to each other, although the mysteries of these connections remain profound.[174] The question whether we first had images in the mind, whether we can protect ourselves against their turning into phantoms, or whether the structures and objects in the world made their impact on our consciousness with sufficient clarity must be kept in mind, but does not impede work in these fields very much.

Paradoxically, as it might seem, the situation is quite different in the social and historical worlds which are definitely human creations and should therefore be amenable to human control. The contrary is the case. Here, consciousness creates phantoms all the time, but the same consciousness drives us to attempt their often lethal transformation into realities (210–212, 427). Franz, a German friend, involved with but also distant from the Nazis, formulates the problem succinctly: "If the human race does not learn to look at the business of death it will not be a viable species: there will have been too much self-deception" (220). Consequently, the second part of the book, aptly entitled "So what do we do", portrays the careers of Eleanor and Max as two zigzag courses especially, but not exclusively, in the Spanish Civil War. That they meet each other there, that Eleanor saves the life of Max, can hardly be taken as proof of the existence of a higher order of life or as an image of some benevolent fate. Their professional careers later in life just confirm that nothing has really changed: Eleanor turns psychotherapist, Max finally changes from a physicist in Cambridge to a professorship in cybernetics "in the north of England". His commitment to cyber-

---

174 This is the famous "three worlds" triangle repeatedly propounded by the British mathematician and physicist Roger Penrose. See for instance Penrose 2005: 18.

netics "arose from his interest in patterns of interaction and control" (542). Yoking together interaction and control is misleading: Patterns of interaction can be explored and described. This does not apply to control. Rather, there is a split between successful control in technological fields and a lack of control in human and social domains. Given the opaque complexity and historical depth into which any action in these domains is willy-nilly embedded, such actions may (they do not have to), even if they obey social rules, produce new contingencies. Scientific and social theories do not help here; they rather increase a sense of helplessness with respect to what appears, pushing aside human intentions, as the self-production of unexpected situations.

The second part keeps cementing this impression with considerable speed. First, the emphasis on and the excitement with the sciences and the possible range of their applications have largely vanished. Dismal political conflicts come to the foreground (in the first part, the deteriorating German Weimar situation could still be seen as an exception). Personal relations, with promiscuity looming large, take on an extremely transitory character. This starts right after the beginning of the second part, when Eleanor reports the bare fact that Rudi "had begun sleeping with me" and casts aside both responsibility and pattern: "In the predicament of fighting to survive, what is my responsibility? (...) We are making patterns in the dust" (297). Certainly, from such a vantage-point the life of a tribe in West Africa below the Sahara looks like an image of "stability", what with its "kinship structures, descent groups, property systems, customs concerning marriage and divorce" (293) and "religious rituals" (295). Plans for crossing the Sahara start out with suspicions on who would save whom in the case of a truck breakdown (300). For Max, who has an offer to go to Cambridge, disorientation at this time (1935, when he is about 25 years old), is complete. Not only does he not know what he *should* do, he does not even know what he *wants* to do (319). Questions whether some person is a Fascist or not bore him (329). Reading "some Freud; some Melanie Klein" (330) is of no avail. On a quite different level, going to Spain does not offer a real alternative either, because he does not know whether he wants to fight (336). Why he finally decides to go, is not made clear. What is clear is that his decision is confirmed when a girlfriend called Caroline promises to sleep with him if he goes (339).

Clearly, *Catastrophe Practice* must have prepared the reader for this *disjunction of person and motivation*. In a first review of her life, Eleanor analyses this disjunction as the result of a *discrepancy of levels in human evolution*. Human evolution falls apart into a state of petrified and obsolete emotions tied up with constantly repeated social (ethnic, regional, national etc) conflicts, and into the abstract knowledge, mainly embodied by the sciences, that, in principle, evolution has made nonsense of habitual emotional and social conflict patterns, that things could and should be quite different. On the boat from Africa to Spain Eleanor ruminates on waves and a possible pattern of her life (I think the pattern is rather impossible, because the eternal repetition of the same – rather remote from Nietzsche's eternal recurrence of the same – is mired in trivialities: The political fights in Weimar Germany, including even the fate of Rosa Luxemburg, pop up like "some eternal Punch and Judy" show, "orating and always orating". There are the university boys and their fraternity duels, with "their childish faces cut and sewn up again like cheeses". There are the betrayals in the fights between Communists and Nazis and so on. "Could not the human race just get this sort of thing over and done with, [...] not hurry on to a true revolution? [...] But might we not consciously one day be able to make contact [...] with whatever was necessary for evolution" (354–355)?

If evidence were needed for such reflections, Max provides it once again negatively with his stubborn search for patterns and the reason he gives for it. Patterns there are, and therefore guides through the maze, "because there is the ability to see patterns" (366). This looks like the converse of the old proverb that things which must not be, cannot be: Things which we want to exist, must exist. Significantly, from this point onward and in contrast to the bald statements leading up to it, reflections amounting to philosophical thoughts concerning action increase in number. In terms of evolution, Max assumes the cogency of the idea that there must have been "so many almost unimaginable coincidences". A complex mechanism like the eye cannot be the result of random mutation and natural selection (427). It is only some overarching evolutionary pattern which would explain it. Establishing such a pattern is undermined from the outset by what might be called a combination of *epistemological asymmetry* and *mutation gap*: We must assume that the universe created consciousness. But we must also assume that consciousness, in some way and to an indeterminate degree, creates the universe. To imagine that these two creative movements could converge towards a unified picture of both universe and mind presupposes, in Max' feverish logic, some basic mutation of the mind, "some Noah's Ark in the mind, if there are to be held the results of all these almost unimaginable coincidences." For such a mutation to be viable, a catastrophe in the technical sense would have had to occur in the modes and conditions of human action and thought (429, c. f. 508). That Eleanor and Max are at least capable of thinking such thoughts, makes them into the hopeful monsters of the title (445), into beings born before their time like, perhaps, Kammerer's toads and salamanders.

So-called history does not inspire hope in that respect. "Between 1936 and 1939 the politics of Europe went freewheeling downhill towards hell [...] human politics ran out of control" (461). Eleanor engages in seminars in which people try to "get in touch with some operational level of this so-called reality". There are "Eastern techniques" for that; their drawback is that they "encourage a mystical turning away from the world rather than a dealing with it". There are Christian techniques, unable to convince her that putting oneself in the hands of a religious authority has more to do with reality than using one's own hands for that purpose. There is Jung's active imagination, provoking the question why games between consciousness and the unconscious should have to do with reality (497).

The questions then remains whether Eleanor and Max are able to reduce or even bridge the mutation gap. One way in that direction certainly consists in the use of advanced scientific theories and terminology for the interpretation and, as much or little that is possible for the orientation of their private lives. Here, Heisenberg's uncertainty principle takes on special importance. As a boy, Max is told about quantum mechanics by the German exchange student Hans (another of his mother's affairs) and tries to apply it to his experiments with the salamanders: "I thought – Perhaps [sic] their tongues move in the jumps that Hans used to talk about; the jumps of those particles that are on one level and then instantaneously they are on another" (72). A very common image is that of Max and Eleanor as a couple being like those particles in Heisenberg's theory. They are seldom together, cannot be observed as a couple but nevertheless are deeply bound to each other. Eleanor is the first to use this picture: "I tried to imagine what you might be doing. We had not yet got the image, had we, of those particles that if you do this to this one here then that happens to that one there –" (132). Later in the novel Max varies the mode of application: "Perhaps we will bump into each other like two of those particles which, if they have bumped into each other once, may never be quite not as if bumping into each other again" (227). Towards the end of the novel Max and Eleanor realise that they have to be separate to give their relation endurance and a deeper meaning. Max quotes Eleanor to the reader: "You said 'You think we can only do what we have to do, become active, if we are sometimes in a practical sense separate'" (488)? Finally, the correlator credits them with achieving a new definition of marriage: "In marriage, why should it not be life-giving to be sometimes apart: what else is pattern'" (534)?

It little matters whether these interpretations and application of the uncertainty principle are 'correct' or not. What emerges from the *life style* of Eleanor and Max (the term *pattern* would claim too much) is indeed a new *amalgamation of intimacy and distance*, that is to say a partial *neutralization* of *personal* and, by extension, *social emotional conflicts* into which the hysterical and schizophrenic charges of conscious processes are all too often invested and projected. Moreover, Eleanor and Max seem to be able to gather around themselves a group of young people to whom they might pass on their willingness to be mutants of the mind. Mosley calls this constellation a "transmission of learning" (544).

4 Hysterical Consciousness and the Beginnings of Institutional Degeneration in Autobiographical Writings

The five texts discussed above represent biographical models on the levels of both consciousness (in the stylized form of "as-if"-processes) and of history. Because of the as-if-signals especially in *Catastrophe Practice*, no content of consciousness can be called an integral part of personality. Because of its – in the ordinary sense – chaotic and catastrophic character, the same must be said of history. Violent ('hysterical') emotional efforts at identification and appropriation flare up and fall flat or fade away inconsequentially. At the same time, the scientific commitment in *Hopeful Monsters* above all makes for a fairly high degree of representational transparency. Since no identification takes place, it is a *transparency without status*. In NM's autobiographical texts war, politics and love, mired in empirical confusion, do not attain the same degree and kind of transparency. Instead, the personal confusion in what is called the business of getting on with life initiates a complementary process of deterioration in social institutions. Following Karl Polanyi, we could call it *institutional degeneration*.[175]

In his autobiographical texts, NM transforms one crucial *experience* into an *axiom* which he repeats several times. Experience and axiom nail down the absolute difference between life in war and life in peace times. "Humans seem at home in war. They feel lost when among the responsibilities of peace. In war they are told what to do; they accept that they have to 'get on with it'. In peace it seems uncertain what they have to do; they have to discover what the 'it' is to get on with". (Mosley 2009: 1; see Mosley 2006: ix, 157)

In both war and peace, to be sure, consciousness may get charged to the hysterical or schizophrenic level. War may provoke a maximum in that respect, because it presents maximum risks – getting wounded or killed. And NM is aware, of course, of the likelihood of wars turning into the madness of senseless bloodbaths – the fighting on Monte Cassino in the winter of 1943 showed signs of that (Mosley 2007: chapter 4 and 2007: 45: "In old age I find it difficult to acknowledge the awfulness of much of my diary of this time"). But if conditions are not too bad, it seems possible that maximum danger produces an uncanny inner calm or, as NM describes a fight with multiple chances of getting killed, "a strange exhilaration. We felt invulnerable, heroic [...] It was all quite like, yes, an apotheosis of a mad apocalyptic children's game" (2007: 109; see also 2007: ix

---

175 For institutional degeneration see Polanyi 1957: 96.

https://doi.org/10.1515/9783110581836-023

about war being senseless and necessary, squalid and fulfilling, terrifying and sometimes jolly). Similarly, for a junior officer to be on effective terms with his platoon what was required was more than a reliance upon orders. "It was a two-way trust that had something of the nature of love" (2007: 57). We may of course, and perhaps we should reject this picture of war as an inadmissible idealization. NM himself later speaks of sometimes "traumatic fighting" (2009: 5). But it can still serve as a hypothetical counterimage to NM's characterization of peace times. The uncertainties of civil life are not deadly. But they tend to keep consciousness in an unproductive and mostly stressful state of constant alarm and unrest. NM alludes to that very emphatically with a quotation from T. S. Eliot on people in civil life: "In even the most intelligent people I meet, or whose books I read, there is a complete lack of unity in behaviour and thought, in faith and reason" (2007: 41). NM experiences the first paradox of peace as "the strings of sexuality and social customs" tying him "into knots" (2009: 2), that is to say as *offers of experience withdrawn while presented* as "allurements" (2009: 3). Married life in the rural wilderness of Wales may look for a while as a respite from ordinary stress. But it is mostly hard work with few rewards. Doing largely without the amenities of civilization does not amount to genuine romanticism. Rather, depression and states of emptiness lurk around the corner, smokescreens covering that up are in constant need (1996: 17–26). Soon "feelings of futility" and depression are increasing to an extent "that it was almost impossible to get out of bed" (2009: 18). It soon dawns upon NM that such states of mind, for which there hardly is a language (1996: 28), easily spread across *all* of social life.

There seem to be two areas in which the descent into a psychological point zero can be avoided: love (including sexuality) and religious belief. The trouble is that these areas are incompatible with each other. (In that respect, NM does not, I think, stick to his program of "efforts at truth", Mosley 1996.) The incompatibility is not removed by distinguishing sharply between Church and faith. Certainly, conflicts between the institution of the Church and the innermost 'religious' feelings are an almost permanent part of religious history. In Christianity, with Protestantism, they have even provoked the founding of a new denomination. But, to some greater or smaller extent, the content of faith is created by the Church, much as the development of the Church may violate its original teachings later on. It is therefore partly interesting, partly amusing, partly annoying to watch NM working as editor of a religious magazine (*Prism*) and engaging in amorous pursuits out of wedlock.[176] His first leading article entitled "What's

---

[176] NM's *Experience and Religion. A Lay Essay in Theology*, Elmswood Park, Il.: Dalkey Archive

Wrong with the Church?" attacked the Church as a mere organization prescribing moral rules, a kind of trades-union of the lily-livered and respectable. It seemed to have little to do with the teaching of Jesus, to say nothing of the Holy Spirit, completely forgotten. God had given humans freedom; Jesus in his turn is supposed to have really taught that each person must find his or her way in life, that the Holy Spirit was there so that "those who watched and listened to what was going on around them, would find what was to be done" (2009: 63 – 65). This certainly represents a highly selective gleaning of Christian teaching. It is clear that a Church, however 'latitudinarian', could not exist with such teachings, so that NM's Christianity collapses into a club for individual ethical preferences. Even so, there must have been a period in which NM accepted the Church as an institution; at one point in *Efforts at Truth* he remarks that his book *Experience and Religion* (1965, 2006) "did turn out to be for me a signing-off from the regular routines of organised religion; though I had not, I think, intended this at the time" (1996: 176 – 177). Generally, NM does not sufficiently take into consideration that his *observational detachment as a professional writer* always yields many more possibilities of action than any *organized practice* would be able to manage or cope with. He does not sufficiently appreciate or take advantage of his own insight: "To be a novelist one had to observe the multifariousness of experience rather than to be committed to one view of it; but how could this be reconciled with the Christian idea of 'good' – especially the idea of a good family?" (1996: 76). While one need not begrudge NM the pleasures of philandering, it is in no way Christian nor sensitive to escape the frictions of marriage and one adultery with a flight to Paris in the company of a third woman and the comment: "[…] both Rosemary [the wife] and Natalie [the mistress] who was still in my flat were anxious about what had become of me; so I became on quite good terms with each of them again […] You can risk a few jumps in life as if it were a work of art". (2009: 92 – 93)

Yes, we can. But given this relatively simple hedonism, one wonders why one is supposed to follow NM's meanderings on Christianity as experience and as the institution of the Church. It all boils down to the opinion, hardly surprising or original, of a Christian friend according to whom the "Church has a long history

---

Press 2006 (originally published 1965), does not, in spite of the title, discuss the tensions between Church and Faith, but concentrates on the (loosely conceived) Christian religion and its function in the modern world. I would not really consider it as an essay in *theology*. NM's own comments on and fairly long quotations from this work in 1996: 172–177) end on a very skeptical note: "In the penultimate chapter of the book I seem to be trying to say everything all at once again – a chorus into the wind, the song blowing on whatever might be its way" (1996: 176). Since I am not using this book systematically, it does not figure in the bibliography.

of horror as well as of holiness, but it endures, because it is founded on the truth, which is Jesus Christ" (Mosley 1996: 31). With NM, however, one is almost driven to despair because of the confusing quantity of varying judgments on the Church, the vagueness of religious experience and the opportunistic position he takes on love and (the institution of) marriage. He does not offer a *multiplicity of possible perspectives*, but an *intentional blurring of issues*.

5 The Failure of Rules and the Unleashing of Hysterical Consciousness: Oswald Mosley and Fascism

On the surface, OM presents the picture of his father as the English gentleman who follows the rules while enjoying, perhaps a bit excessively but without provoking scandals, his hobby-horses, that is to say the pursuit of politics and of women. But on the real operational level, we see the transitionality of consciousness running completely out of control: Fascism in particular, in spite of what looks like the formulation of programmatic political goals, represents pure, *undirected transitionality:* Asserting political goals, OM lets his phantasms run wild. That is why Christopher Ricks, in his review of the biography written by NM already quoted (Ricks 1983) can speak of the nullity of Fascism with respect to its so-called political ideas. That is why the description of one of the speeches of his father by NM can probably be taken as prototypical. The "person who had been so serene and unresentful in prison [OM had been imprisoned during the war as a security risk] was now once more acting like an insecure racist". More precisely:

> His speech was for a time rational; and it was then difficult to tell if people were listening. He then changed key and went off in scathing style telling stories of black people's supposedly primitive eating habits; of the way in which some black men were said to keep teenage white girls in their attics". (2009: 68)

Occasionally, NM seems to doubt that his father's "extravagant" political commitments are meant seriously (1996: 20). But that is not really the crucial issue. OM, starting out as a liberal, rather tries out one political orientation after another in order not to do politics but, as I would maintain, to find the best form for the unleashing of a hysterical consciousness. The claim of this book is that this is, whether with politics or something else, a fairly general phenomenon. I am dealing with OM here because he embodies that phenomenon in a particularly emphatic and clear form. One might risk the assumption that OM gives way to that unleashing in such powerful forms because the discrepancy between the rules he thought he was following and his real desires had become too wide. To some extent, he may have known about that; it would help to make the impression (which he seems to have conveyed frequently) of a clown performing his antics more plausible.

Certainly, OM does not present his consciousness in any immediacy. But his stylizations are such that they must appear as often grotesquely distorted forms

https://doi.org/10.1515/9783110581836-024

of the truth. One might classify OM's speculations about gathering "some idea on the pattern of God" from the available evidence as part of old-age wisdom. It is clear, OM thinks towards the end of his life, that we have to place ourselves in the service of "a progressive movement from lower to higher forms", thus assisting and serving the proved process and purpose of God (quoted in Mosley 1983: 257). But in political terms, the phantasms of self-overestimation and the plans for the improvement of mankind are indeed beyond the pale: "The existing rulers of the earth are responsible for this darkness of humanity [...] So I must give myself to this task [...] my voice can now reach beyond the confines of one country [...] I must do this thing because no other can" (quoted in Mosley 1983: 284). OM fantasizes about a "Thought-Deed man who will be capable of high service to the people in the conception and execution of the great design" (1983: 285, see 286–287 on his views of Hitler as equivalents of "wilful self-destruction").

To say that once more: It would be a mistake to downgrade such phrases as old-age rant running wild because no longer hedged in by the compulsions of political action or practical work. In milder forms the phantasms were prefigured in the fact that "for all his passion for politics, [he] had never found a style by which he could appear wholly committed" (Mosley 1983: 3). While one certainly can change party adherence and party loyalties, OM's trajectory from an Independent via the varieties of Conservative and Labour towards fascism does not constitute a progressive clarification of political commitments, but rather the *progressive dissolution of the bonds* which, in some way, ought to relate political ideas and political action with one another. Whatever its real danger for Great Britain especially during World War II might have been: With OM, the Fascist program, while appearing to be related to the political scene, was rather moving towards *naked transitionality* (or "nullity" in Christopher Ricks' term), to phantasms not really connected with the political and social objects they seemed to point to.

I have read, consequently, NM's biography of his father as a collection of evidence to that effect. While NM cannot be expected to describe his intentions along these lines, it seems clear that, judging also from the reaction of friends, there was something strange about OM's political steps right from the beginning. NM describes that for instance as "a confusion, barely conscious, not just about the nature of the political game, but about the nature of language and even about human nature itself" (Mosley 1982: 129). One can confuse OM's steps with higher, as it were idealistic ambitions which the ordinary party politician was not capable of. OM must also be suspected of demanding "practical remedies" in order not to have to say precisely what they were supposed to consist in, must be accused of "the extraordinary position" of "preparing for a crisis by finding himself able to do nothing about it when it came" (Mosley 1982, chapter 17, "The Mosley Manifesto", especially 167–172, 193 and 197: "The affairs of the New Party went their own bizarre way"). In this way one could explain that holding a political office was cut off by speedy resignation (1982: chapter 15, "Resignation", 143–147) or that the New Party he founded before embarking on fascism lasted for less than a year. OM's "disillusionment with his establishment friends" was felt by these friends as the extraordinary difficulty of bringing him "to the point". To them, he seemed to be creating loopholes all the time by which he could escape from the obvious meaning of his words (1982: 47). For OM, it was easy, too easy to counter such criticism with the assertion that he must remain free to promote his principles and the "triumph of the causes for which I stand" (quoted 1982: 48). It was less easy to shield himself against a more sophisticated criticism, especially criticism which came from friends like the very analytical letter of Bob Boothby, a letter in which the conditions for political work in the context of the existing, but not monolithic party system were set up with admirable clarity.[177] I suppose that means that (not only) politicians have to develop a *style* with which to *handle the elasticity of rules*. Such a style would help to develop a *flexibly significant transitionality* of consciousness and perhaps prevent the fall into its naked variety. Simply ('mechanically') following the rules may work in a context like the one of Eton or to some extent in the army; but even there NM begins to be interested in what is beyond (1983: 139, 142).

NM eventually puts forward a characterization of fascism which comes very close to the naked transitionality I have been talking about above: "Fascism is a form of activity where what is usually contained in games becomes reality; where what is logic is forced into flesh; where rules are broken and not replaced" (1982: 212; for "logic" I would say "phantasms in logical form"). This must be read as a characterization of OM's fascism. Small wonder that "orthodox fascists" could not handle "the most outlandish fascist of all", dressed up as he was for fascism but not playing the "ruthless fascist game" and therefore also called "a kosher fascist" (1982: 213). Small wonder also that OM's language in a book like *The Greater Britain* (1932) became "almost openly without content" (1982: 221).

The second volume of the biography offers variations on the themes of the first. OM is held to have one of the most brilliant brains in England which for some reason he did not use properly (1983: 20). In an Albert Hall speech record-

---

177 Boothby (1900–1986), quoted Mosley 1982: 144–145, see a second Boothby letter 151–153, and a third one 171; see also Harold Nicolson's warning not to "get mixed up with the fascist crowd", 206. Boothby's second letter ends with the remark: "no one, not even you, can break all the rules at once".

ed on gramophone OM's voice "comes out lashing like some great sea: it is pulverising: it is also, from a human being, like something carried far away beyond sense" (51). Alternatively, he may sometimes write in a style which seemed "almost knowingly to be parodying *The Book of Revelation*" (158). Major General Fuller, asked to write a review on the state of the British Union of Fascists, judged that the movement "has grown up on enthusiasm rather than to plan" (88). As a consequence, Mosley worked out organizational and disciplinarian measures in such detail that this kind of order came to look more like a phantasm itself than a feasible practice (91).

Fascism, then, in OM's case, should primarily be viewed as the form, or the *formal pseudo-concretizations* of a hysterical consciousness which did not find better ways of realizing transitionality. One of these better ways might have consisted in devoting some thought to the so-called rules. Apart from technical contexts, most rules do not exist and cannot be followed in the unambiguous clarity which the very word seems to ascribe to them. "To describe the activities and states of a human system, then, we must map out its tendencies or possibilities, not its rules."[178] In OM's "personality landscape", novelty (or what appeared as such) continued to overtake a flexible kind of orderliness. OM's philandering may have been within the limits of a mild and wide interpretation of the term. But it may also have been a wild, that is to say *uncontrolled form* of transitionality. I am aware that I am getting close here to psychoanalytical modes of interpretation which I do not, however, really need. My approach cannot do without assumptions concerning the existence of the unconscious; but it does not need assumptions concerning its content. To a large extent, fascism and philandering, in the direct way pursued by OM, resemble *closed systems* of orientation. In reality, they were driven by undirected confusion. That is why NM could not really penetrate his father's consciousness. His own mode of transitionality, therefore, took the form of a *contrast program*, multiplying perspectives of *observation*, not *action*, as a writer and preventing them from just copying the chaos of consciousness by surrounding the perspectives with the *halo* of a very *soft version of Christianity*.

It is to be feared that OM is not the only case of someone *borrowing forms*, seemingly 'realistic' and concrete, for the meanderings of a hysterical consciousness. Hannah Arendt, for one, has denied that Hitler had any concrete political or military plans. He was rather chasing after some purely imaginary inventions (see fn. 8 above). That may be going too far, but the remark certainly nails down

---

178 Lewis and Junyk 1998: 44, 52.

the confusion between *naked, wild forms of transitionality* and the *channelling of hysterical energy into directed and perhaps even controlled modes.*

6 Tentative Conclusions

The *Catastrophe Practice* series of Nicholas Mosley and his (auto)biographical work provide us with the strongest and most concrete forms of the transitionality of consciousness sketched in the first part of this book with the help of neurobiology and related disciplines. Its impact makes itself felt with particular force because it appears to bolster a systems-theoretical view of a self-referential consciousness. At the same time, however, it imparts a twist and spin to that view which threatens to make nonsense of the self-referential basis. While not disputing its validity, it unhinges the notion of self-referentiality, telling us that we cannot decide which of those thoughts which emerge and disappear so quickly can be called our own. A *shift* takes place from a *self-referential to a self-alienating* conception of consciousness. In this situation, I have proposed to follow suggestions by Edgar Morin and Julian Jaynes concerning the 'hysterical' and 'schizophrenic' consciousness, using the terms not in a pathological sense but rather as affective surrogates, as emotional charges capable of appropriating thoughts and making them 'one's own'. A *quasi-autonomy* of consciousness emerges which is not sufficiently aware of its lack of consistency and orientation. In the quasi-autonomous mode consciousness may handle its transitions into elementary products of thought (for instance of the poetic kind) with sufficient care. But, with respect to larger 'realities out there', its quasi-autonomy falls back into (technically speaking) chaos.

This chaos, the turbulences of the mind, will tend to produce catastrophes in both the technical and the common sense. It will be provoked into a hectic, sometimes successful search for the happiness of (re)solutions. But if we adopt the broad historical perspective of products of thought evolving from unifying total conceptions to highly pluralistic models of thought (leaving out the many intermediate forms here), if we accept the thesis that this evolution is accompanied by a weakening of satisfactorily oriented action and frantic efforts at (ill placed) ethical compensations, then the technical, non-apocalyptic concept of catastrophe must be privileged. This concept demonstrates its usefulness particularly as a tool of evaluation of the 'ideological' and practical difficulties which Western societies experience with respect to – not only – Muslim warmongers and the whole range of phenomena mostly labelled terrorism. One could blame the varieties of liberalism for that situation; in the wake of liberalism self-evident standards have been hollowed out and lost their binding power. William J. Bennett held Bill Clinton responsible for the "death of outrage" and the assault on American ideals. It would be possible to transform his accusations – habitual lying, abuse of power, corruption in (the highest) office, skulduggery,

https://doi.org/10.1515/9783110581836-025

half-truths, stonewalling, contempt for the law – into the diagnosis of a *general cultural situation*, mostly Western, *of a more or less paralysing loss of the enforceability of standards.*[179] In this respect, it is not enough ("crucial", Bennett says) to "pay tribute" and "public affirmation" to "principles and standards, categorical norms, notions of right and wrong" (Bennett 1998: 9–10). Public affirmation for instance encourages the hypocrisy which has infested confessions of loyalty and adherence to principles and norms for a long time already. Also, bashing liberalism(s) will not do. Liberal energies have been far too long and far too strongly inscribed in both the developmental logic of products of thought and the complexities of social evolution. Minor corrections are possible, indeed necessary and have turned into a typical political activity. But no full turnaround of direction is possible. In the perspectives adopted here, the big deal for Western societies (with others exposed more or less to similar problems) emerges as the question whether we can somehow *reconcile liberal trends with the acceptance, never completely legitimized by argument and reasons, and the enforceability of standards.* It is an *interplay of tolerance and strictness* for which, to say the least, we have rarely found the right mixture because we have not practiced it sufficiently. In retrospect, most of my 'literary' examples, by contrast, can be seen as *trial runs* of such interplays meant to open up a view of, at the same time, highly attractive *and* highly problematic possibilities for forms of transitionality from a hysterically tinged consciousness to products of thought and risky, but basically humane action.

---

179 Bennett 1998: 5–8.

Works Cited

Adorno, Theodor W. 1962. *Eingriffe. Neun kritische Modelle*. Frankfurt am Main: Suhrkamp.

Adorno, Theodor W. 1970. *Ästhetische Theorie*. Ed. Gretel Adorno and Rolf Tiedemann. Gesammelte Schriften, vol. 7. Frankfurt am Main: Suhrkamp.

Ahlstrom, Sydney E. 2004. *A Religious History of the American People*. 2nd ed. New Haven and London: Yale University Press.

Albert, Hans. 1998. *Marktsoziologie und Entscheidungslogik. Zur Kritik der reinen Ökonomik*. Tübingen: Mohr Siebeck.

Ash, Timothy Garton. 2016. *Free Speech: Ten Principles for a Connected World*. New Haven and London: Yale University Press.

Arnold, Matthew. 1979. *The Complete Poems*. Ed. Kenneth Allott, 2nd ed. by Miriam Allot. London and New York: Longman.

Bajohr, Hannes. (ed.). 2013. *Judith N. Shklar. Der Liberalismus der Furcht*. Trans. Hannes Bajohr. Berlin: Matthes & Seitz.

Bajohr, Hannes. 2013. "'Am Leben zu sein heißt Furcht zu haben'. Judith Shklars negative Anthropologie des Liberalismus". In: Bajohr (ed.). *Judith Shklar. Der Liberalismus der Furcht*. Berlin: Matthes & Seitz. 131–167.

Barthes, Roland. 1984. "The Grain of the Voice". In: *Image. Music. Text*. Trans. Stephen Heath. London: Fontana. 179–190.

Bayne, Tim. 2015. "Introspective Insecurity". In: Metzinger, Thomas and J. M. Windt (eds.). *Open MIND*: 3(T) Frankfurt am Main: MIND Group. Doi: 10.15502/9783958570214.1/18-18/18.

Bender, John. 1987. *Imagining the Penitentiary. Fiction and the Architecture of Mind in Eighteenth-Century England*. Chicago and London: The University of Chicago Press.

Bender, John. 2012. *Ends of Enlightenment*. Stanford: Stanford University Press.

Bender, John and Michael Marrinan. 2014. *Kultur des Diagramms*. Berlin: Akademie Verlag.

Benhabib, Seyla. 2013. "Judith Shklars dystopischer Liberalismus". In: Bajohr, Hannes (ed.). *Judith Shklar. Der Liberalismus der Furcht*. Berlin: Matthes & Seitz. 67–86.

Bennett, William J. 1998. *The Death of Outrage. Bill Clinton and the Assault on American Ideals*. New York: The Free Press.

Berque, Augustin. 1986. "Das Verhältnis der Ökonomie zu Raum und Zeit in der japanischen Kultur". In: Barloewen, Constantin von and Kai Werhahn-Mees (eds.). *Japan und der Westen*, 3 vols. Frankfurt am Main: S. Fischer. Vol. 1. 21–37.

Blake, Caesar R. 1960 *Dorothy M. Richardson*. Ann Arbor: University of Michigan Press.

Böhme, Gernot. 1985. *Anthropologie in pragmatischer Hinsicht*. Frankfurt am Main: Suhrkamp.

Böhme, Gernot. 2017. *Bewusstseinsformen*. 2nd ed. München: Wilhelm Fink.

Bollenbeck, Georg. 2007. *Eine Geschichte der Kulturkritik. Von J. J. Rousseau bis G. Anders*. München: C. H. Beck.

Blumenberg, Hans. 1964. "Wirklichkeitsbegriff und Möglichkeit des Romans". In: Hans Robert Jauß (ed.). *Nachahmung und Illusion* (Poetik und Hermeneutik I). München: Wilhelm Fink. 9–27.

Borek, Richard (ed.). 2017. *500 Jahre Reformation. Die Welt nach Luther in Wort, Bild und Briefmarken*. Braunschweig: Verlag Borek.

Boswell, James. 1999. *The Life of Samuel Johnson. LL.D.* Ware: Wordsworth Classics.

https://doi.org/10.1515/9783110581836-026

Brandstetter, Gabriele and Gerhard Neumann (eds.). 2011. *Genie – Virtuose – Dilettant. Konfigurationen romantischer Schöpfungsästhetik.* Würzburg: Königshausen & Neumann.

Briggs, Asa. 1985. *A Social History of England.* Harmondsworth: Penguin Books.

Briggs, John and F. David Peet. 2001. *Die Entdeckung des Chaos. Eine Reise durch die Chaos-Theorie.* 7th ed. München: Deutscher Taschenbuch Verlag.

Bronfen, Elisabeth. 1999. *Dorothy Richardson's Art of Memory. Space, Identity, Text.* Trans. Victoria Appelbe. Manchester, New York: Manchester University Press.

Brown, Courtney. 1995. *Chaos and Catastrophe Theories.* Sage University Paper Series on Quantitative Applications in the Social Sciences, 07–107. Thousand Oaks, CA: Sage.

Byatt, A. S. 1981. *The Virgin in the Garden.* Harmondsworth: Penguin Books.

Byatt, A. S. 1991. *Possession. A Romance.* London: Vintage.

Byatt, A. S. 1992. *Angels & Insects.* London: Vintage.

Cannadine, David. 1992. *The Decline and Fall of the British Aristocracy.* London: Penguin Books.

Cannadine, David. 2000. *Class in Britain.* London: Penguin Books.

Claessens, Dieter. 1980. *Das Konkrete und das Abstrakte. Soziologische Skizzen zur Anthropologie.* Frankfurt am Main: Suhrkamp.

Clark, Christopher. 2013.*The Sleepwalkers. How Europe Went to War in 1914.* London: Penguin Books.

Collins, Philip. 1971. *Dickens and Crime.* London: Macmillan.

Curley, Thomas M. 1998. *Sir Robert Chambers: Law, Literature and Empire in the Age of Johnson.* Madison: University of Wisconsin Press.

Damasio, Antonio R. 2000. *The Feeling of what Happens. Body and Emotion in the Making of Consciousness,* New York: Mariner Books.

Damasio, Antonio R. 2010. *Self Comes to Mind. Constructing the Conscious Brain.* London: Vintage Books.

Dennett, D. C. 1969. *Content and Consciousness. An Analysis of Mental Phenomena.* London: Routledge & Kegan Paul.

Dennett, D. C. 2015. "Why and How Does Consciousness Seem the Way It Seems?" In: Metzinger, Thomas and J. M. Windt (eds.). *Open MIND:* 3(T) Frankfurt am Main: MIND Group. Doi: 10.15502/9783958570245, 1/11–11/11.

Devereux, Georges. 1998. *Angst und Methode in den Verhaltenswissenschaften.* 4th ed. Frankfurt am Main: Suhrkamp.

Dickens, Charles. 1955. *Our Mutual Friend.* London and Glasgow: Collins.

Dickens, Charles. 1963. *Bleak House.* London and Glasgow: Collins.

Diderot, Denis. 1962. *Œuvres romanesques.* Ed. Henri Bénac. Paris: Garnier Frères.

Diderot, Denis. 1964. *Œuvres philosophiques.* Ed. Paul Vernière. Paris: Garnier Frères.

Diderot, Denis. 1968. *Œuvres esthétiques.* Ed. Paul Vernière. Paris: Garnier Frères.

Dodds, Eric Robertson. 1962. *The Greeks and the Irrational.* Berkeley and Los Angeles: University of California Press.

Dower, John W. 1999. *Embracing Defeat. Japan in the Wake of World War II.* New York: W. W. Norton.

Durand, Gilbert. 1969. *Les structures anthropologiques de l'imaginaire. Introduction à l'archétypologie générale.* Paris, Bruxelles, Montréal: Bordas.

Durrell, Lawrence. 1968. *Tunc.* London: Faber and Faber.

Dux, Günter. 1982. *Die Logik der Weltbilder. Sinnstrukturen im Wandel der Geschichte.* Frankfurt am Main: Suhrkamp.

Eagleton, Terry. 1982. *The Rape of Clarissa. Writing, Sexuality and Class Struggle in Samuel Richardson.* Minneapolis: University of Minnesota Press.

Edelman, Gerald M. 1992. *Bright Air, Brilliant Fire. On the Matter of the Mind.* New York: Basic Books.

Edelman, Gerald M. 2004. *Wider Than the Sky. The Phenomenal Gift of Consciousness.* New Haven and London: Yale University Press.

Edelman, Gerald M. and Giulio Tononi. 2000. *A Universe of Consciousness. How Matter Becomes Imagination.* New York: Basic Books.

Eliot, George. 1961. *Middlemarch.* 2 vols. London: J. H. Dent.

Eliot, T. S. 1977. "Hamlet and His Problems" (1921). In: *The Sacred Wood.* London: Faber & Faber. 81–87.

Eliot, T. S. 1974. "The Waste Land" (1922). In: *Collected Poems 1909–1962.* London: Faber and Faber. 61–86.

Enderwitz, Anne. 2015. *Modernist Melancholia: Freud, Conrad, and Ford.* Basingstoke: Palgrave Macmillan.

Fauconnier, Gilles and Mark Turner. 2002. *The Way We Think. Conceptual Blending and the Mind's Hidden Complexities.* New York: Basic Books.

Feyerabend, Paul. 1982. *Science in a Free Society.* London: Verso.

Feyerabend, Paul. 1980. *Erkenntnis für freie Menschen.* Frankfurt am Main: Suhrkamp.

Feyerabend, Paul. 1995. *Zeitverschwendung.* Frankfurt am Main: Suhrkamp.

Feyerabend, Paul. 1999. *Wider den Methodenzwang.* Revised and enlarged 7th German ed. Frankfurt am Main: Suhrkamp.

Fox, Stacey. 2008. *The Idea of Madness in Dorothy Richardson, Leonora Carrington and Anaïs Nin*, PhD Dissertation School of Social and Cultural Studies / English and Cultural Studies, The University of Western Australia.

Frazer, James G. 1967 (1922). *The Golden Bough. A Study in Magic and Religion.* Abridged Edition. London, Toronto: Macmillan.

Frye, Northrop. 1968. *Anatomy of Criticism. Four Essays.* New York: Atheneum.

Furet, François and Denis Richet. *Die Französische Revolution.* München: C. H. Beck.

Garcia, Tristan. 2016. *La Vie intense. Une Obsession moderne.* Paris: Flammarion.

Gehlen, Arnold. 1959. *Die Seele im technischen Zeitalter. Sozialpsychologische Probleme in der industriellen Gesellschaft.* Hamburg: Rowohlt.

Gehlen, Arnold. 1961. "Vom Wesen der Erfahrung". In: *Anthropologische Forschung. Zur Selbstbegegnung und Selbstentdeckung des Menschen.* Reinbek bei Hamburg: Rowohlt. 26–43.

Gehlen, Arnold. 1971. "Über kulturelle Kristallisation". In: *Studien zur Anthropologie und Soziologie.* 2nd ed. Neuwied und Berlin: Luchterhand. 283–300.

Gehlen, Arnold. 1973. *Moral und Hypermoral. Eine pluralistische Ethik.* 3rd ed. Frankfurt am Main: Athenäum.

Gehlen, Arnold. 1975. *Urmensch und Spätkultur. Philosophische Ergebnisse und Aussagen.* 3rd. ed. Frankfurt am Main: Athenaion.

Gehlen, Arnold. 1978. *Wirklicher und unwirklicher Geist.* Gesamtausgabe, vol. 1. ed. Lothar Samson. Frankfurt am Main: Vittorio Klostermann. 113–381.

Gellhaus, Axel. 1995. *Enthusiasmos und Kalkül. Reflexionen über den Ursprung der Dichtung.* München: Wilhelm Fink.

Genazino. Wilhelm. 2011. *Das Glück in glücksfernen Zeiten. Roman.* München: Deutscher Taschenbuch Verlag.

Geyer, Christian (ed.). 2004. *Hirnforschung und Willensfreiheit. Zur Deutung der neuesten Experimente.* Frankfurt am Main: Suhrkamp.

Glaubitz, Nicola. 2003. *Der Mensch und seine Doppel. Perspektiven einer anthropologischen Denkfigur in Philosophie und Roman der schottischen Aufklärung.* Sankt Augustin: Gardez!

Gluck, Andrew L. 2007. *Damasio's Error and Descartes' Truth. An Inquiry into Consciousness, Epistemology, and Metaphysics.* Scranton and London: University of Scranton Press.

Goetz, Rainald. 2015. *Johann Holtrop. Abriss der Gesellschaft.* 2nd ed. Berlin: Suhrkamp.

Goldmann, Lucien. 1964. *Pour une sociologie du roman.* Paris: Gallimard.

Grebogi, Celso and James A. Yorke (eds.).1997. *The Impact of Chaos on Science and Society.* Tokyo, New York, Paris: United Nations University Press.

Gregory, Horace. 1967. *Dorothy Richardson. An Adventure in Self-Discovery.* New York: Holt, Rinehart & Winston.

Groethuysen, Bernhard. 1978. *Die Entstehung der bürgerlichen Welt- und Lebensanschauung in Frankreich.* Vol. 1: Das Bürgertum und die katholische Weltanschauung. Vol. 2: Die Soziallehren der katholischen Kirche und das Bürgertum. Frankfurt am Main: Suhrkamp.

Hahn, Marcus and Erhard Schüttpelz (eds.). 2009. *Trancemedien und Neue Medien um 1900. Ein anderer Blick auf die Moderne.* Bielefeld: transcript.

Hanscombe, Gillian E. 1982/83. *The Art of Life: Dorothy Richardson and the Development of Feminist Consciousness.* London: Owen, Athens: Ohio University Press.

Hartmann, Nicolai. 1949. *Das Problem des geistigen Seins. Untersuchungen zur Grundlegung der Geschichtsphilosophie und der Geisteswissenschaften.* 2nd ed. Berlin: Walter de Gruyter.

Havelock, Eric A. 1978."The Alphabetization of Homer". In: Havelock and Jackson P. Hershbell (eds.). *Communication Arts in the Ancient World.* New York: Hastings House. 3 – 21.

Havelock, Eric A. 1982. *The Literate Revolution in Greece and its Cultural Consequences.* Princeton: Princeton University Press.

Havelock, Eric A. 1986. The *Muse Learns to Write. Reflections on Orality and Literacy from Antiquity to the Present.* New Haven and London: Yale University Press.

Hegel, Georg Wilhelm Friedrich. 1970. *Phänomenologie des Geistes.* Berlin: Ullstein.

Hegel, Georg Wilhelm Friedrich. 1975. *Aesthetics. Lectures on Fine Art.* Trans. T. M. Knox. 2 vols. Oxford: Clarendon Press.

Heise, Jens. 1989. "*Nihonron* – Materialien zur Kulturhermeneutik". In: Ulrich Menzel (ed.). *Im Schatten des Siegers: Japan,* 4 vols. Frankfurt am Main: Suhrkamp. vol. 1. 76 – 97.

Henrich, Dieter. 2011. *Werke im Werden. Über die Genesis philosophischer Einsichten.* München: C. H. Beck.

Hermand, Jost. 1989. "Schwundformen des Liberalismus: Zur ästhetischen Fronde im Zweiten Kaiserreich". In: Manfred Pfister (ed.). *Die Modernisierung des Ich. Studien zur Subjektkonstitution in der Vor- und Frühmoderne.* Passau: Wissenschaftsverlag Richard Rothe. 111 – 121.

Hildesheimer, Wolfgang. 1980. *Mozart.* Frankfurt am Main: Suhrkamp.

Hill, C. P. 1977. *British Economic and Social History 1700–1975*. 4th ed. London: Edward Arnold.

Hobsbawm, E. J. (1962). *The Age of Revolutions. Europe 1789–1848*. London: Weidenfeld and Nicolson.

Hotta, Eri. 2013. *Japan 1941. Countdown to Infamy*. New York: Vintage Books.

Houellebecq, Michel. 1998. *Les Particules élémentaires*. Paris: Flammarion.

Hume, David. 1963. *An Enquiry Concerning Human Understanding and Selections from A Treatise of Human Nature*, La Salle, Ill.: Open Court Publishing Company.

Hume, David. 1975. *Enquiries concerning Human Understanding and concerning the Principles of Morals*. 3rd ed. Ed. P. H. Nidditch, Oxford: At the Clarendon Press.

Hume, David. 1978. *A Treatise of Human Nature*. 2nd ed. Ed. P. H. Nidditch. Oxford: At the Clarendon Press.

Huxley, Aldous. 1986. *The Devils of Loudun*. New York: Carroll & Graf.

Iser, Wolfgang. 2006. *How to Do Theory*. Oxford: Blackwell.

James, Henry. 1963. *The Portrait of a Lady*, Harmondsworth: Penguin Books.

James, Henry. 1966. *The Golden Bowl*. Harmondsworth: Penguin Books.

James, Henry. 1967. *The American Scene*. With an Introduction by Irving Howe. New York: Horizon Press.

James, William. 2015. *The Principles of Psychology*. CreateSpace Independent Publishing Platform.

Jaspers, Karl. 1946. *Allgemeine Psychopathologie*. 4th ed. Berlin, Heidelberg: Springer-Verlag.

Jaspers, Karl. 1960. *Psychologie der Weltanschauungen*. 5th ed. Berlin, Göttingen, Heidelberg: Springer-Verlag.

Jaynes, Julian. 2000. *The Origin of Consciousness in the Breakdown of the Bicameral Mind*. Boston, New York: Houghton Mifflin.

Joas, Hans and Klaus Wiegandt (eds.). 2005. *Die kulturellen Werte Europas*. Frankfurt am Main: Fischer Taschenbuch Verlag.

Johnson, Paul. 1988. *Intellectuals*. New York: Harper & Row.

Kamper, Dietmar. 1981. *Zur Geschichte der Einbildungskraft*. München: Carl Hanser Verlag.

Kaplan, Sydney Janet. (1975). *Feminine Consciousness in the Modern British Novel*. Urbana and London: University of Illinois Press.

Kaulen, Hildegard. 2017. "Wortschwall im Gehirn". In *Frankfurter Allgemeine Zeitung* online (www.faz.net, accessed May 11, 2017).

Kierkegaard, Sören. 1975. *Entweder – Oder*. Ed. Hermann Diem and Walter Rest. München: Deutscher Taschenbuch Verlag.

Klein, Jürgen and Gunda Kuttler. 2011. *Mathematik des Begehrens*. Hamburg: Shoebox House.

Kluxen, Kurt. 1976. *Geschichte Englands. Von den Anfängen bis zur Gegenwart*. 2nd ed. Stuttgart: Kröner.

Knowlson, James. 1996. *Damned to Fame. The Life of Samuel Beckett*. London: Bloomsbury.

Koestler, Arthur. 1978. *Janus. A Summing Up*. New York: Random House 1978.

Kofler, Leo. 1976. *Zur Geschichte der bürgerlichen Gesellschaft*. 6th ed. Darmstadt und Neuwied: Luchterhand.

Konersmann, Ralf. 2008. *Kulturkritik*. Frankfurt am Main: Suhrkamp.

Konner, Melvin. 1982. *The Tangled Wing. Biological Constraints on the Human Spirit*. New York: Holt, Rinehart and Winston.

Koselleck, Reinhart. 1973. *Kritik und Krise. Eine Studie zur Pathogenese der bürgerlichen Welt.* Frankfurt am Main: Suhrkamp.

Krieger, Murray. 1994. *The Institution of Theory.* Baltimore: The Johns Hopkins University Press.

Kröner, Franz. 1970. *Die Anarchie der philosophischen Systeme.* Leipzig: Felix Meiner 1929, augmented and improved ed. Graz: Akademische Druck- und Verlagsanstalt.

Lackey, Michael. 2016. *The American Biographical Novel.* New York, London: Bloomsbury Academic.

Lackey, Michael (ed.). 2014. *Truthful Fictions. Conversations with American Biographical Novelists.* New York, London: Bloomsbury Academic.

Lang, Hermann. 2015. *Der gehemmte Rebell. Struktur, Psychodynamik und Therapie von Menschen mit Zwangsstörungen.* Stuttgart: Klett-Cotta.

Le Carré, John. 2009. *Tinker, Tailor, Soldier, Spy.* London: Hodder and Stoughton.

LeGoff, Jacques. 1986. *Die Intellektuellen im Mittelalter.* Stuttgart: Klett-Cotta.

Leo, Friedrich. 1908. *Der Monolog im Drama. Ein Beitrag zur griechisch-römischen Poetik.* Berlin: Weidmannsche Buchhandlung.

Leroi-Gourhan, André. 1988. *Hand und Wort. Die Evolution von Technik, Sprache und Kunst.* Frankfurt am Main: Suhrkamp. (French original *Le geste et la parole*, 2 vols. Paris: Albin Michel 1964/65; American ed. *Gesture and Speech.* Cambridge, MA: MIT Press 1993).

Lewes, George Henry. 1879. *Problems of Life and Mind.* Boston: Houghton, Osgood and Company.

Lewis, Mark D. and Natalka Junyk. 1997. "The Self-Organization of Psychological Defenses". In: Masterpasqua, Frank and Phyllis A. Perna (eds.). *The Psychological Meaning of Chaos. TranslatingTheory into Practice.* Washington, DC: American Psychological Association. 41–73.

Lorenz, Konrad. 1963. *Das sogenannte Böse. Zur Naturgeschichte der Aggression.* Wien: Dr. G. Borotha-Schoeler Verlag.

Lorenz, Konrad. 1973. *Die acht Todsünden der zivilisierten Menschheit.* München, Zürich: Piper.

Lorenz, Konrad. 1983. *Der Abbau des Menschlichen.* München, Zürich: Piper.

Lovejoy, A. O. 1936. *The Great Chain of Being. A Study of the History of an Idea.* Cambridge, Mass. and London: Harvard University Press (22nd printing 2001).

Löwith, Karl. 1964. *Von Hegel zu Nietzsche. Der revolutionäre Bruch im Denken des 19. Jahrhunderts. Marx und Kierkegaard.* 5th ed. Stuttgart: W. Kohlhammer.

Lukács, Georg. 1965. *Die Theorie des Romans. Ein geschichtsphilosophischer Versuch über die Formen der großen Epik.* Neuwied und Berlin: Luchterhand.

Lukács, Georg. 1967. *Der junge Hegel. Über Beziehungen von Dialektik und Ökonomie.* 3rd ed. Neuwied und Berlin: Luchterhand.

Lukács, Georg. 1972. *Ästhetik.* 4 vols. Neuwied und Berlin: Luchterhand.

Luhmann, Niklas. 1984. *Soziale Systeme. Grundriß einer allgemeinen Theorie.* Frankfurt am Main: Suhrkamp.

Luhmann, Niklas. 1995a. "Die Autopoiesis des Bewußtseins". In: Luhmann, Niklas. 1995. *Soziologische Aufklärung 6. Die Soziologie und der Mensch.* Opladen: Westdeutscher Verlag. 55–112.

Luhmann, Niklas. 1995b. "Wie ist Bewußtsein an Kommunikation beteiligt?" In: Luhmann, Niklas. 1995. *Soziologische Aufklärung 6. Die Soziologie und der Mensch.* Opladen: Westdeutscher Verlag. 37–54.

Luhmann, Niklas. 1995c. "Die Tücke des Subjekts und die Frage nach den Menschen". In: Luhmann, Niklas. 1995. *Soziologische Aufklärung 6. Die Soziologie und der Mensch.* Opladen: Westdeutscher Verlag. 155–168.

Luhmann, Niklas. 2000. "Das Medium der Religion. Eine soziologische Betrachtung über Gott und die Seelen". In: *Soziale Systeme*, 6. 39–51.

Luhmann, Niklas und Peter Fuchs. 1989. "Von der Beobachtung des Unbeobachtbaren: Ist Mystik ein Fall von Inkommunikabilität?" In: *Reden und Schweigen*. Frankfurt am Main: Suhrkamp. 70–100.

Macaulay, Thomas Babington. 1849. *History of England from the Accession of James the Second.* 2 vols. Leipzig: Bernhard Tauchnitz.

Mantel, Hilary. 2009. *Wolf Hall.* London: Fourth Estate.

Mantel, Hilary. 2010. *A Place of Greater Safety.* London: Fourth Estate.

Mantel, Hilary. 2013. *Bring Up the Bodies.* London: Fourth Estate.

Maruyama, Masao. 1988. *Denken in Japan (Nihon no shisô).* Frankfurt am Main: Suhrkamp.

Meltzer, Heinz Matthias. 1974. *Der Monolog in der Tragödie der frühen Stuart-Zeit.* Bern, Frankfurt am Main: Lang 1974.

Metzinger, Thomas and Jennifer M. Windt. 2015. "What does it mean to have an open MIND?" In: Metzinger and Windt (eds.). *Open MIND:* 3(T) Frankfurt am Main: MIND Group. Doi: 10.15502/9783958571044. 1/28-28/28.

Meyer, Hans. 1947–1950. *Geschichte der abendländischen Weltanschauung.* 5 vols. Paderborn: Ferdinand Schöningh.

Mill, John Stuart. 1991. *On Liberty and Other Essays.* Ed. John Gray. Oxford: Oxford University Press.

Moody, A. D. 1963. *Virginia Woolf.* Edinburgh and London: Oliver and Boyd.

Morin, Edgar. 1969. *Le Vif du Sujet.* Paris: Éditions du Seuil.

Morin, Edgar. 1973. Le paradigm perdu: La nature humaine. Paris: Éditions du Seuil.

Mosley, Nicholas. 1982. *Rules of the Game. Sir Oswald and Lady Cynthia Mosley 1896–1933.* London: Secker & Warburg.

Mosley, Nicholas. 1983. *Beyond the Pale. Sir Oswald Mosley 1933–1980.* London: Secker & Warburg.

Mosley, Nicholas. 1989. *Imago Bird.* Elmswood Park, IL: Dalkey Archive Press.

Mosley, Nicholas. 1990. *Serpent.* Elmswood Park, IL: Dalkey Archive Press.

Mosley, Nicholas. 1991. *Judith.* Elmswood Park, IL: Dalkey Archive Press.

Mosley, Nicholas. 1996. *Efforts at Truth.* London: Minerva Paperback.

Mosley, Nicholas. 2000. *Hopeful Monsters.* Champaign, IL: Dalkey Archive Press.

Mosley, Nicholas. 2001. *Catastrophe Practice.* Champaign, IL: Dalkey Archive Press.

Mosley, Nicholas. 2007. *Time at War.* London: Phoenix Paperbacks.

Mosley, Nicholas. 2009. *Paradoxes of Peace or The Presence of Infinity.* Champaign, IL: Dalkey Archive Press.

Nassehi, Armin. 1992. "Wie wirklich sind Systeme? Zum ontologischen und epistemologischen Status von Luhmanns Theorie sozialer Systeme". In: W. Krawietz and M. Welker (eds.). *Kritik der Theorie sozialer Systeme. Auseinandersetzungen mit Luhmanns Hauptwerk.* Frankfurt am Main: Suhrkamp. 43–70.

Ong, Walter J. 1977. *Interfaces of the Word. Studies in the Evolution of Consciousness and Culture*. Ithaca and London: Cornell University Press.

Osterhammel, Jürgen. 2013. *Die Verwandlung der Welt. Eine Geschichte des 19. Jahrhunderts*. München: C. H. Beck.

Penrose, Roger. 2005. *The Road to Reality. A Complete Guide to the Laws of the Universe*. New York: Alfred A. Knopf.

Pfeiffer, K. Ludwig. 1988. "Vertreibung des Geistes – Deutsche Fallstudien zur Selbstdemontage Alteuropas". In: Rainer Geißler and Wolfgang Popp (eds.). *Wissenschaft und Nationalsozialismus*. Essen: Blaue Eule. 79–101.

Pfeiffer, K. Ludwig. 2002. *The Protoliterary. Steps toward an Anthropology of Culture*. Stanford: Stanford University Press.

Pfeiffer, K. Ludwig. 2009. "Von der Imagination zum Imaginären (und womöglich zurück)". In: Huber, Jörg, Gesa Ziemer, Simon Zumsteg (eds.). *Archipele des Imaginären*. Zürich: Edition Voldemeer, Wien, New York: Springer. 131–146.

Pfeiffer, K. Ludwig. 2015. *Fiktion und Tatsächlichkeit. Momente und Modelle einer funktionalen Textgeschichte*. Hamburg: Shoebox House.

Pocock, J. G. A. 1985. *Virtue, Commerce, and History: Essays on Political Thought and History, Chiefly in the eighteenth Century*. Cambridge: Cambridge University Press.

Pöppel, Ernst. 2000. *Grenzen des Bewußtseins. Wie kommen wir zur Zeit, und wie entsteht Wirklichkeit?* Frankfurt am Main: Insel.

Pörtner, Peter. 2000. *"mono* – Über die paradoxe Verträglichkeit der Dinge. Anmerkungen zur Geschichte der Wahrnehmung in Japan". In: Elberfeld, Rolf and Günter Wohlfahrt (eds.). *Komparative Ästhetik. Künste und ästhetische Erfahrungen zwischen Asien und Europa*. Köln: edition chōra. 211–226.

Polanyi, Karl. 1957. *The Great Transformation. The Political Origins of Our Time*. Boston: Beacon Press.

Proust, Marcel. 1954. *À la recherche du temps perdu*. 3 vols. Ed. Pierre Clarac and André Ferré, Paris: Gallimard.

Quine, Willard Van Orman. 1960. *Word and Object*. Cambridge, MA: The M. I. T. Press.

Quine, Willard Van Orman. 1963. *From a Logical Point of View. 9 Logico-Philosophical Essays*. 2nd ed. New York: Harper & Row.

Quine, Willard Van Orman. 1971. *Ontological Relativity and Other Essays*. 2nd ed. New York: Columbia University Press.

Radkau, Joachim. 1998. *Das Zeitalter der Nervosität. Deutschland zwischen Bismarck und Hitler*. München: Carl Hanser.

Radkau, Joachim. 2017. *Geschichte der Zukunft. Prognosen, Visionen, Irrungen in Deutschland von 1945 bis heute*. München: Carl Hanser.

Ramachandran, V. S. 2011. *The Tell-Tale Brain. Unlocking the Mystery of Human Nature*. London: William Heinemann.

Redlich, Fredrick C. and Daniel X. Freedman. 1966. *The Theory and Practice of Psychiatry*. New York: Basic Books.

Richards, I. A. 1969. *Coleridge on Imagination*. Bloomington & London: Indiana University Press.

Richardson, Dorothy. 1979. *Pilgrimage*. 4 vols. London: Virago.

Richardson, Samuel. 2004. *Clarissa, or, The History of a Young Lady*. Ed. Angus Ross. London: Penguin Books.

Ricks, Christopher. 1983. "Dark Tom" (Review of Nicholas Mosley's two-volume biography of his father Sir Oswald Mosley *Rules of the Game* and *Beyond the Pale*). *London Review of Books*. 5(22/23). 3–5.

Robinson-Valéry, Judith (ed.). 1993. *Funktionen des Geistes. Valéry und die Wissenschaften.* Frankfurt am Main, New York, Paris: Campus.

Roth, Gerhard. 1996. *Das Gehirn und seine Wirklichkeit. Kognitive Neurobiologie und ihre philosophischen Konsequenzen.* 5th ed. Frankfurt am Main: Suhrkamp.

Roth, Gerhard. 2003. *Fühlen, Denken, Handeln. Wie das Gehirn unser Handeln steuert.* Frankfurt am Main: Suhrkamp.

Rothacker, Erich. 1965. *Logik und Systematik der Geisteswissenschaften.* München: R. Oldenbourg (first published 1927).

Ruelle, David. 1991. *Chance and Chaos.* Princeton: Princeton University Press.

Sachs, Gunter. 1997. *Die Akte Astrologie. Wissenschaftlicher Nachweis eines Zusammenhangs zwischen den Sternzeichen und dem menschlichen Verhalten.* München: Wilhelm Goldmann Verlag.

Sayers, Dorothy L. 1970. *Gaudy Night.* London: Hodder and Stoughton.

Schadewaldt, Wolfgang. 1926. *Monolog und Selbstgespräch. Untersuchungen zur Formgeschichte der griechischen Tragödie*, Berlin: Weidmannsche Buchhandlung.

Schelling, F. W. J. 1979. *System des transzendentalen Idealismus.* Leipzig: Philipp Reclam jun.

Schelsky, Helmut. 1979. *Auf der Suche nach Wirklichkeit. Gesammelte Aufsätze zur Soziologie der Bundesrepublik*, München: Wilhelm Goldmann Verlag.

Schmitt, Arbogast. 2012. *Modernity and Plato: Two Types of Rationality.* Trans. Vishwa Adluri. Rochester, NY: Camden House.

Schoeck, Helmut. 1964. *Die Soziologie und die Gesellschaften. Problemsicht und Problemlösung vom Beginn bis zur Gegenwart.* 2nd ed. Freiburg / München: Karl Alber.

Schopenhauer, Arthur. 1977. *Werke in 10 Bänden* (Zürcher Ausgabe). Zürich: Diogenes.

Schücking, Levin Ludwig. 1948. *Essays über Shakespeare, Pepys, Rossetti, Shaw und Anderes.* Wiesbaden: Dieterich'sche Verlagsbuchhandlung.

Schücking, Levin Ludwig. 1964. *Die puritanische Familie in literar-soziologischer Sicht.* 2nd ed. Bern und München: Francke.

Schüttpelz, Erhard. 2009. "Medientechniken der Trance. Eine spiritistische Konstellation im Jahr 1872". In: Hahn, Marcus and Erhard Schüttpelz (eds.). *Trancemedien und Neue Medien um 1900. Ein anderer Blick auf die Moderne.* Bielefeld: transcript. 275–309.

Schulz, Sabine (ed.). 2012. *"Leben Sie wohl für immer." Die Affäre Hume-Rousseau in Briefen und Zeitdokumenten.* Zürich: diaphanes.

Shelley, Percy Bysshe. 1963. "A Defence of Poetry". In: *English Critical Essays.* (Nineteenth Century). Ed. Edmund D. Jones. London: Oxford University Press. 102–138.

Shklar, Judith N. 1989. "The Liberalism of Fear". In: Nancy L. Rosenblum (ed.). *Liberalism and the Moral Life.* Cambridge, Mass.: Harvard University Press. 21–38.

Singer, Wulf. 2015. "The Ongoing Search for the Neuronal Correlate of Consciousness". In: Metzinger and Windt (eds.). Doi: 10.15502/9783958570344, 1/30-30/30.

Sloterdijk, Peter. 2006. *Zorn und Zeit. Politisch-psychologischer Versuch.* Frankfurt am Main: Suhrkamp.

Snell, Bruno. 1965. *Dichtung und Gesellschaft. Studien zum Einfluß der Dichter auf das soziale Denken und Verhalten im alten Griechenland.* Hamburg: Claassen.

Snell, Bruno. 2011. *Die Entdeckung des Geistes bei den Griechen*. 9th ed. Göttingen: Vandenhoeck & Ruprecht.

Stafford, Barbara Maria. 1994. *Artful Science. Enlightenment, Entertainment, and the Eclipse of Visual Education*. Cambridge, MA: Harvard University Press.

Stang, Richard. 1959. *The Theory of the Novel in England 1850–1870*. New York: Columbia University Press, London: Routledge & Kegan Paul.

Storr, Anthony. 1992. *Music and the Mind*. London: HarperCollins.

Tóibín, Colm. 2005. *The Master*. London: Picador.

Topitsch, Ernst. 1969. *Mythos, Philosophie, Politik*. Freiburg: Rombach.

Trevelyan, George Macaulay. 1947. *Geschichte Englands*. 2 vols. 3rd ed. München: Leibniz Verlag.

Trollope, Anthony. 1980. *An Autobiography*. Ed. Michael Sadleir and Frederick Page, with an Introduction and Notes by P. D. Edwards. Oxford: Oxford University Press.

Turner, Mark. 1996. *The Literary Mind*. New York. Oxford: Oxford University Press.

Turner, Mark (ed.). 2006. *The Artful Mind: Cognitive Science and the Riddle of Human Creativity*. Oxford: Oxford University Press.

Tyrrell, R. Emmett, Jr. 2012. *The Death of Liberalism*. Nashville: Thomas Nelson.

Valéry, Paul. 1957–1960. *Œuvres*. Ed. Jean Hytier. 2 vols. Paris: Gallimard.

Valéry, Paul. 1957–1961. *Cahiers*. 29 vols. Ed. C.N.R.S. [Centre national de recherche scientifique] Préface de L. de Broglie. Paris: C.N.R.S.

Valéry, pour quoi? 1987. Bruxelles: Les Impressions Nouvelles.

Vondung, Klaus and K. Ludwig Pfeiffer (eds.). 2006. *Jenseits der entzauberten Welt*. Vol. 1 of *Mysticism and Modernity*. 4 vols. München: Wilhelm Fink.

Vondung, Klaus. 2016. "Gnosis und Apokalypse als Interpretamente der Moderne im Werk von Eric Voegelin". In: Hans-Jörg Sigwart (ed.). *Staaten und Ordnungen. Die politische und Staatstheorie von Eric Voegelin*. Baden-Baden: Nomos. 115–133.

Ward. J. A. 1961. *The Imagination of Disaster. Evil in the Fiction of Henry James*, Lincoln, NE: University of Nebraska Press.

Weber, Max. 1922. *Gesammelte Aufsätze zur Religionssoziologie I*. Tübingen: J. C. B. Mohr (Paul Siebeck).

Weber, Max. n. d. *Religion und Gesellschaft. Gesammelte Aufsätze zur Religionssoziologie*. Frankfurt am Main: Zweitausendeins.

Weischedel, Wilhelm.1966. *Die philosophische Hintertreppe. Von Alltag und Tiefsinn großer Denker*. München: Nymphenburger Verlagshandlung.

William and Henry James: Selected Letters. 1997. Ed. by Skrupskelis, Ignas K., Elizabeth M. Berkeley, and John J. McDermott. Charlottesville, VA: University of Virginia Press.

Williams, Raymond. 1963. *Culture and Society. 1780–1950*. Harmondsworth: Penguin Books.

Williams, Raymond. 1973. *The Country and the City*. New York: Oxford University Press.

Winning, Joanne. 2000. *The Pilgrimage of Dorothy Richardson*. Madison: University of Wisconsin Press.

Williford, Kenneth. 2015. "Representationalisms, Subjective Character, and Self-Acquaintance". In: Metzinger, Thomas and J. M. Windt (eds.). *Open MIND:* 3(T) Frankfurt am Main: MIND Group. Doi: 10.15502/9783958570054, 1/27-27/27.

Wilson, Edward O. 2004. *On Human Nature*. Cambridge, MA, London: Harvard University Press (originally 1978).

Witzel, Frank. 2015. *Die Erfindung der Roten Armee Fraktion durch einen manisch-depressiven Teenager im Sommer 1969*. Berlin: Matthes & Seitz.

Wolff, Robert Paul. 1969. *The Poverty of Liberalism*. Boston: Beacon Press.

Index

Action 4, 6–10, 28–29, 54, 62, 67, 75–77, 90, 111, 115, 120, 125, 138, 144, 148, 152–156, 160, 166, 169–170, 173, 177–178, 180, 182, 185–187, 191–197, 206–207, 212, 215, 217–220
– French Revolution and motivation of 123–124
– norms of 8–9, 75, 90
– orientation of 4, 7–8, 39, 90–91
– Tudor history and motivation of 123
Adorno, Theodor W. 11, 55, 132, 155, 177, 187
Ahlstrom, Sydney E. 27
Andersen, Hendrik 139–140
Antigone 180
Arendt, Hannah 6, 171, 217
Aristotle 26, 98, 151, 172
Arnold, Matthew 23, 127

Bach, Johann Sebastian 34
Bachelard, Gaston 64
Bacon, Francis 72–73
Bajohr, Hannes 165, 171, 173
Balzac, Honoré de 84, 173
Bardot, Brigitte 143
Barthes, Roland 70
Bayne, Tim 16–17
Beatles, the 156, 159
Beckett, Samuel 91, 116, 119
Bender, John 147, 171, 173–174
Benhabib, Seyla 165, 173
Benn, Gottfried 76
Bennett, William J. 133, 219–220
Bentham, Jeremy 147
Berensmeyer, Ingo VII, 120
Bergson, Henri 153
Berkeley, George 6–7
Berque, Augustin 29
Bettelheim, Bruno 53
Binding power of ideas 159, 177
Blackstone, Sir William 147–148
Blake, Caesar R. 92
Bloch, Ernst 155
Blumenberg, Hans 11

Boccaccio, Giovanni 73
Böhme, Gernot 17, 62–63, 76, 137, 186
Boleyn, Anne 121–122
Bollenbeck, Georg 3
Boothby, Robert 216
Borek, Richard 7
Boswell, James 192
Bourdieu, Pierre 155
Brandstetter, Gabriele 70
Breton, André 63
Briggs, Asa 169
Briggs, John 1
Bronfen, Elisabeth 92, 94
Brown, Courtney 1
Browning, Robert 82, 86
Buber, Martin 157
Burke, Edmund 166
Byatt, Antonia S. 71, 78–80, 82–87, 89–90
Byron, George Gordon Noel (Lord Byron) 137

Camerata (Florence) 79–80
Camus, Albert 155
Cannadine, David 39
Cardaillac, Jean Jacques Séverin de 38
Carlyle, Thomas 120, 127
Carnap, Rudolf 24
Carré, John le (David John Moore Cornwell) 177
Carus, Carl Gustav 104
Catastrophe 1, 41, 75, 115, 119, 155, 159, 191–202, 206–207, 210, 219
Cave, Terence 3
Certainty 67, 99, 115, 126–127, 130, 204
Chambers, Sir Robert 147–148
Chaos 1, 32–33, 57, 75, 96, 134, 141, 155, 186, 217, 219
Chomsky, Noah 19
Christianity 101, 146, 211–212, 217
Claessens, Dieter 56, 64, 116
Claessens, Karin 116
Clark, Christopher 119
Coleridge, Samuel Taylor 62, 116

Collins, Philip Arthur William   128
Complexity   7, 10, 19, 21, 24, 34, 41,
  49–50, 54, 57, 60, 62, 80, 83, 106, 108,
  110, 118, 140, 151, 153, 172–173, 206
Condillac, Étienne Bonnot de   133
Conrad, Joseph   24, 81
Consciousness *passim*
– alienation   15, 66, 85, 118, 193, 198, 219
– and awareness   15–19, 28, 49, 65, 67,
  83–84, 89, 92, 98, 104, 120, 150, 159,
  164, 181, 194–195, 199–200, 219
– and experience   16, 18, 21, 25, 27, 32,
  34, 41, 49, 56, 65–66, 73, 101, 104–
  105, 109, 153, 155, 179, 181, 194, 210,
  212
– and systems theory   18–19
– bicameral   1, 55, 66–69, 71, 73–74, 78,
  142
– drama and situational crisis   59, 65, 132
– fluctuations of   37–48
– hysterical, schizophrenic   1–2, 4, 11–12,
  58–59, 62, 66–67, 74, 90, 95, 108,
  115, 133, 137, 142, 151, 164, 166, 168–
  169, 192, 198, 201–204, 208, 210, 214,
  217–219
– processes, products   1–3, 10–11, 15–16,
  18–19, 23–24, 27, 47–51, 54–55, 58,
  62–65, 74, 79, 90, 93, 95, 100–103,
  106, 110, 112, 115, 117, 132, 138, 148–
  151, 155, 164, 168, 171, 173, 182, 191,
  193, 195, 199–200, 208, 210
– self-observation of   18–22, 33, 105, 127,
– Western, Japanese thought   3–4, 7–9,
  27–28, 49, 75, 85, 94–95, 97–98,
  108, 115–116, 133, 146, 148, 159, 162,
  177, 187, 194, 219–220
– Cost-benefit analysis   141–154
Cromwell, Thomas   120–123, 126
Culture and seriousness   59, 137–138, 201
Curley, Thomas H.   147–148

Damasio, Antonio R.   34, 49–54, 56, 124,
  193
Dante Alighieri   68, 72–73, 80
Danto, Arthur C.   94
Danton, Georges Jacques   125
Darwin, Charles   55, 88, 138

Defoe, Daniel   147
Dennett, Daniel C.   17, 83
Descartes, René   16, 98, 152–153
Desmoulins, Camille   124–125
Destutt de Tracy, Antoine Louis Claude de
  133
Devereux, Georges   8, 66, 75, 145–146,
  148, 177, 194
Dickens, Charles   2, 127–132, 134–135,
  140, 157
– the unconscious, fixed ideas and violence
  12, 16–17, 87, 104–105, 127, 130–132,
  137–138, 159–160, 191, 208, 217
Diderot, Denis   173–175, 177–179, 181, 199
Dodds, Eric Robertson   55, 66
Dogma, dogmatism   2, 4, 6, 38, 100, 128,
  134, 146, 151, 177
Donne, John   7
Doors   159
Dower, John   30
Drama, dramatic   1, 18, 20–21, 33–35,
  41–42, 49, 51, 58, 61–89, 115, 126,
  133–134, 142, 153, 155–156, 164–169
– and forms   5, 76, 132, 142, 147
– poetry and/as dramatic form   65, 115
– séances as failed drama   86–87
Dujardin, Edouard   32
Dumas, Alexandre (père)   201
Durand, Gilbert   58, 63–64
Dürer, Albrecht   95
Durrell, Lawrence   97, 118
Dux, Günter   4

Eagleton, Terry   35
Edelman, Gerald M.   25, 27, 32, 50–52, 60
Eibl-Eibesfeldt, Irenäus   54–55
Einstein, Albert   204
Eliot, George   21–23, 103–106, 109, 127
Eliot, Thomas Stearns   58–59, 64, 79–80,
  157, 211
Emerson, Ralph Waldo   26–27
Emotions   25, 32, 35, 54, 59, 68, 70,
  79–80, 91, 95, 99, 125, 129, 137, 152,
  156–157, 172–173, 175, 184, 199, 202,
  206
Enderwitz, Anne   24
Enforceability   163, 187, 220

Engels, Friedrich   133
Enlightenment   55, 126, 155, 158, 164, 171–184
– and life forms   171, 184
Epistemological asymmetry   207
Erikson, Erik H.   66
Esposito, Elena   116
Ethics   see action, norms of, orientation of
Euclid   153
Evolution   1–7, 11, 19, 21, 24, 32–33, 50–67, 88, 108, 157, 203, 207–208, 219–220
– discrepancy of levels in   206

Fabre d'Églantine (Philippe-François-Nazaire Fabre)   124
Farinelli (Carlo Broschi)   69
Fascism   214, 216–217
Fauconnier, Gilles   17–18
Feuerbach, Ludwig   157
Feyerabend, Paul   11, 125, 141–146, 148, 160–161
– traditions according to   142–143
Fichte, Johann Gottlieb   26–27
Fiction, fictitiousness, fictionality   36, 108, 117–118
Fielding, Henry   111, 147
Fischer-Dieskau, Dietrich   70
Flavius Josephus   199
Fodor, Jerry   19
Fox, Stacey   110
Frazer, James George   64
Freedman, Daniel X.   2
French Revolution   120, 123–124, 166–167, 171, 185
Freud, Sigmund   24, 59, 63, 66, 74, 158, 204, 206
Frye, Northrop   118, 126
Fuchs, Peter   73
Fuchs, Thomas   76
Fuller, John Frederick Charles   217
Furet, François   123, 126

Garcia, Tristan   2
Garton Ash, Timothy   154
Gehlen, Arnold   6–10, 16, 19–20, 89, 135, 141, 145, 149, 160, 164

Gell, Alfred   61
Gellhaus, Axel   5, 72
Genazino, Wilhelm   2
Gendolla, Peter   VII
George III (King)   167
Geyer, Christian   51
Gibbon, Edward   73
Gissing, George   118
Glaubitz, Nicola   185
Gluck, Andrew L.   25–26
Godmer, Corinne   78
Goethe, Johann Wolfgang von   27, 37
Goetz, Rainald   2
Goldmann, Lucien   117
Goldsmith, Oliver   162
Grebogi, Celso   1
Gregory, Horace   92
Groethuysen, Bernhard   111
Gumbrecht, Hans Ulrich   179

Hahn, Marcus   74
Hanscombe, Gillian E.   92
Harcourt, Sir William   169
Hardy, Thomas   163
Hartmann, Eduard von   105, 138
Hartmann, Nicolai   57
Havelock, Eric A.   68
Hearn, Lafcadio   94
Hegel, Georg Wilhelm Friedrich   57, 95, 101, 112, 119, 134–136, 179–181, 194
Heise, Jens   29
Heisenberg, Werner   141, 204, 208
Henrich, Dieter   153
Henry VIII (King)   120, 123
Hermand, Jost   165
Hildesheimer, Wolfgang   134
Hill, C. P.   169
History   104, 119, 123, 165, 204
– biography and   123, 126
– of ideas   4–5
– how-questions   119
– why-questions   119
Hitler, Adolf   6, 215, 217
Hobbes, Thomas   67, 185–186
Hobsbawm, Eric J.   8–9, 116
Hobson, J. A.   165
Hogarth, William   69, 85

Holbach, Paul Henry Thiry d' 176
Homer 65–66, 68, 77
Honneth, Axel 171
Horkheimer, Max 55, 177, 187
Hotta, Eri 30
Houellebecq, Michel 115, 146
Howe, Irving 47, 140
Humboldt, Wilhelm von 144, 165, 180
Hume, David 18, 32–33, 35, 73, 163, 175–
178, 181–186, 191–192
– and the politics of culture 184
Huxley, Aldous 21, 54, 69

Ideology 6, 10–11, 133, 146, 166, 180
Imagination, imaginary 39, 40, 44, 53,
56–63, 72, 100–101, 121–122, 182
Individuality 16, 20, 144, 157, 191, 197–
202
– and extended consciousness 49, 52, 193
– and periphery of systems 18, 128
– autobiographical self 34, 51
– exhausted self 66
Institutional degeneration 210
Introspection 103–105
Iser, Wolfgang 75, 141

James, Henry 37–49, 65, 102, 105–107,
110, 117, 138–140
– aesthetic and/as moral dimensions 43,
45, 65
– ascriptive blurring 106
– body and consciousness 40
– dialogue and consciousness 40, 44
– imagination of disaster 42–43, 49
– status and consciousness 39
– style of oratory 47
– symbolic and social binding power 42
James, William 19–20, 32–33, 37–49,
62, 65, 81, 83, 106, 139, 155, 157
– inside dynamics of the mind 37
Jaspers, Karl 11, 21, 25–27, 134–136, 173
Jaynes, Julian 1, 15–18, 55, 60–61,
65–74, 76–77, 81, 142, 219
Joas, Hans 7
John (King John 'Lackland') 148
Johnson, Paul 26–27
Johnson, Samuel 147–148, 192

Jonson, Ben 89
Joyce, James 25–26, 32, 91, 93, 116
Junyk, Natalka 217

Kammerer, Paul 204, 207
Kamper, Dietmar 62
Kaplan, Sydney Janet 92
Kaulen, Hildegard 78
Keats, John 81, 86
Kierkegaard, Sören 76, 134–137
Kinks, the 159
Kleist, Heinrich von 76
Kluxen, Kurt 168
Knowlson, James 91
Knox, T. M. 135
Koestler, Arthur 2
Kofler, Leo 99
Konersmann, Ralf 3–4
Konner, Melvin 31
Koselleck, Reinhart 185
Kray, Ralph VII
Kretschmer, Ernst 76
Krieger, Murray 3
Kröner, Franz 24

Lacan, Jacques 31, 159
Lackey, Michael 117, 121, 139
Laclos, Choderlos de 124
Lang, Hermann 31
Langer, Susanne K. 194
Lauri-Volpi, Giacomo 70
Le Vasseur, Thérèse 176
LeGoff, Jacques 134
Leo, Friedrich 77
Leonardo da Vinci 152–153
Leroi-Gourhan, André 56–58, 60, 64, 74,
196
Levinas, Emmanuel 157
Lewes, George Henry 103–105, 127
Lewis, Mark D. 217
Lhermitte, François 149
Liberalism 164–165
– as *Weltanschauung* 165
Lichtenberg, Georg Christoph 85
Life forms 4, 45, 145–146, 177, 179, 181
– and existential categories 179
Life insurance 116

Liszt, Franz   69
Locke, John   47, 73
Lorenz, Konrad   2, 54 – 55
Lovejoy, Arthur O.   11
Löwith, Karl   135 – 138
Ludwig, Jo(sef)   21, 165
Luhmann, Niklas   10, 18 – 21, 73, 76, 128
Lukács, Georg   98 – 99, 117, 181
Lyotard, Jean-François   119

Macaulay, Thomas Babington   165 – 166
Mantel, Hilary   119 – 123, 125 – 126, 171, 185
Marat, Jean-Paul   123
Marrian, Michael   174
Maruyama, Masao   28 – 29
Marx, Karl   10, 133, 135 – 136, 157 – 158
Meltzer, Heinz Mathias   77
Menn, Dietrich   204
Metzinger, Thomas   17 – 18, 65, 91
Mey, Reinhard   198
Michel Angelo (Michelangelo Buonarroti)
   73
Michelet, Jules   88
Mill, John   37
Mill, John Stuart   127, 141, 144 – 145, 165,
   169, 185
– custom in   144
– individuality in   145
Milton, John   68, 72 – 73
Mnouchkine, Ariane   201
Models of thought   2, 5 – 8, 11, 23, 56,
   75 – 76, 115, 136, 158 – 160, 163, 170,
   174, 178 – 179, 187, 219
Molière (Jean-Baptiste Poquelin)   137, 173,
   201
Monod, Jacques   75, 194
Monologue   78
Moody, A. D.   109
More, Thomas   122
Moreschi, Alessandro   70
Morin, Edgar   1, 15, 34, 56, 58 – 62, 66 – 67,
   74, 89, 95, 108, 133, 137, 142, 151, 198,
   219
Mosley, Nicholas   9, 12, 15, 23, 75, 189,
   191, 193 – 194, 197, 199 – 200, 203,
   209 – 211, 213 – 217, 219
– and acting   193, 195, 197, 200 – 202, 214

– and alienation of consciousness   15, 193,
   198
– and rational experience   194
– and transitionality   195, 197, 200
– art and human beings   194
– as-if-qualities in   195, 210
– sex and religious belief   211
Mosley, Oswald   6, 12, 15, 189, 191, 214 –
   217
– and phantasms of self-overestimation
   214 – 215
– and undirected transitionality   214 – 215
– fascism and pseudo-concretization of hysterical consciousness   217
Mozart, Wolfgang Amadeus   137
Murphy's Law   197
Music   69, 79, 96, 156
– and binding power   158 – 159
– opera   68, 80, 137
Musil, Robert   119
Mustafà, Domenico   70

Narratives   62
Nassehi, Armin   149
Nazism   5 – 6
Neumann, Gerhard   70
Neurobiology   49 – 61, 66 – 69, 74 – 75
– and adequacy of emotions in *Hamlet* and
   Macbeth   59
– and evolutionary pressures   57 – 59
– and the arts   34, 49, 53
– binding problem   51
– descriptive gap   25
– explanatory gap   25 – 27
– material basis and consciousness   24 – 25
– reduction of claims   52 – 53
Newton, Isaac   153
Nicolson, Harold   216
Nietzsche, Friedrich   118, 137, 195, 207
Novalis (Georg Philipp Friedrich von Harden-
   berg)   65
Novel   117, 147, 155
– anthropomorphic commitments of   117 –
   118
– biographical   12, 35, 77, 90 – 92, 105,
   115 – 117, 120 – 122
– cognitive elasticity of   121

Ong, Walter J. 68
Orléans, Philippe d' 124
Osler, Douglas J. 147
Osterhammel, Jürgen 105, 119
Owen, Robert 88

Paganini, Niccolò 69
Paine, Thomas 167
Pascal, Blaise 27
Peet, F. David 1
Penrose, Roger 205
Penty, A. J. 127
Performance 16–17, 29, 47, 68, 70, 72, 183, 199–200
Petrarch (Francesco Petrarca) 73
Pfeiffer, K. Ludwig 58, 85, 89, 92, 105, 133, 137, 146
Pitt, William (the Elder) 167
Plato 26, 71–72, 98, 151, 158, 172
Pocock, John Greville Agard 185
Polanyi, Karl 116, 163, 210
Pope, Alexander 33, 110
Pöppel, Ernst 79
Pörtner, Peter 29
Pound, Ezra 79
Price, Richard 167
Priestley, John 167
Proust, Marcel 34, 70, 119

Quine, Willard Van Orman 187

Racine, Jean 70, 78–79
Radkau, Joachim 1–2
RAF (Rote Armee Fraktion) 155–156
Ralegh, Walter 81
Ramachandran, Vilayanur S. 16, 24, 50–51
Raphael (Raffaello Sanzio di Urbino) 73
Reality concepts 11
Réaumur, René-Antoine Ferchault de 88
Redlich, Fredrick C. 2
Reformation 6–7
Relativity 27, 75, 85, 98, 172, 187, 204
– theory of 204
Renan, Ernest 135
Richards, Ivor Armstrong 62
Richardson, Dorothy 76, 90–102, 108–110

– consciousness and 'aesthetic' perception 94–97
– consciousness and consistency 90, 97, 100
– consciousness and the sense of the real 99, 101
– consciousness and writing 100–101
Richardson, Samuel 34–36, 65, 91–92, 102, 108, 111, 175
– social values and dynamics of consciousness 91
Richet, Denis 123, 126
Ricks, Christopher 6, 214–215
Ringen, Stein 39
Robespierre, Maximilien 124–125
Robinson-Valéry, Judith 149
Roland de la Platière, Jean-Marie 125–126
Roland de la Platière, Jeanne-Marie 125–126
Rolling Stones, the 159
Rorty, Richard 155
Roth, Gerhard 50–51
Rothacker, Erich 175
Rousseau, Jean-Jacques 3, 73, 76, 126, 175–178, 181–182
Ruelle, David 1

Sachs, Gunter 143
Sartre, Jean Paul 63, 76, 194, 201
Sayers, Dorothy L. 111–112
Schadewaldt, Wolfgang 77
Schelling, Friedrich Wilhelm Josef 23, 62
Schelsky, Helmut 161–163
Schiller, Johann Christoph Friedrich von 84, 100, 117
Schmitt, Arbogast 98–99, 151–152, 158, 172
Schnell, Ralf VII
Schoeck, Helmut 15
Scholasticism as style of thought 134
Schopenhauer, Arthur 6–8, 89
Schreber, Daniel Paul 74
Schücking, Levin Ludwig 2, 111
Schulz, Sabine 176–177
Schulz-Buschhaus, Ulrich VII
Schüttpelz, Erhard 74, 87
Schwitzgebel, Eric 16

Scott, Sir Walter   116
Shakespeare, William   26–27, 33–34, 49,
   52–53, 55, 68, 72–73, 78–80, 85, 110,
   134, 150, 194
Shelley, Percy Bysshe   26, 62, 71–73, 77,
   84
Shklar, Judith   165, 171–173
Simmel, Georg   24
Simon, Claude   119
Singer, Wolf   24, 50
Skinner, Quentin   185
Sloterdijk, Peter   157
Smith, Adam   28, 35
Snell, Bruno   65–66, 68
Spanish Civil War   75, 203, 205
Speenhamland   169
Spencer, Herbert   138
Stafford, Barbara Maria   174
Stang, Richard   117
Stevens, Wallace   76, 82, 133
Storr, Anthony   79
Swedenborg, Emanuel   26–27
Systems and self-reference   16, 87, 128–
   129
– deterioration of self-reference   128

Tennyson, Alfred   31–32, 82, 86–87
Texts   5, 26, 31, 34, 37, 57, 70, 76, 78, 82,
   85, 155, 159, 173, 184
– competition of   31, 34
– discourse and style of thought   33–34
– discursive power of   31
– legal discourse   9, 74, 146–147
– oral performance   47–48, 68
Theory, theories   1, 4–5, 7, 11, 23, 28,
   75–76, 85, 117, 133, 141–145, 156–158,
   160–161, 178, 206
– multiplicity of   34, 141, 213
Thom, René   1, 149
Titian (Tiziano Vecellio)   95
Tóibín, Colm   138–140
Tolstoy, Leo   32
Tononi, Giulio   50–52
Topitsch, Ernst   64
Total conception   5, 160
Transitionality   3, 5, 12, 17, 21, 68, 71, 73,
   76–77, 80–81, 90–91, 97, 115, 130,

132, 135, 140, 156, 159, 191, 195, 197,
   200, 202, 204, 214–220
Trevelyan, George Macaulay   166–168
Trollope, Anthony   117–118
Turner, Mark   17–18, 50–52, 90
Tylor, Edward   87
Tyrrell, R. Emmett, Jr.   169

Vaihinger, Hans   118
Valéry, Paul   141, 148–153, 155
– knowing and doing in   151
– language and thought in   150–151
– living systems and theory in   151
– theory, logic and transfer of energy   153
– theory and theorizing in   149, 151–153
– transformations in consciousness in   153
Verdi, Giuseppe   70
Vernière, Paul   174
Vivas, Eliseo   3
Voltaire (François-Marie Arouet)   73, 178–
   179
Vondung, Klaus   VII, 4, 92

Wallace, Alfred Russel   55, 88
Walzer, Michael   165
Ward, Joseph Anthony   42
Weber, Max   27, 98–99
Weischedel, Wilhelm   153
Wells, Herbert George   92
Weltanschauung   5–11, 21, 23, 38, 76, 90,
   117, 127, 130, 132–136, 138, 140–141,
   143, 145, 154, 158, 160, 163, 165–166,
   168–170, 174–175, 178, 187
– difficulties of   6, 11, 16, 100, 127
Wicht, Wolfgang   VII
Wiegandt, Klaus   7
Wilberforce, William   116
Wilde, Oscar   61, 139
Wilkes, John   168
Williams, Bernard   165
Williams, Raymond   127, 162–163, 169
Williford, Kenneth   17–18
Wilson, Edward O.   24, 55, 92, 142
Windt, Jennifer M.   17–18, 65, 91
Winning, Joanne   92
Witzel, Frank   11, 155–160, 163–164
Wolff, Robert Paul   145

Wolsey, Thomas 120
Woolf, Virginia 108
Woolson, Constance Fenimore 139
Wordsworth, William 79 – 80, 95

Yeats, William Butler 7
Yorke, James A. 1

Zapf, Hubert VII
Zeeman, Sir Erik Christopher 1